Space Law and Policy

Series Editor

Maria A. Pozza, Gravity Lawyers
Christchurch, New Zealand

Space activities across the Asia-Pacific, specifically in Australia and New Zealand, are increasing and diversifying. Over the last decade, countries in this region have seen significant growth within their national space industries and economies which in turn benefit their wider societies due to the downstream application and use of, space-related technologies, products, and services. This phenomena presents not only a great opportunity for these countries, but also represents a situation necessitating considered and fit-for-purpose space law and policy. Robust yet flexible regulatory regimes are needed if countries in the Asia-Pacific, such as Australia and New Zealand, are to benefit from the strategic and commercial advantages associated with a presence in outer space and functioning domestic space sector. These regulatory regimes must respond to, and address, numerous challenges ranging from adherence to international legal obligations to issues of geo-political space security and military concerns through to questions about how best to regulate and support commercial space endeavours. These myriad factors will have an impact upon how countries develop, implement, and refine their space laws and policies. This series offers a unique perspective from this region and intends to act as a source of knowledge and guidance for space actors across government, the private sector and academia in the pursuit and furtherance of their respective space activities and operations. The contributors to this series are all experts in their field who share a common interest in strengthening space governance via the promotion and development of space law and policy.

Joel A. Dennerley • Maria A. Pozza
Editors

The Business of Outer Space

Commercial and Legal Issues

Springer

Editors
Joel A. Dennerley
Canberra, ACT, Australia

Maria A. Pozza
Gravity Lawyers
Christchurch, New Zealand

ISSN 2662-9054 ISSN 2662-9062 (electronic)
Space Law and Policy

ISBN 978-981-95-2033-6 ISBN 978-981-95-2034-3 (eBook)
https://doi.org/10.1007/978-981-95-2034-3

This Springer imprint is published by the registered company Springer Nature Singapore Pte Ltd.
The registered company address is: 152 Beach Road, #21-01/04 Gateway East, Singapore 189721, Singapore

Foreword

The Business of Outer Space: Commercial and Legal Issues

Outer Space is often portrayed as the Final Frontier, characterised as a lawless region of untouched, isolated heavenly bodies within an inconceivably vast and empty void. At once something devoid of value and far removed from our everyday lives, and at the same time an orbital Wild West ready for rapacious land grabs by companies and conflict between superpowers.

The reality, however, is very different from this caricaturised view of space. Indeed, as this incredible book so engagingly and comprehensively conveys, space is in fact well-regulated with both international and domestic laws as well as normative behaviours between and by companies and nations. The activities underpinned by these frameworks establish space as a domain set to be worth over a trillion dollars in the next two decades, but also the ultimate high ground of critical import for national security. It is therefore almost inevitable that it will be a contested region in the context of global geostrategic competition.

The incredible valuations attributed to space are due to the services it provides and facilitates for us back on Earth. From global telecommunications to emergency response using the latest Earth Observation technologies, all of which underpin our everyday lives. On any given day, you may check the weather forecast, use maps on your phone to guide you to your meeting, and even get cash out of an ATM. You have used the global space sector in each of these examples. We are the beneficiaries of decades of government and private sector investment that have developed these awe-inspiring capabilities.

What is the market structure and governance framework that allows billion-dollar companies to safely trade and provide such services? A far-reaching study, this work describes the historical journey that has seen space become an everyday part of our lives and takes the reader right to the cutting edge of this rapidly developing sector. The space market provides a framework in which astonishingly advanced capabilities can be acquired in competitive cost comparisons with access delivered by payload to space, akin to ridesharing to the local shops. In just one example, at my own organisation, Swinburne offers high school students a chance to design and build their own scientific experiments that private rocket providers then fly to the International Space Station. A few decades ago, this would have been the preserve of Superpowers alone, and now it is routine for schools across Australia.

It is safe to say that space has always inspired, with the ability to reach orbit and beyond seen as the gold standard of technological and national achievement. Now, thanks to the development of NewSpace or Space 2.0, innovation by the commercial sector occurs on time scales of months rather than decades, as seen in the historical context of national space programs. This makes the current Return to the Moon a race, not between superpowers, but start-ups. We live in a world in which there is profit, not just prestige, to the exploration and, yes, exploitation of space with off-world mining (particularly of water from the Moon) rapidly moving from science fiction to science fact. If proactively well-regulated, this will be a boon for all humanity. If left to reactive legislation and declining normative behaviours, we will see the tragedy of the commons play out across the vastness of the void surrounding our world and beyond.

Pro Vice-Chancellor, Flagship Initiatives, Swinburne Research Alan R. Duffy
Swinburne University,
Hawthorn, Australia

Acknowledgements

I would like to extend my heartfelt thanks to my co-editor, Dr Maria Pozza, whose legal expertise has been invaluable throughout the development of this book. Her insights and contributions have greatly enriched the content and quality of this work. Maria's extensive understanding of space law and policy has been instrumental in shaping the direction and scope of this book.

I am also profoundly grateful to the authors of the book's chapters. Your scholarly contributions and commitment to advancing the understanding of commercial space activities have been essential to the success of this book. Each chapter reflects your deep knowledge and innovative thinking, providing a comprehensive and nuanced exploration of the legal issues associated with the commercial space industry. A special thanks to Mamum from Springer for her support and guidance throughout the editing and publishing process. Another special thanks must go to Prof. Alan Duffy for his endorsement of this book and for his tireless efforts in promoting the Australian space industry. Finally, a very special thanks goes out to Dr Andrew Nicholls whose care and advice sustained me this past year.

Finally, I would like to acknowledge the broader community of scholars, practitioners, and enthusiasts in the field of space law and policy. Your ongoing efforts to explore and address the complex legal and regulatory challenges of space activities inspired and drove the work presented in this book. It is my hope that this book will contribute to the ongoing dialogue and development in this dynamic and rapidly evolving field.

Joel A. Dennerley

Contents

About the Editors and Contributors

About the Editors

Joel A. Dennerley, BA, LLB (Hons), M App Dat An. Joel is a management consultant and is the co-editor of the book Risk Management in Outer Space Activities: An Australian and New Zealand Perspective.

Maria A. Pozza, LLB (Hons), BVC (ICSL), PG Dip Legal Research & Skills, M Inst, PhD. Dr Pozza is the director and principal lawyer of Gravity Lawyers, New Zealand, which specialises in the international regulation, and New Zealand regulation, of space activities. She is the co-editor of the book Risk Management in Outer Space Activities: An Australian and New Zealand Perspective.

Contributors

Art Cotterell The Australian National University, Canberra, Australia

Joel A. Dennerley, Canberra, ACT, Australia

Mark Giddings LK Law, Adelaide, SA, Australia

Thomas Graham Swinburne University of Technology, Melbourne, VIC, Australia

J. Lauren Napier Northumbria University, Newcastle, UK

Christopher J. Newman Northumbria University, Newcastle, UK

Bradley Robb ALARP Solutions, Adelaide, Australia

Dale Stephens The University of Adelaide, Adelaide, SA, Australia

Aaron Young ALARP Solution, Canberra, Australia

An Introduction to Commercial Space Activities

Joel A. Dennerley

1 Introduction to the Space Industry

1.1 Overview and Definitions

Outer space is open for business. The current era of space exploration and use, sometimes referred to as NewSpace or Space 4.0, is characterised by new business paradigms, disruptive technologies, start-ups, public-private partnerships, and the increasing commercialisation of space activities (Martin, 2015, p. 6; European Space Agency [ESA], 2016). From our current vantage point in the first quarter of the twenty-first century, the space industry will be a driving force in how the rest of this century unfolds. In areas such as materials science and manufacturing to telemedicine and epidemiology, the space industry is facilitating economic and technological progress and offering us solutions to problems that were previously out of reach. As of 2022, the global space economy was estimated to be worth USD 384 billion (BryceTech, 2023), with economic forecasting suggesting that it may grow to over USD 1 trillion by 2040 (Morgan Stanley, 2020; Deloitte, 2020a). Much of this growth is attributable to the increasing commercialisation of outer space, where space companies and businesses are developing and offering new goods and services to different markets, investors, consumers, and clients. As a result, space technologies, goods, and services are increasingly important in many parts of society

The views of the authors are the authors' alone and are intended to provide commentary and general information, and do not represent the views of any organisation. This chapter should not be relied upon as a substitute for professional legal advice or for any other purpose.

J. A. Dennerley (✉)
Canberra, ACT, Australia
e-mail: info@gravitylawyers.co.nz

J. A. Dennerley, M. A. Pozza (eds.), *The Business of Outer Space*, Space Law and Policy, https://doi.org/10.1007/978-981-95-2034-3_1

and throughout the broader economy. From satellite imagery used to monitor and respond to natural disasters to the Global Positioning System (GPS) accessed by most smartphones, the space industry provides commercial value across a broad range of business offerings. Nevertheless, with such a diverse set of business activities, it can be difficult to define what the space industry is and what commercial space activities entail. Therefore, we will now turn to a brief discussion on this point.

One broad definition of 'space activities' includes 'any human activities conducted in, having an effect in, or intended to have an effect in the outer space domain' (Dennerley et al., 2022, p. 5). When space activities are conducted by commercial entities producing goods and/or services for profit, these would be considered commercial space activities. Activities of this kind are broadly considered to form part of the space industry, which encompasses various economic space activities. It is important to note that the space economy includes not only space products and services but also governmental space budgets, commercial infrastructure, and the activities of space-adjacent industries (Space Policy Online, 2022). Therefore, for the purposes of this book, the space industry can loosely be understood as the collection of organisations (both government and non-government) that partake in, contribute to, or support space activities (definition above) by supplying and/or consuming goods and/or services (both commercial and non-commercial). An example might be a firm supplying electronic components that form part of a satellite or its payload, a launch service provider that launches and deploys a satellite into orbit, or a government department that purchases Earth observation data sets from the owner of a satellite. When these sorts of space industry activities are undertaken by commercial entities seeking profit, they would be considered commercial space activities.

The above definitions appear broad, but this is because it is challenging to say with certainty what definitively counts as 'commercial space activities'. To highlight this issue, it is worth mentioning here specific characteristics of 'commercial activities' which may assist us in determining the scope and content of the business uses of outer space. To begin, it might be proposed that to be truly commercial in nature, space activities must operate within a 'free-market' economic system where presumably the prices for various space-related goods and services are determined by the forces of supply and demand with minimal to no governmental coercion.[1] This can be problematic because certain space technology is considered dual-use (Johnson-Freese, 2018), meaning that it can be utilised for civilian and military purposes (European Commission, 2018). An example might be a remote sensing satellite that is used to map soil types for use in agriculture (civilian) whilst at the same time being used for surveillance and reconnaissance (military). This being the case, there are governmental controls, such as the International Traffic in Arms Regulation (ITAR), and the Export Administration Regulations (EAR) in the United States (US) (U.S. Department of State, n.d.; Bureau of Industry and Security (BIS), U.S. Department of Commerce, n.d.) which place restrictions on things like the sale,

[1] For a detailed discussion see Davidian (2021, p. 553), Peeters (2021, p. 211).

export, and access to dual-use space technologies (Straub & Vacek, 2014, p. 351). Mechanisms like ITAR serve an important role in prohibiting certain actors from obtaining military technologies (Straub & Vacek, 2014, p. 352) while at the same time, regulatory regimes such as this might be viewed as curtailing certain free-market principles because government intervention places conditions on transactions between sellers and buyers. Despite what one thinks about such intervention, this highlights that at least parts of the space economy are not 'free' in the sense of being an 'unregulated system of economic exchange' (Orlitzky, 2021). Indeed, as Harari points out, 'in its extreme form, belief in the free market is [...] naïve [...] There simply is no such thing as a market free of all political bias' and intervention (2015, p. 329). This point is true of the commercial space industry.

Furthermore, space activities, such as the launching of space objects or the operation of satellites, are considered hazardous and risky endeavours (see generally Pozza & Dennerley, 2022; Dennerley, 2018), meaning governments will likely want to strictly control any commercial space activity that poses a risk to public safety, national security, or international relations.[2] Under Article VI of the United Nations (UN) space treaty entitled the Treaty on Principles Governing the Activities of States in the Exploration and use of Outer Space, Including the Moon and Other Celestial Bodies[3] (Outer Space Treaty), which is the foundational text of international space law, States bear 'international responsibility for national activities in outer space' (Outer Space Treaty, Art. VI). This responsibility extends to 'non-governmental entities', understood more commonly to be a nation's commercial or private space actors (Dempsey, 2016, p. 6). Article VI goes on to stipulate that '[t]he activities non-governmental entities [...] shall require authorisation and continuing supervision' by the State (Outer Space Treaty, Art. VI). This approval and oversight is typically done via licencing and permitting regimes (Dempsey, 2016, p. 6), often with terms, conditions, and requirements incumbent upon commercial space actors who are obliged to perform or refrain from certain things, as well as update government bodies about various events throughout their space mission's lifecycle.[4] This form of national space regulation is becoming the norm for many space-faring nations, with the UN General Assembly calling for States to 'consider enacting and implementing national laws [for] the activities in outer space of non-governmental entities' (United Nations General Assembly [UNGA], 2004). At the time of writing, 42 countries had enacted some form of domestic space law or regulation (United

[2] See for example Part 3 of the Australian Government's Space (Launches and Returns) Act (2018), where the minister may consider issues of 'security, defence or international relations' when deciding whether to grant approval for various kinds of space activities.

[3] For further details about the treaty, see Treaty on Principles Governing the Activities of States in the Exploration and Use of Outer Space, Including the Moon and Other Celestial Bodies (Outer Space Treaty) (1967), 610 UNTS 205. As at 1 January 2022, the status of the Outer Space Treaty is 112 ratifications and 23 signatures (United Nations Committee on the Peaceful Uses of Outer Space [UNCOPUOS], 2022).

[4] See for example ss 9, 37, 41, 50, and 120 of the Australian Space (Launches and Returns) Act (2018); ss 10, 18, 26, 34, 41, and 48 of New Zealand's Outer Space and High-altitude Activities Act (2017); s 5 of the United Kingdom's Outer Space Act (1986).

Nations Office for Outer Space Affairs [UNOOSA], 2022). However, in reality, government intervention in space activities makes many markets in the space economy 'regulated markets' rather than free markets. This fact is important if we are to grasp the contemporary nature of commercial space activities and the important role that governments play in the context of the space industry. Moreover, governments often supply significant funding for space projects, missions, products, and services by way of direct investment, service procurement, or grants to space companies and businesses, many of whom rely on governments for their revenue or financial support (Ben-Itzhak, 2022; Space Policy Online, 2022). In addition, commercial space activities are often tied to government (and military) policies, programs, and initiatives. This means that in many parts of the space economy, there is a nexus between commercial entities offering space-related goods and/or services, and governments and militaries as the consumers (and funders) of these activities, or as the owners of space technologies (Organisation for Economic Co-operation and Development [OECD], 2021, p. 6).

However, this is not to say that private space entities do not trade, transact, or contract with other private space entities or even the general public. An excellent example of this is satellite television which made up roughly one-quarter of the global space economy's worth in 2019, being valued at USD 92 billion (BryceTech, 2020). Customers around the globe can easily consume television programming transmitted directly to their location by communications satellites orbiting the Earth. These satellites are often owned and operated by private firms, which invest their money and resources to provide these broadcasting services. Indeed, when attempting to characterise commercial space activities, some have highlighted that commercial activities necessitate the requirement for there to exist some commercial entity that generates and/or invests its capital into its space activities while taking on associated economic and business risks (Space Policy Online, 2022). For instance, the US National Space Policy highlights that, in the context of the policy, a commercial space entity is understood as bearing 'a reasonable portion of the investment risk' (Office of Space Commerce, 2020, p. 20). The policy goes on to specify that for space activities to be termed 'commercial', entities must be sanctioned to engage in these activities and that these entities will operate in response to market drivers such as the desire to generate profits and minimise costs (Office of Space Commerce, 2020, p. 20).

What the above discussion is getting at is that the notion of what constitutes 'commercial space activities' is not settled but is contested and ever-changing (Odom, 2021, p. 9). We will unlikely ever obtain a universal or precise definition, but this is less of a problem than it may first appear. Any definition is likely too narrow and inflexible to fully capture the dynamic and varied nature of commercial space activities. Novel space activities and technologies will soon emerge, and older space industry paradigms and approaches will fade and be replaced. If the history of the space industry (Sect. 1.2 below) has taught us anything, it is that its industry characteristics will undoubtedly change. What is undeniable, however, is that there is an inevitable drift toward the commercialisation of space activities driven in large part by a series of industry trends that will be explored in Sect. 1.3 below

(International Trade Administration [ITA], 2022a). The reader should take away from this section that the aforementioned characteristics of commercial space activities represent a broad set of traits unique to the current space era. This book is focused on commercial and legal aspects relevant to this era and will therefore not adopt any strict definitions. With such rapid change occurring in the space industry today, it would not be wise to adopt one definition of commonly used terms such as commercial space activities, space industry, or space economy. Instead, this book will present the reader with data, research, analysis, and commentary about recent space activities in the hopes that you will come away with a greater understanding of some of the commercial and legal issues relevant to the business uses of outer space. The book will do this by presenting a series of topical case studies on commercial and legal issues of particular relevance to various space activities. The reader can consult Sect. 3 below for an overview of the case studies covered by the book's chapters.

1.2 Brief Historical Background

This section will outline some of the key historical events, milestones, and dates relevant to commercial space activities, with a particular focus on the US. This section does not provide a comprehensive account of the historical development of the space industry or space economy but will rather chart a high-level historical timeline which will allow the reader to better understand the evolving business uses of outer space. The timeline outlined here is one of many different historical space narratives. The reader is encouraged to seek out other accounts and use the sources cited throughout to delve deeper into specific topics of interest.

Pinpointing the beginnings of the commercial uses of outer space, let alone the beginnings of the space industry, is difficult to do. Nevertheless, ever since the first human-made object entered outer space, the *Bumper-WAC* sounding rocket in 1949 (National Aeronautics and Space Administration [NASA], 2008), governments were quick to dominate space activities (Ben-Itzhak, 2022). In the early years of the space industry, governments, and by extension their national space agencies and militaries, set the mission agendas, determined the national approach to space exploration, and appropriated the necessary resources to reach the space domain (Harrison, 2012). These trends fall into what might be termed the 'first phase' or the 'early era' of the space industry's development (Peeters, 2021, p. 206; ESA, 2016). This era was 'government led' and only counted as its members a small group of space-faring nations globally, all of which had the political, economic, and technological power required to operate space programmes (ITA, 2022a; OECD, 2020, p. 4). Important milestones in this early era included events such as the Soviet Union's successful launch of *Sputnik 1* in 1957, which was the first artificial satellite launched into Earth's orbit. *Sputnik*'s influence ushered in the Space Age, which saw the Cold War superpowers invest considerable resources into acquiring 'the most advanced [space] technology (Sheehan, 2007, pp. 7, 9; Dennerley, 2022, p. 109).

Ever since these early days, governments have partnered with commercial entities[5] who have provided many of the goods, services, capabilities, and know-how needed to access, explore, and exploit outer space (Robison Hasani, 2021, p. 27). For example, the National Advisory Committee for Aeronautics (NACA),[6] which was the predecessor of the National Aeronautics and Space Administration (NASA), awarded contracts to private manufacturers for the building of the *X-15* aircraft's airframe and rocket engine (Heracleous et al., 2019, p. 2). The practice of contracting out for the provision of technical goods and/or services to private entities was continued by NASA after it was first formed in 1958 (Heracleous et al., 2019, p. 2). It was also about this time that certain organisations began showing a keen interest in private space endeavours, particularly in the field of satellite communications (Lal, 2013, p. 28).

Arguably the first commercial space markets were telecommunications and satellite television (Peeters, 2021, p. 210; Dempsey, 2016, p. 15). Research and development company Bell Telephone Laboratories helped to instigate the commercial space age when in 1962, they successfully transmitted the first live television signal using the *Telstar 1* communications satellite,[7] which was launched by NASA in what was the first privately funded space mission (NASA, 2012; Ben-Itzhak, 2022). *Telstar 1* was launched into orbit by a *Thor-Delta* rocket designed by the aerospace manufacturer the Douglas Aircraft Company. The same year, President John F. Kennedy signed into law the Communications Satellite Act of 1962 which established a public-private corporation, known as the Communications Satellite Corporation (COMSAT), and which formed a regulatory regime for the private ownership of commercial satellites (Communications Satellite Act, 1962; Ben-Itzhak, 2022). COMSAT was tasked with establishing and operating a commercial, 'global satellite communications network' (Schwartz, 1965, pp. 350-351). Two years later, in 1964, COMSAT became a founding member of the International Telecommunications Satellite Organization, or INTELSAT, a public-private international consortium formed to develop and operate a constellation of communications satellites that would provide global broadcasting services (Intelsat, 2022a, 2022c). In 1965, INTELSAT's first satellite, Intelsat 1, was launched, being the first 'commercial communications satellites' to be placed into a geosynchronous orbit (GSO) around the Earth (Intelsat, 2022b). Only a decade after forming, INTELSAT comprised 86 Member States, all contributing to the consortium's funding and sharing in its profits (Britannica, 2014).

While the commercial satellite market was growing, the seeds were being sown for the commercial space transportation, or space launch market. Whilst early Space Age rockets were built and launched almost exclusively for government space

[5] For instance, during the early pioneering stages of rocketry, innovators, scientists, and engineers were helped along in their research and development by private donations and philanthropy (Lal, 2013, p. 28).

[6] The NACA was established in 1915 to undertake aeronautical research and was later absorbed into NASA in 1958. For a history of the NACA, see NASA (2019b).

[7] Telstar 1 was developed for the American Telephone and Telegraph Company (AT&T).

missions, commercial entities were contracted to design and manufacture such rockets. In the US during the 1970s, these rockets, also known as expendable launch vehicles (ELV),[8] were procured by government entities, such as NASA, from private US manufacturers and then launched by private contractors under the space agency's supervision (Federal Aviation Administration [FAA], 2022, p.1). As the commercial satellite market grew, countries and corporations would contract with NASA to launch their communications satellites giving the US Government an early monopoly over the launch market (FAA, 2022, p. 1). In the late 1970s, the US Government began to move away from using ELVs. Instead, it turned toward NASA's fleet of Space Shuttles for the transportation of government and commercial satellites into space, with the first Space Shuttle launched in 1981 (FAA, 2022, p. 1).[9] As a partially reusable spacecraft that could be repeatedly used to ferry astronauts and cargo into space and repair satellites in orbit, the Space Shuttle changed the way space nations accessed and used[10] space by providing 'regular access' to Low Earth Orbit (LEO) (Odom, 2021, p. 10; NASA, 2017b; Deloitte, 2022a, p. 4). In 1978 the US Government implemented a policy mandating that every client (both government and non-government) had to use the Space Shuttle for launches, effectively removing all other domestic ELV alternatives (McLucas, 1991, p. 90). This policy was eventually challenged by the European Space Agency (ESA), which was formed in 1975, and which developed the *Ariane* rocket to deliver commercial satellites into space. *Ariane*, which was first launched in 1979, represented a viable competitor to the Space Shuttle. In 1980, the world's first commercial launch service provider, Arianespace, was formed by ESA and the French space agency the National Centre for Space Studies (CNES) to operate the *Ariane* rocket and manage its commercial launch programme (ESA, 2022b). In the US, the 1986 Space Shuttle *Challenger* disaster led to a reversal in government policy, resulting in ELVs being reintroduced as commercial alternatives to the Space Shuttle (McLucas, 1991, pp. 93–95; FAA, 2022, p. 3).

Still in the US, the first privately owned and operated rocket, the *Conestoga 1*, was successfully launched by Space Services, Inc. of America (SSIA) in 1982 (FAA, 2022, p. 1). As the customer base for the commercial space launch market grew, President Ronald Regan signed into law the Commercial Space Launch Act of 1984 (Commercial Space Launch Act, 1984). Amongst other things, the purposes of the Act were to stimulate the growth of America's commercial space industry and to support the development of its private space launch market. The Act also made it quicker and easier to obtain a commercial launch licence (see Commercial Space Launch Act, 1984). The first commercial launch licence was issued to SSIA for its suborbital launch of the *Starfire 1* rocket in 1989. That same year, the *Ariane 4* ELV delivered the largest geosynchronous communications satellite at that time, Intelsat

[8] An ELV is a launch system, such as a rocket, that is only capable of being launched once.

[9] The Space Shuttle Program lasted until 2011 (NASA, 2017b).

[10] Not to mention many modules of the International Space Station were launched by the Space Shuttle.

VI, into orbit (McLucas, 1991, p. 93). A year later, in 1990, another important piece of American legislation was enacted—the Launch Services Purchase Act of 1990, which required 'NASA to purchase launch services [...] from commercial providers' (see Launch Services Purchase Act, 1990). The same year the *Pegasus* rocket placed a satellite into LEO. *Pegasus* was developed by Orbital Sciences Corporation[11] and launched by NASA from beneath an aircraft in-flight, becoming the first privately developed launch vehicle to be used (Northrop Grumman, 2022). The 1980s and 1990s saw 'a number of mergers and acquisitions of aerospace [and defence] companies' leading to a 'space sector dominated by a handful of large multinational giants' (see Sherborne, 2022, p. 22). The late 1990s and early 2000s saw increased competition in the satellite communications market, leading to the privatisation of several noteworthy commercial operators and owners of satellite telecommunications systems, including INTELSAT, the International Maritime Satellite Organization (INMARSAT), and the European Telecommunications Satellite Organization (EUTELSAT) (Baumann et al., 2018, p. 931).

In the twenty-first century, space tourism became a reality when, in 2001, Dennis Tito became the first tourist to visit space staying aboard the International Space Station (ISS), which had begun its construction 3 years earlier in 1998. The ISS, which has been crewed continuously since 2000, has served many purposes, including acting as a location for commercial space activities in LEO (Deloitte, 2022a, p. 6). In America in 2004, President George W. Bush signed an Executive Order that established a Presidential Commission[12] 'to obtain recommendations [regarding] implementation of [a] new vision for space exploration' (President's Commission on Implementation of United States Space Exploration Policy [President's Commission], 2004, p. 10). Two key recommendations included: 'the need to restructure and transform NASA; and [...], the need to promote new models of private sector involvement' [in commercial space activities] (see President's Commission; Sherborne, 2022, p. 23). The framework for regulating commercial human spaceflight was strengthened when President George W. Bush signed into law the Commercial Space Launch Amendments Act of 2004, which, amongst other things, established safety standards for commercial human spaceflight and sought to promote the growth of the industry (see Commercial Space Launch Amendments Act, 2004). Also in 2004, Mike Melvill became the first person to pilot a privately built spacecraft, the *SpaceShipOne*, into space (Britannica, 2016). In 2005, NASA started to implement the Presidential Commission's recommendations, and by 2006, NASA had launched the Commercial Orbital Transportation Services (COTS) program which was a public-private partnership between the space agency and private industry for the development and procurement of space transportation services for crew and cargo to the ISS (Lal, 2013, p. 34; Robison Hasani, 2021, p. 28). The COTS program represented a paradigm shift in the way the government worked

[11] *Pegasus* is now manufactured and launched by Northrop Grumman.

[12] The commission is sometimes referred to as the 'Aldridge Commission' after its chairman, E.C. Aldridge Jr.

with industry over the course of managing space projects and missions. This was because NASA did not specify any detailed technical requirements in its request to industry, opting to outline instead the broad capabilities that it needed and leaving it open to companies to specify the details and approaches to delivering these capabilities in alignment with their own unique business models, products, and services (NASA, 2017a). Additionally, NASA achieved cost reductions and increased efficiencies by ensuring that any of its commercial partners shared in the 'costs of the COTS system development and demonstration' (NASA, 2017a). At the time, these were novel approaches for space project management (Lambright, 2015, p. 31), which have since become a standard model for public-private collaboration across many commercial space activities.

In 2008, Space Exploration Technologies Corp. (SpaceX), which was founded in 2002, successfully launched the *Falcon 1* rocket, the first 'privately funded liquid-fuelled rocket' (Cobb, 2019). From 2010/2011 to the present, NASA has been operating the Commercial Crew Program (CCP), which has built a US commercial space transportation capability by contracting out spacecraft manufacturing and operation for crewed missions to the ISS (NASA, 2019a; Heracleous et al., 2019, p. 2). The CCP has seen numerous American private firms design, create, and operate spacecraft and space transportation services to and from LEO and the ISS, aiming to deliver 'safe, reliable and cost-effective' access to space (NASA, 2019a). The CCP is yet another example of a paradigm shift for public-private space ventures due to the way in which NASA has worked with private industry. In the context of the CCP, companies will own and control the spacecraft and its associated infrastructure and have the opportunity to present the space transportation capability or service model that they believe best fits NASA's mission requirements (NASA, 2019a). This approach has provided the innovation needed to secure regular and efficient access to space. Indeed, after a total of 135 missions, NASA's fleet of Space Shuttle was retired in 2011 (NASA, 2017b), further reinforcing the need for industry to step up and service commercial contracts for space transportation needed by government and industry alike (Deloitte, 2022a, p. 7). In 2012, while servicing a contract for NASA, SpaceX's *Dragon* capsule became the first private spacecraft to dock with the ISS in a mission to deliver it cargo (Lal, 2013, p. 25; Cobb, 2019). Further milestones were made in rocketry when in 2015, Blue Origin successfully launched and returned its *New Shepard* vertical takeoff, vertical landing (VTVL) launch vehicle (Blue Origin, 2015). This feat represented significant progress in the domain of reusable launch vehicles, which, unlike ELVs, can be fully or partially reused after a flight.

The year 1972 saw the last crewed mission to the Moon, but now in the twenty-first century, humanity has once again set its sights on returning to the lunar surface. In 2017, President Donald J. Trump signed Space Policy Directive 1, which detailed that the US would lead a return to the Moon with other 'commercial and international partners' (White House, 2017; Gibney, 2019, p. 436). This return is being orchestrated as part of NASA's Artemis program, which will see the space agency partner with other governments and the private space industry to return humans to the lunar surface by 2025. In 2018, NASA launched the Commercial Lunar Payload

Services (CLPS) program, which is ongoing, and which is designed to procure 'lunar delivery services' from companies that will transport things like scientific instruments, tools, power supplies, rovers, and other cargo to the Moon (NASA, 2022). At the time of writing, 14 companies are part of the CLPS program, all of which have been tasked with delivering different payloads (NASA, 2022). In addition, further exploration of the solar system is being planned by ESA, which has outlined its Terrae Novae programme, which aims to explore deep space and return its discoveries to Earth's society while at the same time '[stimulating] a more vibrant and dynamic commercial space ecosystem' (ESA, 2022a, p. 13). Furthermore, access to space for the private citizen got closer in 2021 when Virgin Galactic and Blue Origin began offering suborbital space tourism flights (Deloitte, 2022c, p. 3). In 2022, the Axiom Mission 1 (Ax-1) saw the first 'all-commercial' group of astronauts travel to the ISS in a privately financed and operated mission (The Guardian, 2022; Deloitte, 2022c, p. 3). Finally, in 2024, the privately built *Odysseus* spacecraft (built by the US company Intuitive Machines) achieved touchdown on the Moon, with this being the first time a commercial space object has visited the lunar surface (The Guardian, 2024).

If the history of the space industry has taught us anything, it is that governments have regularly partnered with private industries in order to realise their space ambitions. Companies in the space industry's early era typically came from aerospace and defence industries, but as Sect. 2 of this chapter will show, there is now a more diverse cohort of space businesses operating in different markets with new customer bases. However, there is, and will continue to be, a role for governments as the 'partner, facilitator […] regulator [and] customer of' space companies and businesses (Australian Space Agency [ASA], 2021, p. 4). Nevertheless, in the twenty-first century, we are witnessing an accelerating commercialisation of space activities where the government and 'military industrial space sector[s]' (Martin, 2015, p. 3) are now being supported more fully by, and in some cases fully outsourcing to commercial space entities. To explore this phenomenon, this chapter will now turn to an examination of current space industry trends.

1.3 Industry Trends

This section is dedicated to describing and analysing a series of contemporary space industry trends and recent areas of growth and change. It will focus on the current general direction in which the space industry is developing, with a particular focus on commercial space activities. As highlighted in the previous section, the makeup of the space industry is largely a blend of governmental and non-governmental organisations, with increasing diversification and growth in the number and type of commercial space actors. Space programs and policies such as NASA's COTS, CCP, and CLPS represent new ways of administering public-private partnerships (PPP), where government and corporations alike share in the financing, design, delivery, operation, and maintenance of space projects and missions. In space PPPs, governments often determine their mission goals and requirements and leave it open to businesses to determine what space products and/or services will best achieve these goals and satisfy the mission's requirements. This is a radical change to how space programs were traditionally managed during the early era of space exploration, where for instance NASA, acting in the prime contractor role, defined and undertook most aspects of 'capability development' (Martin, 2015, p. 23). The modern commercial approach to PPPs sees government cost share with industry, where mission financing is controlled through the use of fixed price contracts, with payments being released to companies upon the successful completion of specified milestones (Martin, 2015, p. 23). Particularly in the case of recent programs like NASA's COTS, new commercial arrangements have allowed governments to manage their budgets and risk and have allowed the private sector to secure a foothold in the space industry, as well as help establish space supply chains, enhance technical capabilities, and grow business confidence in the long-term viability of the LEO economy (NASA, 2017a). This in turn allows governments and space agencies, such as NASA, to focus on different aims, such as the exploration of deep space (Lambright, 2015, p. 31), and to instead purchase access to LEO from space transportation companies, such as SpaceX, as well as many other affiliate companies that make up the emerging LEO economy (Cobb, 2019). This new approach to spaceflight sees private companies 'sell a delivery service' to destinations in LEO and beyond (Gibney, 2019, p. 435).

Within most established space nations, government investment in space activities still represents most of the capital inflow into these nations' respective space economies (OECD, 2020, p. 3). This current role of government as the investor in, and customer of, commercial space entities and their activities, is a key factor in the development of the modern LEO economy. LEO spans the altitude range between 160 and 2000 km above the Earth's surface[13] and can be visualised 'as a spherical expanse [around] the Earth' (Dennerley, 2022, p. 113). Therefore, the LEO economy broadly encompasses commercial space activities that occur in this orbital region,[14] such as commercial space transportation services (including space tourism), on-orbit servicing of space objects, and the operation and use of a range of different commercial satellites (Deloitte, 2022a, p. 3). The LEO economy is still establishing itself. However, continued commercial space activities will likely assist in developing more intricate LEO 'trade networks' and increasingly connected space supply chains (Marais, 2022). Transportation is critical to the growth of the LEO economy, namely affordable, consistent, and frequent access to space. This is where the launch industry comes in. Historically, the prohibitive cost of launch meant that only governments with dedicated space budgets could afford the cost of placing objects into outer space. More recently, and especially over the last decade, the costs

[13]As a reference point, the ISS orbits the Earth in LEO at an average altitude of 400 km.

[14]Arguably the LEO economy also encompasses upstream and downstream commercial space activities. These include those products and/or services that enable spacecraft, satellites, crew, and cargo to get into LEO, as well as the products and/or services generated by having these assets in orbit, such as internet and data services.

associated with launching have been on the decline (Cobb, 2019). This has been driven in large part by several factors,[15] with an interesting one being the trend toward greater technology and hardware reusability. Previously, a large portion of a space mission's budget was dedicated to designing and manufacturing the rocket itself, which in the case of ELVs, was only capable of being used once. A launch vehicle was expensive hardware that could only be flown once because many components were destroyed during the launching process. This constraint had kept launch costs on the high side and acted as a barrier to entry for many space actors. One way to overcome this challenge presented itself in the form of reusable rocket technology. The concept of a reusable spacecraft traces its history back to the late 1950s with the US Air Force's (USAF) *X-20 Dyna-Soar*, a reusable space vehicle designed by Boeing (2022). Despite the X-20 program being cancelled, its space plane design influenced the later Space Shuttle design, which was itself a partially reusable spacecraft. However, during the Space Shuttle era, the cost to move 1 kg (1 kg) to LEO was roughly USD 54,500. This meant that despite the Space Shuttle being able to be reflown, it could cost up to USD 1.5 billion per flight when the orbiter's payload bay was nearly full (Jones, 2018, p. 1). By comparison, the contemporary reusable SpaceX *Falcon 9* can transport 1 kg to LEO for only USD 2720 (Jones, 2018, p. 1; Cobb, 2019). Whilst determining the costs of launching from a 'price per kilogram' perspective has several drawbacks (Driscoll, 2021), what this fact demonstrates is the decline in launch costs that has occurred from the 1980s through to today. Indeed, the example above shows that over this period, commercial launching to LEO[16] has been reduced 'by a factor of 20' (Jones, 2018, p. 1). Part of the reason for this is that reusable launch vehicles, such as the *Falcon 9*, can have their 'most expensive [components reused] which in turn drives down the cost[s]' associated with getting objects into outer space (SpaceX, 2022). Other trends in rocket design and manufacturing include the greater use of commercial off-the-shelf components, which are sourced from a relatively globalised supply chain of different providers, and which are interoperable and integrate into simplified launch vehicle designs, which in turn minimises the launcher's overall components count and increases its speed of production (see Jones, 2018, p. 3-4; Harrison, 2012, p. 186).

Additionally, more and more launch sites and facilities are being built and are now open for commercial launching (see BryceTech, 2021). With increasing revenues from launch activities worldwide, more capital is reinvested into 'technology and operations [which in turn drives down the] per-kg launch cost [facilitating greater] access to space' (Deloitte, 2022b, p. 6). With more competition in the launch market, launch service providers (LSP) are exploring new business models and approaches to servicing their new and expanding customer base. For instance, some LSPs are exploring the viability of offering end-to-end launch services to

---

[15] For a discussion of these factors see Jones (2018).

[16] It is important to note that this is launching to LEO, not transportation to the ISS which typically costs more.

customers, where the LSP works with the client throughout a large portion of the launch journey, assisting them with things like launch feasibility studies, obtaining the necessary launch approvals, sourcing various launch hardware, navigating global supply chain logistics, through to on-site preparation and finally orbital deployment of the customer's payload (see Equatorial Launch Australia, n.d.; Southern Launch, n.d.). This sort of offering provides much greater value to customers, who can increase their speed to launch and reduce mission costs by working with a single LSP for much of their space project. Additionally, there is interest in the 'creation of shared spaceports [and launch] infrastructure' as a way of scaling launch operations via 'multi-user activities' much like how an airport operates (Deloitte, 2022c, p. 13).

Another key trend that has driven costs down, and at the same time increased access to space is miniaturisation. This phenomenon is most apparent in the satellite market, where satellites are becoming smaller, making them cheaper to manufacture and quicker to deploy. Small satellites, or smallsats, can be classified in various ways, but the most common method is by their mass, with 600 kilograms or less generally being considered the smallsat's weight range[17] (BryceTech, 2022a, p. 3). Between 2012 and 2021, there were 4676 smallsats launched, with 3588 of these being commercial smallsats, most of which are owned by a small group of private operators (BryceTech, 2022a, pp. 15-16). The trend toward the increasing use of smallsats is being driven by things such as more rapid business development cycles supported by the use of 3D-printed parts, cheap commercial off-the-shelf satellite components, iterative and open-source software development, increasing adoption and harmonisation of industry standards, as well as Satellite-as-a-Service (SataaS) and Ground-Station-as-a-Service (GSaaS) business models (Deloitte, 2020b, p. 2; Werner, 2021). This in turn has meant satellite manufacturers and operators incur less capital expenditure on the design, development, and operation of smallsats, leading to 'lower economies of scale' (Peeters, 2021, p. 213). This transition from large satellites to smallsats[18] has also made ridesharing more frequent (Foust, 2022). Ridesharing occurs when multiple, often smaller payloads such as smallsats, share a single launch vehicle into outer space. Another characteristic of the NewSpace business ecosystem is the proliferation of space start-ups and private investment. In 2021, space-related start-ups generated 'over [USD] $15 billion' in capital from a variety of investors and firms (BryceTech, 2022b, p. 2). A recent trend analysis of the investment in commercial space activities identified that more and more private investment is being made in space start-ups, that 'public markets' have proved to be a major source of finance for space endeavours, and that there is an increase in mergers and acquisitions occurring within the space industry (BryceTech, 2022b, p. 2).

[17] For a further breakdown of the smallsat mass class, see BryceTech (2022a, p. 3).

[18] It is important to note that the satellite market still comprises a mix of large and small satellites but there is an increasing trend toward the use of smallsats for particular purposes and missions.

Easier access to capital and credit is just one of several reasons for the growth and diversification of commercial entities in the contemporary NewSpace era. Other drivers of new and emerging space business paradigms include easier access to innovative products and services from the information and communications technology sector, as well as technology transfers from space-adjacent industries. A good example of this is the use of things like cloud technology to support space missions. Activities such as Earth observation generate massive amounts of data. Indeed, the term 'big Earth data' has been coined to describe the Earth science data collected from space assets, such as remote sensing satellites. Big Earth data well and truly conforms to the characteristics of big data which include high volume, velocity, veracity, and variety of data sets and types. The voluminous stores of space data filling up the world's data centres create the challenge of efficiently collecting, processing, storing, and making this data accessible to end users (see generally Sudmanns et al., 2020). This is where technology like cloud computing and edge processing helps. Edge processing enables imaging devices, scientific instruments, and sensors onboard spacecraft and satellites to process their collected data in situ within the space domain rather than transferring it to a ground-based data centre or server for processing. This reduces the energy and resources needed to transmit the data back to the Earth and increases the speed at which operators and customers receive data and insights. (Daly, 2020). The general characteristics of cloud,[19] being a model for enabling access to 'ubiquitous, convenient, on-demand [...] computing resources' (Mell & Grance, 2011, p. 2) has transformed how space missions and projects are carried out. Cloud infrastructure and networks assist organisations rapidly access, use, and create value from space data by providing 'increased computing power and storage capabilities', making space data easily available to platforms and applications for analysis and decision-making, integrating enhanced cybersecurity controls and reducing the technology management burden on the data's end user (see generally Daly, 2020; Sudmanns et al., 2020, p. 840). Civil space data is also increasingly becoming free, full, and open and is easily accessible via a number of online data portals, hubs, gateways, databases, and data cubes (see, e.g., GIS Geography, 2022). This in turn has enabled a flourishing space data community and marketplace where governments, businesses, researchers, and individuals can access Earth observation and remote sensing imagery for use across a broad set of disciplines and activities such as farming, minerals exploration, urban planning, logistics, natural disaster management, weather forecasting, 'meteorology, epidemiology, hydrology, climate and environmental sciences' (Dennerley, 2022, pp. 108–109; ASA, 2021, p. 8). Technology trends such as these, as well as advanced robotics, artificial intelligence (AI), machine learning (ML), and the internet of things, are finding use and application throughout many parts of the space industry. This section has provided the reader with an overview of some recent space industry

[19] For a description of the essential characteristics of cloud computing see Mell & Grance, 2011, p. 2.

trends. The chapter will now turn to a breakdown of the types of commercial space activities that exist, and these activities' respective markets.

2 Commercial Space Activities and Markets

There are many ways to describe and categorise the space industry and space economy. Traditionally, space activities within the space industry typically fell into one of three (sometimes overlapping) segments, which included:

(i) Spacecraft, satellite, and payload manufacturing, including associated equipment manufacturing, known as the space segment.
(ii) The launch of the aforesaid space segment's objects into orbits around the Earth, including all associated launching activities, known as the launch segment.
(iii) The operation and support of the aforesaid space segment's objects via ground-based systems, known as the ground segment (Dennerley et al., 2022, p. 6).

The above three segments have been commonly used as a way of dividing up the space industry into its component parts. However, other classification systems exist and are being used (see ITA, 2022b). For instance, some choose to group those space economic activities that build space objects and get them into outer space as 'upstream' activities, while the on-orbit operations of these objects and the products and/or services they produce (for instance, data transmissions) as 'downstream' activities (OECD, 2020, p. 5).

For the purposes of this chapter, commercial space activities will be grouped into three non-exhaustive categories—(i) Destination Space, (ii) Destination Earth, and (iii) Supporting Space. They are defined to mean:

(i) Destination Space encompasses those entities that partake in, contribute to, or support commercial space activities[20] by producing and/or providing objects, goods, and/or services designed to go into outer space, including the operation of these objects whilst in outer space.[21]
(ii) Destination Earth encompasses those entities that partake in, contribute to, or support commercial space activities by utilising objects in outer space to produce and/or provide goods and/or services that can be accessed and consumed by end users (customers) on Earth.
(iii) Supporting Space encompasses those entities that partake in, contribute to, or support commercial space activities by producing and/or providing goods and/or services to those entities that fall into the Destination Space and/or Destination Earth categories.

[20] Refer to Sect. 1.1 of this chapter for a definition of space activities and commercial space activities.

[21] For a discussion of what and where outer space is, see Dennerley et al. (2022, pp. 8–11).

From the names of the first two categories above, it is obvious that they are grouped around their respective destinations or the location (outer space and Earth) where these commercial space activities occur or are intended to occur. The last category supports the two former categories through the production and/or provision of specialist goods and/or services. It is important to note that these three categories are non-exhaustive and may overlap. However, in the context of this chapter, they represent one way in which commercial space activities can be grouped and organised so as to gain a clearer picture of how the space industry is structured (see Fig. 1 below).

2.1 Destination Space

2.1.1 Manufacturing

Since 1957, there have been more than 6300 successful rocket launches worldwide which have deployed over 14,450 satellites into various orbits around the Earth, with roughly 6800 of these satellites still operating in outer space at the time of writing (ESA, 2022c). All this space hardware needed to be designed and manufactured

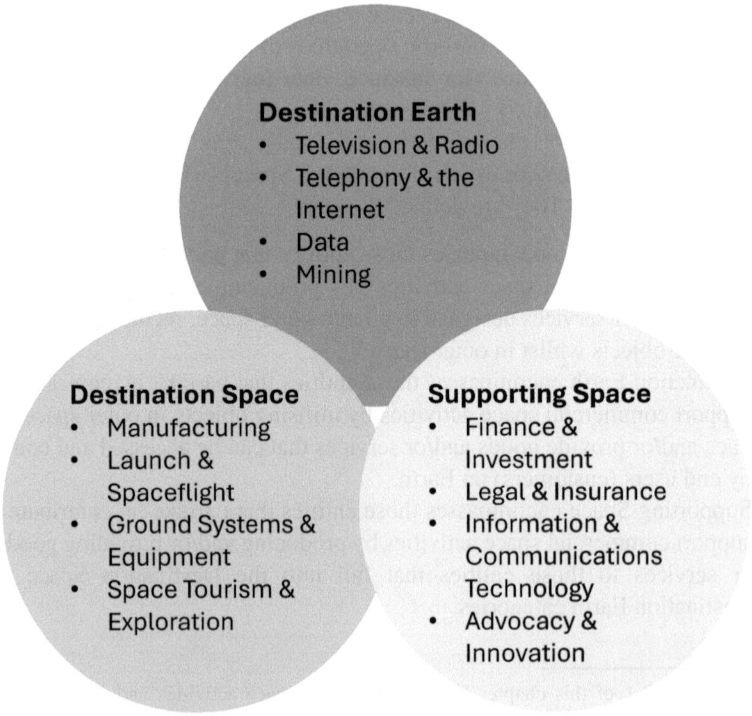

Fig. 1 The chapter's three overlapping non-exhaustive space industry categories

and be supported by critical space infrastructure. The industrial production and assembly of space objects, such as satellites and spacecraft, including their components as well as the space infrastructure and equipment that supports their use, is broadly considered space industry manufacturing. Arguably, this sort of space manufacturing occurs at the start of the space 'value' or supply chain (Baumann et al., 2018, p. 934) and provides customers and buyers with the physical space assets (and ground equipment) critical to their space projects and missions. In reality, space manufacturing is embedded into a complex, diverse, and integrated supply chain involving raw material suppliers, vendors, distributors, wholesalers, retailers, customers, as well as the manufacturing entities themselves (Coyle et al., 2013, pp. 18–23). Currently, over 75 nations operate satellites with the US, Russia, China, Japan, India, and the Europeans making up the largest proportion of satellite owners/operators globally (ITA, 2022a; Union of Concerned Scientists, 2022). These countries have established industrial bases and domestic heavy industries to draw upon for the supply of raw materials and the manufacturing of 'space-oriented' hardware such as spacecraft, satellites, rockets and launchers, related parts, and space infrastructure (Harrison, 2012, p. 183). In addition, there are increasingly interconnected global supply chains where customers can purchase the hardware, components, and related equipment they need to operate space projects and missions, as well as global labour markets of qualified experts with the capability and know-how needed to design and assemble all manner of space objects. Moreover, manufacturing includes not only the production of space objects like satellites and their payloads but also space-related equipment such as 'GPS transceivers and antennae [as well as] satellite dishes and GPS units' (Highfill et al., 2022, p. 3). Just examining the global satellite industry for 2021, satellite manufacturing revenues totalled USD 13.7 billion, with satellite ground equipment revenues totalling USD 142 billion (e.g., satellite TV dishes, GNSS devices/chipsets) (see BryceTech, 2022c).

There are several ways to break apart the space manufacturing market. One method is to group manufacturing into (1) the production of objects, such as launch vehicles and carrier rockets, that transport other objects into space, (2) the production of objects, such as satellites and spacecraft (specifically the bus), that are vehicles that hold and deliver crew and cargo into specific orbits or to a specific location, (3) the production of payloads, such as scientific equipment and instruments onboard a space object, designed for a specific use (for instance telecommunications systems), and (4) the production of ground equipment that connects to and communicates with space objects and enables their control and use (cf., Harrison, 2012, pp. 186–187). Other methods categorise the goods, products, and infrastructure that are produced by 'industry and upstream supply chain inputs' and which enable space activities to take place as falling within the 'infrastructure [or manufacturing] segment' of the space industry (Deloitte, 2022b, p. 6). This includes the production of launch vehicles, satellites, spacecraft and their related parts, ground equipment and infrastructure (such as launch facilities), and even products manufactured on-orbit within the space environment (Deloitte, 2022b, p. 6). This last point is noteworthy because we are beginning to see the manufacturing of objects in space (and eventually on the surface of celestial objects such as the Moon). This is sometimes termed ‘On-Orbit Servicing, Assembly, and Manufacturing’ or OSAM, and includes activities such as the maintenance and repair of functioning objects in orbit like satellites, the removal of objects like space debris from the space environment, or simply the manufacturing of goods and parts, or the constructions of objects in space, taking advantage of the ‘unique physical [...] conditions associated with outer space’ (BryceTech, 2022b, p. 36; Dennerley et al., 2022, p. 7). We are beginning to see the early stages of this type of activity with the additive manufacturing (also known as 3D printing) of spare parts onboard the ISS (Baumann et al., 2018, p. 932; Peeters, 2021, p. 218).

One area of growth in the space manufacturing market will likely be the production of large constellations of smallsats, sometimes called mega-constellations, and their associated ground equipment. Mega-constellations comprise many hundreds to many thousands of networked smallsats in LEO that together form a communication system typically for the provision of internet services. For example, several companies, including SpaceX (Starlink), and the communications company OneWeb, are operating large fleets of commercial smallsats that provide high-speed broadband internet services (BryceTech, 2022a, p. 15; Boley & Byers, 2021).[22] Internet services such as these require the manufacture and distribution of ‘related ground equipment’ such as satellite dishes, modems, and transceivers (Baumann et al., 2018, p. 949). As explained in Sect. 2.2.2 below, satellite internet is a contemporary growth market in the space industry, meaning its associated manufacturing and sale of ground equipment will likely continue to grow into the future.

2.1.2 Launch and Spaceflight

The launch and return of spacecraft, satellites, payloads, crew, and cargo to and from outer space, sometimes referred to as space transportation, including their deployment into specific orbits, or their delivery to specific locations, is loosely considered as falling into the space launch or spaceflight market[23] (George, 2019, p. 182). For example, space launch focuses on moving crew and space objects from the ground, or from within airspace, into outer space, and spaceflight focuses on their transportation to orbit or to specific locations (and their re-entry and return to the Earth). An example of this would include the launch of crew and cargo to space and their subsequent transportation to the ISS (ITA, 2022b), or the transportation of a satellite into space, and its subsequent deployment into a specific orbit. Arguably, spaceflight also includes enabling activities like ‘astronaut training’, as well as on-orbit activities such as space object ‘servicing [or] resupply’ (Deloitte, 2022b, p. 6). As explained previously, new commercial space activities are changing how we conceive of the space industry and its various market components. At present however, the launch or spaceflight market includes things like the design, manufacture,

[22] For a discussion on the risks created by satellite mega-constellations see Boley and Byers (2021).

[23] Space tourism is covered in Sect. 2.1.4 as it is an application of launch and spaceflight.

use, and maintenance of all manner of launch hardware, such as traditional ELVs, 'reusable launcher vehicles, re-entry vehicles', and includes more novel paradigms such as 'commercial spaceports' as well as the establishment, operation, and maintenance of more traditional launch sites and facilities (George, 2019, p. 182). The owners/operators of launch sites, known as LSPs, can generally be categorised as private LSPs, government LSPs, or exist as a hybrid of both (Robison Hasani, 2021, p. 27).

As explained above, since 1957, there have been over 6300 successful launches, with 2021 setting a new record for the most successful launches over 1 year, with 135 in total (Wikipedia, 2022). Also in 2021, 1743 smallsats were launched, representing 37 per cent of the total number of smallsats launched in the 10 years preceding 2021 (BryceTech, 2022a, p. 2). On top of this, an increasing number of launch facilities and launch infrastructure that supports both orbital and suborbital spaceflight is being built and is now operational (see BryceTech, 2021). The current growth in the launch market is likely the result of a confluence of several industry trends. These include decreasing launch costs, greater choice for one's LSP, miniaturisation, and reusability, but also the phenomena of mega-constellations and large-scale space projects. These endeavours necessitate large-scale contracts for the launching of multiple space assets, not to mention that there is increasing demand for launch services being driven by governments wanting the strategic and commercial advantages that come with having an active presence in outer space. This can be seen in the US, where NASA's Commercial Crew and Cargo Program (C3PO) is investing in, and supporting, the development of a domestic commercial transportation industry, with the specific aims of 'stimulating the commercial space industry [to ensure] safe, reliable, cost-effective access to [LEO, in order to meet the demands of] government and private sector customers' (NASA, 2017a). C3PO represents the US Government's desire to shift most of its launch activities to the commercial space industry (Robison Hasani, 2021, p. 27). One key factor for the increase in commercial launching is the demand that stems from the commercial satellite market (Harrison, 2012, pp. 187–188). Launching services in the global satellite industry alone generated revenues of USD 5.7 billion in 2021 (see BryceTech, 2022c). Additionally, human spaceflight in LEO is currently estimated to generate USD 40 billion 'in value' per annum (Deloitte, 2022a, p. 8). With the advent of mega-constellations and space tourism, it is likely that these growth trends will continue well into this decade and beyond.

2.1.3 Ground Systems and Equipment

As a complex technical system-of-systems, spacecraft and satellites require support from ground-based systems for their control, operation, and management when in the outer space domain (Stark et al., 2011, p. 4). The ground-based components of a space system are traditionally known as the ground segment and typically function by sending commands to the object in space and also by receiving information from the object (Stark et al., 2011, p. 4). However, in reality, the ground segment is composed of many different ground-based systems and infrastructures that are used at different points in a space mission's overall project lifecycle, from its preparation to on-orbit operations to post-mission activities (see European Cooperation for Space Standardization [ECSS], 2008, p. 19; Chatel, 2011, p. 467). This means that the ground segment includes things like physical ground stations, mission control centres, in-orbit test sites, terrestrial communications networks, telemetry, tracking and command stations, ground-based assembly and test facilities, and even launch facilities, not to mention the trained staff who work at these facilities (Baumann et al., 2018, p. 941; Chatel, 2011, p. 467).

Ground equipment broadly includes the physical devices and hardware (and software) that connect to, receive transmissions from, and communicate with objects in outer space or are enabled by these space objects (for instance, GPS-enabled smartphones). Ground equipment is used by various end users on Earth and is sometimes termed the user segment. The devices and hardware that form part of the user segment include things like ‘satellite TV dishes, very small aperture terminals (VSATs), satellite phones […] GPS chips’, (Baumann et al., 2018, p. 941), control centre terminals, and 'GNSS devices/chipsets’ (BryceTech, 2022c). Ground equipment revenues in 2021 for the global satellite industry amounted to USD 142 billion (see BryceTech, 2022c). With the proliferation of things like broadband satellite constellations and internet-of-things-enabled smart devices, the user segment will likely see continued financial growth as more and more end users (customers, businesses, governments, and militaries) make increased use of sensors and devices for communications and the internet both in space and here on Earth.

2.1.4 Space Tourism and Exploration

Space tourism includes those ‘human spaceflight activities done for recreational or entertainment purposes’ (Dennerley et al., 2022, p. 7). These activities can be categorised by where the space tourist goes, with sub-orbital tourism occurring at the 'edge of space', orbital tourism taking the tourist into Earth's orbit, and location-specific space tourism transporting the tourist to destinations such as the ISS (see Deloitte, 2022b, p. 8). Contemporary space tourism has been enabled by the launch and spaceflight market, with decreasing launch costs and increases in privately funded spaceflight missions being partly responsible for turning space tourism into more of a ‘viable and self-sustaining commercial enterprise’ (Deloitte, 2022c, p. 3). Space tourism in turn is supporting new growth in the manufacture of launch vehicles and space capsules that are designed exclusively for tourists (Harrison, 2012, p. 189). In 2021, both Virgin Galactic and Blue Origin began operating spaceflights for tourists. Both companies have announced future spaceflights, with Blue Origin having successfully completed six (6) human spaceflights as of 4 August 2022 (Blue Origin, 2022). Soon after, Virgin Galactic announced it would begin ‘revenue-generating’ commercial spaceflight services from June 2023 (Rose, 2023). It is important to note that space tourism is currently only accessible to wealthy individuals, meaning that any tourist demand for commercial human spaceflight will come from a smaller pool of 'high net-worth individuals' (Deloitte, 2022c, p. 11). However, we will likely witness eventual decreases in commercial spaceflight ticket costs as tourist demand rises, and we see cost savings and technology transfers to space tourism companies from the economies of scale created by programs like NASA's CCP which may assist in reducing tourism costs by driving new innovation in things like launch vehicle design, reuse, and operational efficiency (Deloitte, 2022c, p. 5). One additional potential application of space tourism is 'point-to-point travel', where passengers use a launch vehicle to commute from one location on the Earth to another location by transiting through space (Martin, 2015, p. 7).

While space tourism focuses on often shorter trips that eventually return the tourist to the Earth, space exploration encompasses the crewed and uncrewed (robotic) physical exploration of outer space, including celestial bodies such as the Moon and Mars. Typically, these sorts of activities are currently being led by governments and space agencies for scientific purposes, with ESA's Terrae Novae programme aiming to send missions deep into our solar system (ESA, 2022a). Complex, multi-year missions such as this often have commercial components to them, with the Terrae Novae programme being characterised as an 'investment' due to the fact that it will create 'high quality jobs and [...] economic returns [while being a] driver and accelerator for sustainable development' (ESA, 2022a, p. 25). By 2022, the Terrae Novae programme had already generated a 'direct economic impact' of EUR 5.4 billion and had contracted 408 companies and 95 research organisations and generated four commercial services (ESA, 2022a, p. 10).

2.2 *Destination Earth*

2.2.1 Television and Radio

Two important applications of communications satellites[24] are satellite television and radio. Satellite services, such as these, comprise the largest proportion of the commercial space industry (ITA, 2022b). Satellite television, also known as direct broadcast satellite (DBS) television, is the transmission of television programming from a communications satellite in the Earth's orbit directly to an end user's terrestrial location (Fisher et al., 2020). In 2019, satellite television made up roughly one-quarter of the global space economy, being valued at USD 92 billion (BryceTech, 2020). Revenues in this market come from the sale of things like programming subscriptions (pay television), equipment such as receiving antennas (satellite dishes) and set-top boxes, as well as the ongoing maintenance and support services associated with satellite broadcasting. There are currently over one billion

[24] The term 'communications satellite' in the context of this chapter refers to commercial communications satellites which include those manufactured, operated, and used for commercial purposes. This does not exclude the use of commercial communications satellites for military purposes per se, but this chapter does focus more on the civilian use of such satellites (see ITA, 2022b).

subscriptions worldwide to some form of pay television service (Assayag, 2017). Satellite television will likely continue to be a growth market this decade, with a steady increase in the number of pay television subscribers worldwide, as well as the establishment of new television channels, with estimates suggesting that there will be over 53,600 satellite television channels available by 2026 (Assayag, 2017).

Satellite radio, sometimes termed satellite digital audio radio services (SDARS), is a digital broadcasting service where audio signals are transmitted over a wide geographic area to end users[25] (Britannica, 2021). As part of the global space economy, the satellite radio market was valued at USD 6.2 billion in 2019 (BryceTech, 2020). Generally, satellite radio is subscription-based, where consumers purchase a receiver from a broadcasting company and a subscription to their radio programming services (Britannica, 2021). With satellite radio having both increased the accessibility of radio services, especially to customers in remote locations and enlarged the diversity of programming options, satellite radio will likely continue to be a steady growth market this decade.

2.2.2 Telephony and the Internet

Communications satellites are used in the provision of telephony and internet services. Telephony includes the use of satellite telephones, also known as satphones, which are mobile phones that are networked to one another via communications satellites in orbit, as opposed to being connected via terrestrial cell phone towers. There are several leading commercial vendors of satphones, and satphone-related products and services, such as AT&T, INMARSAT, Iridium, etc. These companies often have customer bases in regional or remote parts of the world, where satellite connectivity fares better than landlines or cell towers. In 2019, satellite mobile services worldwide were valued at USD 2 billion (BryceTech, 2020). It has been forecasted that satphone products and services will see steady growth over the next 5 years, with the market set to grow by over USD 137 million (Technavio, 2022).

Satellite internet is wireless internet transmitted by orbiting satellites (typically in LEO) to an end-user location on Earth. This internet technology has existed for several decades; however, over the last 10 years, several companies have planned, built, and operated new satellite systems and constellations to provide global internet access. Notable examples include the satellite internet constellation Starlink which SpaceX operates and the broadband satellite internet constellation operated by OneWeb. As of January 2023, Starlink comprised several thousand satellites and OneWeb several hundred (see Starlink, 2023; OneWeb, 2023). Satellite internet operators such as these have dominated the smallsat market over the last few years, with the two aforementioned companies having launched 1273 out of the 1743 smallsats in 2021 alone—this makes up a 73 per cent 'share of [the total] smallsats

[25] A satellite radio service typically operates via the transmission of a radio signal from a ground-based site to an orbiting satellite, which in turn retransmits the signal back to terrestrial receivers (for instance such as those located in motor vehicles) (see Britannica, 2021).

launched' that year (BryceTech, 2022a, pp. 11, 13). In 2019, satellite broadband worldwide was valued at USD 2.8 billion (BryceTech, 2020). By the end of 2022, Starlink had over 1 million active users of its satellite internet service (Yeo, 2022), with much of this recent growth due to internet services' competitive pricing, ease-of-purchase, easy technical set-up, connectivity in remote geographical regions, high speeds, and low latencies (Deloitte, 2020a). These and other factors will likely drive the continual growth of the satellite internet market.

2.2.3 Data

Assets in space, such as satellites, collect various data sets and types using many different scientific instruments, equipment, sensors, and imaging devices. An example of this is Earth observation (EO), which is the collection of data 'about [the] Earth's physical, chemical and biological systems via remote sensing technologies' (European Commission, 2023). Remote sensing is simply gathering information from afar without making physical contact with the thing or event being observed. In this sense, Earth observation, or remote sensing satellites, image the Earth from space 'by scanning [...] parts of the [electromagnetic] spectrum' (ITA, 2022b), thereby producing photographs, 'measurements and spatial data to monitor and examine' the natural and human-made environment (ASA, 2021, p. 10). The captured EO satellite data is then sent via a downlink transmission to one or more ground stations, where it will be archived, integrated, undergo various levels of processing and transformation, and eventually be analysed by end users for a vast array of different use cases and applications. The application of EO data across society and the economy range from sectors such as farming, minerals exploration, urban planning, logistics, natural disaster management, weather forecasting, 'meteorology, epidemiology, hydrology, climate and environmental sciences' (Dennerley, 2022, pp. 108–109; ASA, 2021, p. 8).

EO satellite data is valuable for several reasons, chief amongst these being that satellites in space can capture large portions of the Earth's surface[26] in a variety of spatial resolutions and wavelengths. By the end of 2022, there were over 1000 EO satellites in orbit (Thorpe, 2022), with each of these satellites creating an increasingly large amount of data that can be exploited for commercial and governmental uses. For example, EO data is utilised to make smarter, faster, and better decisions about how best to prepare for, monitor, and respond to, natural disasters like wildfires and floods, with this data also being used by the insurance industry for risk modelling and claims assessments. EO data also assists farmers in boosting their 'agricultural productivity' by identifying water reserves, monitoring soil and crop health, and informing more efficient 'resource management practices' (see ASA, 2021, pp. 3, 8). Additionally, EO data is used to 'monitor transport networks' such

[26] EO satellites are placed in orbits closer to the Earth like LEO, or further away such as GSO (Thorpe, 2022).

as roads and shipping lanes to improve logistic and supply chain efficiency (Deloitte, 2020a). These are a few real-world uses of EO data that benefit society and the economy. In 2019, commercial remote sensing activities were valued at USD 2.3 billion (BryceTech, 2020). At present, governments are the largest consumers of EO data, and there is an increasingly profitable market for the provision of insights to governments that use EO data sets to inform public policy, support the functions of regulatory bodies, and generally improve administrative decision-making (ASA, 2021, p. 16). Several governments, in partnership with industry, have supported the development of various national and international space data communities and marketplaces, where EO data is made available, often for free, to anyone wanting to use it for commercial, scientific, or research purposes (see Sect. 1.3 above). It is likely that the market for EO and remote sensing data will continue to see strong growth this decade, driven by several factors that include several EO data companies becoming publicly traded entities, increased government focus on climate change and the management of natural disasters as a result of this, EO data's application for defence and national security (maritime and border protection), and EO data's ability to improve 'economic productivity [across a range of different sectors from] agriculture [to] transport' (Deloitte, 2022b, p. 6; ASA, 2021, p. 8).

2.2.4 Mining

Space mining is extracting and utilising valuable resources and materials from objects in space, such as asteroids, moons, or planets. For example, different types of asteroids in our solar system have been identified as containing a high abundance of rare and valuable elements such as gold, platinum, palladium, nickel, iron, cobalt, manganese, etc. (see generally Klas et al., 2015). Space mining in this chapter is found in the Destination Earth category. However, space mining will likely play a role in our global economy and be instrumental in developing a space-based economy where mined raw materials will service deep space exploration missions and lunar and Mars bases. Indeed, there are technical, logistic, and economic issues associated with returning resources and materials from outer space to the Earth, meaning that space mining might first kick-start a 'space-based economy', where raw materials are primarily used for exploration missions and on-orbit activities prior to their eventual return and use in Earth-based economies (Klas et al., 2015, p. 20). This is the case with water, where the extraction of water ice from asteroids and the Moon's poles will likely be a necessary undertaking in the future because access to water will play a vital role in supporting human life in space as well as being utilised to produce propellants (Dahlstrom & Pozza, 2022, pp. 227-228; Peeters, 2021, p. 217).

As an activity, space mining is still in the early and somewhat speculative stages of development, but research and planning are underway. Companies like Moon Express and iSpace have set their sights on the Moon and its lunar resources (Moon Express, 2023; iSpace, 2023). In anticipation of the growth and profitability of the space resources market, countries such as America and Luxembourg have been readying themselves by establishing legal frameworks that will regulate the extraction of space resources, as well as investing in, and partnering with, space mining companies (Tepper, 2019, p. 2; Robison Hasani, 2021, p. 24). Financial modelling estimates that the value of asteroids with 'high concentrations of precious metals' reach into the billions of US dollars, with some asteroids containing roughly USD 50 billion 'worth of platinum' (Tepper, 2019, p. 2; Deloitte, 2022b, p. 7). We will likely continue to see the early stage planning of future space mining missions this decade, with small scientific samples being extracted in the near term from objects such as asteroids[27] and the Moon. Any large-scale commercial space mining operation is still a long way off.

2.3 Supporting Space

2.3.1 Finance and Investment

Space finance and investment represents the capital acquired by space businesses used to undertake their day-to-day space operations and to fund their future growth. Space activities are financed via numerous different public and private funding mechanisms. Governments around the world provide the majority of the financial investment that is directed into the space economy (OECD, 2021, p. 6), typically by funding space policies and programs through the procurement of space-related goods and services, administering competitive tender processes, and issuing grants. For many space companies, governments represent their primary customer base, with the US Government being the largest space industry investor globally (Robison Hasani, 2021, p. 28). Turning toward the private sector, debt and equity financing provided by lenders such as banks, or raising required funds by selling shares, are traditional ways that space businesses have generated the capital needed to finance space activities. Many large and well-known aerospace and defence companies, including some smaller space companies, are publicly traded entities meaning these firms rely on various financial markets to raise money. However, in the NewSpace era, space companies are turning toward different sources of funding. Private investment, by way of venture capital, has been a steadily growing method for raising funds, with cumulative investment in space start-up companies totalling USD 16.6 billion between 2000 and 2018 (Baumann et al., 2018, p. 933). Only a few years later in 2021, USD 15.4 billion was raised by space start-ups alone with USD 9 billion of this being generated by venture capital investments (BryceTech, 2022b, pp. 4, 23). Venture capital, as a private equity financing method, will likely remain a viable means to raise capital, with companies like SpaceX using it to generate USD 2 billion in 2022 (Reuters, 2023).

[27] For example, the Japanese *Hayabusa* spacecraft was the first mission to obtain a material sample from an asteroid that it landed on in 2005 and then returned it to the Earth in 2010 (NASA, 2023).

2.3.2 Legal and Insurance

Space law encompasses the rules that govern and regulate space activities, having application in both international and national settings. International space law governs States and international organisations and is enshrined in a set of five UN multilateral space treaties and five UNGA resolutions.[28] Together, these treaties and resolutions set out primary rules, obligations, and principles, that the subjects of international law, such as States, must observe and comply with when engaged in space activities. Within the national context, there are at present approximately 42 countries with some form of domestic space law or regulation (UNOOSA, 2022), that applies to those space actors (for instance businesses, universities, individuals, foreign nationals, etc.) undertaking space activities in a specific national jurisdiction or related to it. Domestic space law typically takes the form of licencing and permitting regimes that outline what space activities are permissible (or prohibited) and stipulates the conditions under which one may engage in such activities. In reality, domestic space law can cover a wide array of domains, such as regulating the launching (and return) of objects into outer space, the creation and operation of space launch facilities, the allocation and management of radio frequencies (spectrum management), enacting prohibitions on the creation of space debris (and other environmental protections); it can elaborate rules regarding liability and insurance requirements, detail how intellectual property rights are enforced in the context of space activities, highlight duties of consultation and notification, etc.[29]

With this being the case, professional legal and advisory services have emerged as one form of commercial space activity. Space legal services see law firms advising their clients about what legal rights and responsibilities they have in the context of their own space activities. Specifically, space lawyers provide advice to their clients on how to navigate the framework of laws and regulations specific to a legal jurisdiction, explain how to ensure compliance with such laws, represent clients in civil or criminal matters related to space activities, draw up legal contracts and agreements for those parties engaged in space activities, as well as provide advice related to a variety of space business transactions (Department of Industry, Science and Resources, 2023). A separate but often linked service is 'space and satellite insurance, which comprise the provision of insurance products to space actors to protect them, and other parties, by way of certain guarantees and the accessing of compensation in the event of damage, harm or loss that arises in the course of conducting space activities' (Dennerley et al., 2022, p. 7). Often, insurance will be a mandatory requirement under a country's domestic space law and used to cover, or transfer, the financial risks 'of harm or damage that may result from [a] space activity' (Dennerley & Pozza, 2024, p. 143). Numerous global insurers currently offer space and satellite insurance, and with the proliferation of space activities in the

[28] For a full list and complete copies of these space law sources, see United Nations Office for Outer Space Affairs, 2002.

[29] For a detailed discussion of domestic space law in the Australian and New Zealand contexts, see Dennerley and Pozza (2024), Sherborne (2022).

NewSpace era, it is likely that the space insurance market will see steady growth in the coming decade as space businesses seek to ensure they adequately manage the risks associated with their space activities.

2.3.3 Information and Communications Technology

Space activities are highly technical affairs. Space systems, from launch infrastructure to mission control centres, rely on many complex technological systems. Many of these systems are different computer and digital technologies that are broadly characterised as information and communications technology (ICT). Traditionally, space ICT included a wide variety of technologies (hardware and software), tools, techniques, infrastructure, resources, and know-how relevant to the creation, storage, processing, transmission, sharing, linkage, analysis, and archiving (including destruction) of data. Indeed, space ICT has always acted as an enabler for many space industry activities because these activities simply wouldn't be possible without certain computational and digital devices, programs, and systems. One only needs to look at space activities such as Earth observation to see that remote sensing satellites are placed into orbit to collect data about the Earth (see Sect. 2.2.3 on data above), and that the information and insights that this yields, would not be possible without the use of certain ICT systems. Satellite services from Earth observation to satellite broadband and GPS are now considered 'part of the larger digital economy' (Baumann et al., 2018, 939), and this digital economy, in turn, is increasingly reliant on, and interconnected with, the space industry.

In the NewSpace era, it is technology companies that have been forging new approaches to traditional space industry activities, with many technology transfers supporting and enabling novel space products, services, applications, and capabilities. A good example of this is the 'as-a-Service' (aaS) paradigm that has been adopted by, and transferred from, the ICT industry to the space industry. aaS is a business model whereby a company provides a service to its customers without the customer having to be burdened with the services' associated management, operation, and maintenance (for instance the customer will not need to make any significant investments into the service in question nor is there a need for them to organise staffing, facilities, manage assets, etc.). This way, the customer can focus solely on using the service thereby shifting the business focus from ownership and goods to service centricity (Consultancy.eu, 2022) where services are cheaper, more accessible, and available on demand. In the space industry, this business model has found application with Ground-Stations-as-a-Service (GSaaS), where customers operating satellites and/or sensors in orbits such as LEO, can pay to connect to ground stations operated by service providers, thereby eliminating the need to 'build, operate and maintain' their own ground station(s) (Hidalgo, 2023). This significantly reduces mission costs, allows the customer to focus on the space object and its use, provides customers with access to existing and maintained ground infrastructure, and allows the customer to scale up and down operations as required (Hidalgo, 2023). There are several current providers of GSaaS, with Microsoft and Amazon

Web Services (AWS) being two such providers offering a network of fully managed ground stations where customers can operate their space-based assets and transmit/receive satellite data (see Microsoft, 2023; Amazon Web Services, 2023).

As discussed in Sect. 1.3 above, cloud computing is another digital technology that is radically changing how space activities are conducted. Space-based assets, such as satellites, generate prodigious amounts of data. Cloud computing offers solutions to some of the big Earth data challenges associated with the world's massive stores of complex EO data. The key solution that cloud offers is to minimise data storage and processing costs. The aaS business model, discussed above, underpins the cloud service model. The cloud service model sees customers moving from having to self-manage traditional on-premises digital infrastructure to paying an external vendor to supply them either Infrastructure-as-a-Service (IaaS), Platform-as-a-Service (Paas), or Software-as-a-Service (SaaS). These business models provide end users with access to a range of digital services, with some of those relevant to big Earth data being elastic and flexible data storage arrangements, computation and parallel processing of large data sets, analytics tools and platforms, access to application programming interfaces (APIs), having regularly updated cybersecurity services and controls, etc. An example of a dedicated big Earth data 'hosting and processing' platform underpinned by cloud infrastructure is Google Earth Engine, which provides its users with a 'multi-petabyte catalog' of current, and historical, EO data with in-built tools for analysing the data (Google Earth Engine, 2023; Miglarese, 2019). Indeed, the concepts, techniques, and approaches to working with such massive volumes of data, which had originated in the ICT industry, have found their place in the space industry. This is most obvious with data mining, artificial intelligence (AI), and machine learning (ML). Data mining encompasses those techniques used to discover 'interesting patterns and knowledge from [massive] amounts of data' (Han et al., 2012, p. 8) such as EO data. Data mining is often aided by AI and ML. AI is any intelligence demonstrated by machines. ML, which is a subfield of AI, occurs when computers 'improve their performance' (learn) based on data sets made available to them, with the aim of identifying 'complex patterns [and making] intelligent decisions based on the data' (Han et al., 2012, p. 24). ML has implications for the space industry, where, for instance, it can be deployed to analyse satellite imagery to detect disease amongst agricultural crops, estimate crop yields, classify land cover and natural terrain, map human settlements to gauge a region's poverty levels, automate the detection of World Heritage sites from space, as well as a large variety of other Earth Science application (see generally Miglarese, 2019; Lary et al., 2018; ESA, 2023). As these examples demonstrate, there is a technological overlap between the ICT and space industries, where technology transfers and techniques move from one industry to the other, and serve as sources of innovation driving many of the new activities in the NewSpace economy.

2.3.4 Advocacy and Innovation

Space industry groups and associations advocate on behalf of individual space businesses and/or national (and sometimes international) space industries by providing a collective voice and a unified front for their member organisations to interact with each other or specific clients such as governments. Specifically, these sorts of 'association, consortiums or [advocacy] organisations connect space actors [across both the private and public sectors, lobby governments to influence space policy and decision-making], and promote the development and growth of the [...] space industry, or a subset of the industry' (Dennerley et al., 2022, p. 7). Space industry advocates support commercial space activities by working with national governments to shape political and economic factors relevant to the space industry, as well as connecting space actors across business, government, and academia, in both international and domestic settings (see, e.g., Space Industry Association of Australia, 2023).

Innovation in space technology or mission design can come in many guises and can originate from many different parts of the space industry. However, for the purposes of this chapter, it is taken to mean the generation and implementation of practical ideas that introduce novel space goods (technologies), services, techniques, methodologies, etc. This sort of space innovation typically comes from 'academic research and development, which comprise those companies or organisations (for instance universities) undertaking activities that seek to innovate and improve existing space activities or technologies, or introduce new scientific or commercial space-related products, services, applications and capabilities' (Dennerley et al., 2022, p. 7). For example, businesses, universities, or technical institutions may receive funding or grants for the express purpose of scientific research and development with the goal of learning about the space environment, gathering valuable space-related data,[30] improving a specific space technology, optimising a space service, or delivering a new space capability.

3 An Overview of Commercial and Legal Issues

The following chapters in this book present a series of topical case studies on commercial and legal issues of particular relevance to various space activities. These chapters are just a sample of some of the varied and interesting current and emerging trends in the space industry today.

Chapter 2 examines the connection between military and commercial space activities. The dual use nature of space activities and technologies means that commercial space services have an integral role to place within the framework of

[30] For the purposes of this chapter disciplines such as astronomy fit into this space industry category as they typically are associated with a research organisation or the university sector.

military operations. This chapter looks at how commercial space service providers are increasingly being relied upon to provide military space capabilities, and the ways in which the nexus between these two domains overlaps and is tightening. The chapter looks at how international and national laws might serve to regulate commercial space operators in the context of the military uses of outer space and highlights several policy choices that States (and by extension their militaries) should consider when engaging with the commercial space sector.

Chapter 3 examines the risks and opportunities associated with the application of artificial intelligence to the commercial space industry. The chapter covers how AI systems are being integrated into space operations and technologies, and how AI might be applied to future space activities. It also delves into the risks associated with the use of AI in the context of commercial space activities and how these risks might be managed. The chapter has a particular focus on certain regulation and policy—for instance responsible AI principles, the European Union's AI Act, and other AI technical standards. These instruments are designed to regulate the use of AI in the context of the space industry, guide AI's ethical application, manage and mitigate AI related risks, and foster uniformity and interoperability at both international and national levels.

Chapter 4 examines the regulation of satellite constellations. The chapter charts the recent commercial advances in designing, deploying, and operating satellite constellations, which range from tens to sometimes thousands of satellites. The chapter describes how commercial providers of high-speed internet from space, are increasingly embracing the potential of constellations by leveraging the benefits of low-cost production and cheaper access to LEO. Despite the growth of this sector, the chapter highlights the associated legal, environmental, and commercial risks and challenges related to satellite constellations. The chapter pays particular attention to how satellite constellations fit into the current international space legal framework and examines how liability and responsibility might operate in the context of satellite collisions or environmental damage.

Chapter 5 examines the intellectual property (IP) law in the context of the space industry. The chapter discusses the relevance of patent law to space activities and provides a brief history of IP in outer space. The chapter continues by examining the extent to which the intersection between international space law and terrestrial patent law frameworks can provide certainty to space actors on patent protection in the course of undertaking space activities. The ISS serves as this chapter's key example of proven international cooperation especially as it relates to IP law. The chapter also considers future considerations relevant to improving legal certainty with regard to IP and space activities. Finally, the chapter concludes by examining options to strengthen IP law across the space industry.

Chapter 6 examines risk management in the context of the space industry. Specifically, the chapter introduces the notion of a system-of-systems, which entails multiple interrelated and interdependent equipment, elements, or parts (such as systems, subsystems, assemblies, components, etc.) that work together to accomplish specific outcomes. Many space objects, such as satellites, would qualify as a system-of-systems, each entailing varied and complex risks that must be identified, assessed,

Table 1 Chapter reference

Chapter number	Chapter name	Keywords	Intended audience
2	The Connection Between Military and Commercial Space Activities	Space power, international space law, dual use, use of force/armed conflict	Military personnel, policymakers, space lawyers, national security experts
3	Artificial Intelligence, Risk Management, and the Space Industry	Artificial intelligence, risk management, space data, AI regulation, responsible AI, privacy, technical standards for AI	Policymakers, commercial space operators, space data experts, AI service providers, software developers
4	Regulating Satellite Constellations	Satellite constellations, internet from space, environmental regulation, international space law, licences	Satellite operators, space lawyers, policymakers, international organisations, regulatory bodies
5	Patent Law in Outer Space	Intellectual property, patent, trademark, copyright, space law	IP lawyers, space lawyers, policymakers, regulatory bodies, space businesses
6	Space Industry System-of-System Risk Considerations	Systems engineering, system-of-systems, risk management, risk context	Risk management experts, space systems engineers, space lawyers, policymakers, space historians, standards setting bodies

and mitigated. To control these threats, the chapter discusses the concept and practice of system-of-systems hazard analysis and provides several historical examples where risk processes and practices would have been beneficial. Overall, the chapter presents a detailed analysis of the challenges associated with designing and operating complex space missions and objects, and how system-of-systems risk considerations can provide a structured and proactive approach to hazard identification and mitigation (Table 1).

References

Amazon Web Services. (2023). *AWS Ground Station.* https://aws.amazon.com/ground-station/

Assayag, C. (2017, November 8). *Where does the future of satellite TV fit into the future of television?* Viaccess-Orca.

Australian Space Agency. (2021). *Earth observation from space roadmap 2021-2030.* https://www.industry.gov.au/publications/earth-observation-space-roadmap-2021-2030#:~:text=Earth%20observation%20(EO)%20encompasses%20a,and%20the%20infrastructure%20we%20build.

Baumann, I., El Bajjati, H., & Pellander, E. (2018). NewSpace: A wave of private investment in commercial space activities and potential issues under international investment law. *Journal of World Investment & Trade, 19*, 930–950.

Ben-Itzhak, S. (2022, January 11). Companies are commercializing outer space. Do government programs still matter? *The Washington Post.* https://www.washingtonpost.com/politics/2022/01/11/companies-are-commercializing-outer-space-do-government-programs-still-matter/.

Blue Origin. (2015, November 23). *Blue origin makes historic rocket landing*. https://www.blueorigin.com/news/blue-origin-makes-historic-rocket-landing/.

Blue Origin. (2022, August 4). *Blue origin successfully completes 22nd mission to space*. https://www.blueorigin.com/news/ns-22-mission-updates/.

Boeing. (2022). *X-20 Dyna-Soar space vehicle*. https://www.boeing.com/history/products/x-20-dyna-soar.page.

Boley, A. C., & Byers, M. (2021). Satellite mega-constellations create risks in Low Earth Orbit, the atmosphere and on Earth. *Sci Rep, 11*, 10642. https://doi.org/10.1038/s41598-021-89909-7

Britannica, T. Editors of Encyclopaedia. (2014, December 5). Intelsat. *Encyclopedia Britannica*. https://www.britannica.com/topic/Intelsat.

Britannica, T. Editors of Encyclopaedia. (2016, November 28). Michael Melvill. *Encyclopedia Britannica*. https://www.britannica.com/biography/Michael-Melvill.

Britannica, T. Editors of Encyclopaedia. (2021, September 23). Satellite radio. Encyclopedia Britannica. https://www.britannica.com/technology/satellite-radio.

BryceTech. (2020). *2019 Global space economy at a glance*. https://brycetech.com/reports

BryceTech. (2021). *Orbital and suborbital launch sites of the world*. https://brycetech.com/reports.

BryceTech. (2022a). *Smallsats by the numbers 2022*. https://brycetech.com/reports.

BryceTech. (2022b). *Start-up space update on investment in commercial space ventures*. https://brycetech.com/reports.

BryceTech. (2022c). *State of the satellite industry report 2022*. Prepared for the Satellite Industry Association. https://brycetech.com/reports.

BryceTech. (2023). *2022 Global space economy at a glance*. https://brycetech.com/reports.

Bureau of Industry and Security (BIS), U.S. Department of Commerce. (n.d.). *Export administration regulations (EAR)*.

Chatel, F. (2011). Ground segment. In P. W. Fortescue, G. G. Swinerd, & J. P. W. Stark (Eds.), *Spacecraft systems engineering* (pp. 467–494). Wiley.

Cobb, W. W. (2019, March 1). How SpaceX lowered costs and reduced barriers to space. *The Conversation*. https://theconversation.com/how-spacex-lowered-costs-and-reduced-barriers-to-space-112586.

Commercial Space Launch Act. 51 U.S.C. § 50901 et seq. (1984).

Commercial Space Launch Amendments Act. 49 U.S.C. § 70101 et seq. (2004).

Communications Satellite Act. 47 U.S.C. § 701 et seq. (1962).

Consultancy.eu. (2022, March 3). *'As a service' business models: What it is and its benefits*. https://www.consultancy.eu/news/7350/as-a-service-business-models-what-it-is-and-its-benefits.

Coyle, J. J., Langley Jr, C. J., Novack, R. A., & Gibson, B. J. (2013). *Supply chain management: A logistics perspective*. (9th ed.). South-Western, Cengage Learning.

Dahlstrom, E., & Pozza, M. (2022). New risks of future lunar landings. In M. A. Pozza & J. A. Dennerley (Eds.), *Risk management in outer space activities: An Australian and New Zealand perspective*. Springer.

Daly, J. (2020, October 29). *Why cloud and edge are launching the next space race*. IBM. https://www.ibm.com/blogs/industries/ibm-space-tech-cloud-edge-communication-breakthrough/.

Davidian, K. (2021). What makes space activities commercial? *Acta Astronautica, 182*, 547–558.

Deloitte. (2020a). *Space capability positioning Australia at the forefront of the space sector*. https://www2.deloitte.com/au/en/pages/strategy-operations/articles/space-capability.html.

Deloitte. (2020b). *The economics of space transforming life on earth*. https://www2.deloitte.com/content/dam/Deloitte/uk/Documents/consultancy/deloitte-uk-economics-of-space.pdf.

Deloitte. (2022a). *The commercialization of low earth orbit volume 1: The time is now*. https://www2.deloitte.com/content/dam/Deloitte/us/Documents/public-sector/us-gps-the-commercialization-of-leo-vol-1-the-time-is-now.pdf.

Deloitte. (2022b). *The commercialization of low earth orbit volume 2: An orbit for everyone.* https://www2.deloitte.com/content/dam/Deloitte/us/Documents/public-sector/us-gps-the-commercialization-of-leo-vol-2-an-orbit-for-everyone.pdf.

Deloitte. (2022c). *The commercialization of low earth orbit. Volume 3: Making the dream of space travel a reality for private citizens.* https://www2.deloitte.com/content/dam/Deloitte/us/Documents/public-sector/us-gps-the-commercialization-of-leo-vol-3-making-the-dream-of-space-travel-a-reality.pdf.

Dempsey, P. S. (2016). National laws governing commercial space activities: Legislation, regulation, & enforcement. *Northwestern Journal of International Law & Business, 36*(1), 1–44.

Dennerley, J. A. (2018). State liability for space object collisions: The proper interpretation of 'fault' for the purposes of international space law. *The European Journal of International Law, 29*(1), 281–301. https://doi.org/10.1093/ejil/chy003

Dennerley, J. A. (2022). Managing the risks associated with space debris. In M. A. Pozza & J. A. Dennerley (Eds.), *Risk management in outer space activities: An Australian and New Zealand perspective.* Springer.

Dennerley, J. A., & Pozza, M. A. (2024). Regulating commercial space activities in Australia and New Zealand. In L. J. Smith, I. Baumann, & S. Wintermuth (Eds.), *Routledge handbook of commercial space law.* Routledge.

Dennerley, J. A., Young, A., & Pozza, M. A. (2022). An Introduction to risk management in outer space activities. In M. A. Pozza & J. A. Dennerley (Eds.), *Risk management in outer space activities: An Australian and New Zealand perspective.* Springer.

Department of Industry, Science and Resources. (2023). *Space lawyer.* https://www.industry.gov.au/australian-space-discovery-centre/pathways-career-space/space-lawyer.

Driscoll, E. (2021, May 5). *Why "Dollars Per Kilogram" is a poor way to estimate launch costs.* https://spaceflight.com/why-dollars-per-kilogram-is-a-poor-way-to-estimate-launch-costs/.

Equatorial Launch Australia. (n.d.). https://ela.space/.

European Commission. (2018, May 28). *Dual-use trade controls.* https://ec.europa.eu/trade/import-and-export-rules/export-from-eu/dual-use-controls/.

European Commission. (2023, January 12). *Earth observation.* https://joint-research-centre.ec.europa.eu/scientific-activities-z/earth-observation_en#:~:text=Earth%20observation%20is%20the%20gathering,the%20natural%20and%20manmade%20environment.

European Cooperation for Space Standardization. (2008, July 31). ECSS-E-ST-70C Space engineering Ground systems and operations. ECSS Secretariat ESA-ESTEC.

European Space Agency. (2016). *What is space 4.0?* https://www.esa.int/About_Us/Ministerial_Council_2016/What_is_space_4.0.

European Space Agency. (2022a, June). *Terrae Novae 2030+ Strategy Roadmap.* https://esamultimedia.esa.int/docs/HRE/Terrae_Novae_2030+strategy_roadmap.pdf

European Space Agency. (2022b). *Key dates 1960-2018.* https://www.esa.int/About_Us/ESA_history/Key_dates_1960-2018.

European Space Agency. (2022c, November 7). *Space debris by the numbers.* https://www.esa.int/Space_Safety/Space_Debris/Space_debris_by_the_numbers.

European Space Agency. (2023). E*arth observation applications and machine learning for cultural heritage preservation.* https://commercialisation.esa.int/2021/02/earth-observation-applications-and-machine-learning-for-cultural-heritage-preservation/.

Federal Aviation Administration. (2022). *Origins of the commercial space industry.* https://www.faa.gov/about/history/milestones/media/commercial_space_industry.pdf.

Fisher, D. E., Fink, D. G., Marshall, J. F. & Noll, A. M. (2020, January 31). Television. *Encyclopedia Britannica.* https://www.britannica.com/technology/television-technology.

Foust, J. (2022, August 9). SpaceX sees continued strong demand for rideshare missions. *Space News.* https://spacenews.com/spacex-sees-continued-strong-demand-for-rideshare-missions/.

George, K. W. (2019). The economic impacts of the commercial space industry. *Space Policy, 47*, 181–186. https://doi.org/10.1016/j.spacepol.2018.12.003

Gibney, E. (2019). First private Moon lander sparks new lunar space race. *Nature, 566*, 434–436.

GIS Geography. (2022, May 30). *15 Free satellite imagery data sources*. https://gisgeography.com/free-satellite-imagery-data-list/.

Google Earth Engine. (2023). *Google earth engine*. https://earthengine.google.com/.

Han, J., Kamber, M., & Pei, J. (2012). *Data mining concepts and techniques* (3rd ed.). Morgan Kaufmann Publishers.

Harari, Y. N. (2015). *Sapiens. A brief history of humankind*. HarperCollins.

Harrison, G. J. (2012). The commercial space industry and launch market. *Journal of Magnetohydrodynamics, Plasma and Space Research, 17*(3), 183–206.

Heracleous, L., Terrier, D., & Gonzalez, S. (2019). NASA's capability evolution toward commercial space. *Space Policy, 50*, 101330.

Hidalgo, S. (2023). *Ground station as a service: A data guide for space startups*. Cloudflight. https://www.cloudflight.io/en/blog/ground-station-as-a-service-a-data-guide-for-space-startups/.

Highfill, T., Jouard, A., & Franks, C. (2022). *Updated and revised estimates of the U.S. Space Economy*, 2012–2019. Bureau of Economic Analysis US Department of Commerce. https://www.bea.gov/system/files/2022-01/Space-Economy-2012-2019.pdf

Intelsat. (2022a). *About COMSAT*. https://www.intelsat.com/partner/comsat/.

Intelsat. (2022b). *Meet Intelsat 1*. https://www.intelsat.com/meet-intelsat-1/.

Intelsat. (2022c). *Our story*. https://www.intelsat.com/about-us/our-story/.

International Trade Administration. (2022a). *Commercial space market overview*. https://www.trade.gov/commercial-space.

International Trade Administration. (2022b). *Commercial space overview*. https://www.trade.gov/commercial-space

iSpace. (2023, January 14). *About us*. https://ispace-inc.com/aboutus.

Johnson-Freese, J. (2018). Space and national security. In D. S. Reveron, N. K. Gvosdev, & J. A. Cloud (Eds.), *The Oxford handbook of U.S. National Security*. Oxford University Press. https://doi.org/10.1093/oxfordhb/9780190680015.013.36

Jones, H. W. (2018, July 8–12). *The recent large reduction in space launch cost* [Paper Presentation]. 48th International Conference on Environmental Systems, Albuquerque, New Mexico. https://ttu-ir.tdl.org/handle/2346/74082.

Klas, M., Tsafnat, N., Dennerley, J., Beckmann, S., Osborne, B., Dempster, A. G., & Manefield, M. (2015). Biomining and methanogenesis for resource extraction from asteroids. *Space Policy, 34*, 18–22. https://doi.org/10.1016/j.spacepol.2015.08.002

Lal, B. (2013). A brief history of government policies to promote commercial space. *Journal of the Washington Academy of Sciences, 99*(3), 25–41.

Lambright, W. H. (2015). Launching commercial space: NASA, cargo, and policy innovation. *Space Policy, 34*, 23–31. https://doi.org/10.1016/j.spacepol.2015.05.005

Lary, D. J., Zewdie, G. K., Liu, X., Wu, D., Levetin, E., Allee, R. J., Malakar, N., Walker, A., Mussa, H., Mannino, A., & Aurin, D. (2018). Machine learning applications for earth observation. In P.-P. Mathieu & C. Aubrecht (Eds.), *Earth observation open science and innovation* (ISSI scientific report series) (Vol. 15). Springer. https://doi.org/10.1007/978-3-319-65633-5_8

Launch Services Purchase Act. 42 U.S.C. § 2451 et seq. (1990).

Marais, E. (2022, April 9). Axiom launch: why commercial space travel could be another giant leap for air pollution. *The Conversation*. https://theconversation.com/axiom-launch-why-commercial-space-travel-could-be-another-giant-leap-for-air-pollution-180990.

Martin, G. (2015). *NewSpace: The emerging commercial space industry*. NASA Ames Research Center.

McLucas, J. L. (1991). *Space commerce*. Harvard University Press.

Mell, P., & Grance, T. (2011). *The NIST definition of cloud computing. Special Publication 800-145*. National Institute of Standards and Technology. https://nvlpubs.nist.gov/nistpubs/Legacy/SP/nistspecialpublication800-145.pdf.

Microsoft. (2023). *Azure orbital ground station*. https://azure.microsoft.com/en-au/products/orbital/#layout-container-uid189e.

Miglarese, A. H. (2019, April 23). How Earth observations, cloud computing, and machine learning enables global development solutions. *Medium*. https://medium.com/radiant-earth-insights/how-earth-observations-cloud-computing-and-machine-learning-enables-global-development-solutions-9ad1c2e60762.
Moon Express. (2023, January 14). *Redefine Possible*. https://moonexpress.com/.
Morgan Stanley. (2020). *Space: Investing in the Final Frontier*. https://www.morganstanley.com/ideas/investing-in-space.
National Aeronautics and Space Administration. (2008). *First human-made object to enter space*. https://www.nasa.gov/mission_pages/explorer/bumper.html.
National Aeronautics and Space Administration. (2012). J*uly 12, 1962: The day information went global*. https://www.nasa.gov/topics/technology/features/telstar.html.
National Aeronautics and Space Administration. (2017a). *Commercial orbital transportation services (COTS)*. https://www.nasa.gov/commercial-orbital-transportation-services-cots.
National Aeronautics and Space Administration. (2017b). *Space Shuttle Era*. https://www.nasa.gov/mission_pages/shuttle/flyout/index.html.
National Aeronautics and Space Administration. (2019a). *Commercial crew program—essentials*. https://www.nasa.gov/content/commercial-crew-program-the-essentials.
National Aeronautics and Space Administration. (2019b). *The National Advisory Committee for Aeronautics*. https://www.nasa.gov/ames/the-national-advisory-committee-for-aeronautics
National Aeronautics and Space Administration. (2022). Commercial Lunar payload services overview. https://www.nasa.gov/content/commercial-lunar-payload-services-overview
National Aeronautics and Space Administration. (2023). *Hayabusa*. https://www.jpl.nasa.gov/missions/hayabusa
Northrop Grumman. (2022). *Pegasus*. https://www.northropgrumman.com/space/pegasus-rocket/
Odom, B. C. (2021, March 17–19). *NASA and the rise of commercial space* [Paper presentation]. NASA and the Rise of Commercial Space: A Symposium to Examine the Meaning(s) and Context(s) of Commercial Space. https://www.nasa.gov/sites/default/files/atoms/files/space_portal_brian_odom.pdf.
Office of Space Commerce. (2020, December 9). *National Space Policy of the United States of America*. https://www.space.commerce.gov/policy/national-space-policy/.
OneWeb. (2023, January 11). *Our story*. https://oneweb.net/about-us/our-story
Organisation for Economic Co-operation and Development. (2020, October 7). *Measuring the economic impact of the space sector key indicators and options to improve data*. Background paper for the G20 Space Economy Leaders' Meeting (Space20). Saudi Arabia.
Organisation for Economic Co-operation and Development. (2021, September 20-21). *Space economy for people, planet and prosperity*. OECD paper for the G20 Space Economy Leaders' Meeting. Italy.
Orlitzky, M. (2021, December 22). Free market. *Encyclopedia Britannica*. https://www.britannica.com/topic/free-market.
Outer Space Act. (1986).
Outer Space and High-altitude Activities Act. (2017).
Peeters, W. (2021). Evolution of the space economy: Government space to commercial space and new space. *Astropolitics, 19*(3), 206–222. https://doi.org/10.1080/14777622.2021.1984001
Pozza, M. A., & Dennerley, J. A. (2022). *Risk management in outer space activities: An Australian and New Zealand perspective*. Springer.
President's Commission on Implementation of United States Space Exploration Policy. (2004). *A journey to inspire, innovate, and discover*. https://www.nasa.gov/pdf/60736main_M2M_report_small.pdf.
Reuters. (2023, March 23). Saudi, UAE investors plan to invest in SpaceX—the information. *Reuters*. https://www.reuters.com/business/aerospace-defense/saudi-uae-investors-plan-invest-spacex-information-2023-03-22/#:~:text=The%20funding%20round%20is%20expected,venture%20capital%20firm%20Space%20Capital.

Robison Hasani, K. (2021). The next Frontier of the global commons. In M. de Zwart & S. Henderson (Eds.), *Commercial and military uses of outer space* (pp. 19–32). Springer Nature. https://doi.org/10.1007/978-981-15-8924-9_3

Rose, G. (2023, June 16). *Virgin Galactic announces start of commercial spaceflight service*. https://www.virgin.com/about-virgin/latest/virgin-galactic-announces-start-of-commercial-spaceflight-service.

Schwartz, H. (1965). Governmentally appointed directors in private corporation: The communications satellite act of 1962. *Harvard Law Review, 79*(2), 350–364.

Sheehan, M. (2007). *The international politics of space*. Routledge Taylor & Francis Group.

Sherborne, A. K. E. (2022). The commercialisation of space: An overview of legal risks and considerations. In M. A. Pozza & J. A. Dennerley (Eds.), *Risk management in outer space activities: An Australian and New Zealand perspective*. Springer.

Southern Launch. (n.d.). https://www.southernlaunch.space/.

Space (Launches and Returns) Act. (2018).

Space Industry Association of Australia. (2023). *About the SIAA*. https://www.spaceindustry.com.au/about/.

Space Policy Online. (2022, October 11). *Commercial space activities*. https://spacepolicyonline.com/topics/commercial-space-activities/.

SpaceX. (2022). *Falcon 9*. https://www.spacex.com/vehicles/falcon-9/.

Stark, J. P. W., Swinerd, G. G., & Tatnall, A. R. L. (2011). Introduction. In P. W. Fortescue, G. G. Swinerd, & J. P. W. Stark (Eds.), *Spacecraft systems engineering* (pp. 467–494). Wiley.

Starlink. (2023, January 11). *World's most advanced broadband satellite internet*. https://www.starlink.com/technology.

Straub, J., & Vacek, J. J. (2014). Reforming regulation of basic and small business research and education in space technologies under ITAR (International Traffic in Arms Regulations) and EAR (Export Administration Regulations). *Journal of Space Law, 39*(2), 351–378.

Sudmanns, M., Tiede, D., Lang, S., Bergstedt, H., Trost, G., Augustin, H., Baraldi, A., & Blaschke, T. (2020). Big Earth data: disruptive changes in Earth observation data management and analysis? *International Journal of Digital Earth, 13*(7), 832–850. https://doi.org/10.1080/17538947.2019.1585976

Technavio. (2022, November 26). *Satellite phone market size to increase by USD 137.43 Million: 33% growth to originate from APAC—Technavio*. https://www.prnewswire.com/news-releases/satellite-phone-market-size-to-increase-by-usd-137-43-million-33-growth-to-originate-from-apac%2D%2D-technavio-301687206.html.

Tepper, E. (2019). Structuring the discourse on the exploitation of space resources: Between economic and legal commons. *Space Policy, 49*, 101290. https://doi.org/10.1016/j.spacepol.2018.06.004

The Guardian. (2022, April 9). First all-private astronaut team lifts off for ISS in milestone SpaceX flight. *The Guardian*. https://www.theguardian.com/science/2022/apr/09/first-all-private-astronaut-team-lifts-off-for-iss-in-milestone-spacex-flight.

The Guardian. (2024, February 23). US returns to lunar surface for first time in over 50 years: 'Welcome to the moon'. *The Guardian*. https://www.theguardian.com/science/2024/feb/22/us-moon-landing-odysseus-intuitive-machines.

Thorpe, E. (2022, November 12). *Earth Observation Satellites Imagery: Types, Application, And Future Trends*. https://orbitaltoday.com/2022/03/05/earth-observation-satellites-imagery-types-application-and-future-trends/.

Treaty on Principles Governing the Activities of States in the Exploration and Use of Outer Space, Including the Moon and Other Celestial Bodies (Outer Space Treaty) 1967, 610 UNTS 205.

U.S. Department of State. (n.d.). International Traffic in Arms Regulations (ITAR).

Union of Concerned Scientists. (2022, May 1). *UCS Satellite Database*. https://www.ucsusa.org/resources/satellite-database.

United Nations Committee on the Peaceful Uses of Outer Space. (2022, March 28). *Status of international agreements relating to activities in outer space as at 1 January 2022*, 61st sess, UN Doc. A/AC.105/C.2/2022/CRP.10*. https://www.unoosa.org/res/oosadoc/data/documents/2022/aac_105c_22022crp/aac_105c_22022crp_10_0_html/AAC105_C2_2022_CRP10E.pdf.

United Nations General Assembly. (2004, December 10). *Resolution adopted by the general assembly*, UN GAOR 59th sess, agenda item 74, UN Doc. A/RES/59/115.

United Nations Office for Outer Space Affairs. (2002). *United Nations treaties and principles on outer space*, ST/SPACE/11.

United Nations Office for Outer Space Affairs. (2022). *National Space Law.* https://www.unoosa.org/oosa/en/ourwork/spacelaw/nationalspacelaw/index.html.

Werner, D. (2021, June 24). Software-as-a-Service model takes the space sector by storm. *Space News*. https://spacenews.com/space-as-a-service-model/

White House. (2017, December 11). *Presidential memorandum on reinvigorating America's human space exploration program.* https://trumpwhitehouse.archives.gov/presidential-actions/presidential-memorandum-reinvigorating-americas-human-space-exploration-program/.

Wikipedia. (2022, November 11). *2021 in spaceflight.* https://en.wikipedia.org/wiki/2021_in_spaceflight#:~:text=2021%20saw%20several%20spaceflight%20related,in%20space%20at%20one%20time.

Yeo, A. (2022, December 19). *SpaceX's Starlink announces it now has 1 million users.* https://mashable.com/article/starlink-spacex-1-million-users#:~:text=Apparently%20a%20lot%20of%20people,Elon%20Musk's%20internet%20service%20provider.&text=SpaceX%20has%20announced%20that%20its,over%201%20million%20active%20subscribers

Joel A. Dennerley, BA, LLB (Hons), M App Dat An., is a management consultant and is the co-editor of the book *Risk Management in Outer Space Activities: An Australian and New Zealand Perspective.*

The Connection Between Military and Commercial Space Activities

Dale Stephens and Mark Giddings

1 Introduction

Military ascendancy in the space domain is a goal of many States (see Lopez, 2019; Fallon, 2022; Brunner, 2021). Increasingly, States include within their military forces a dedicated space element, and their pursuit of space power finds expression in their military doctrine (see United States Department of Defense, 2020; Office of General Counsel, 2023, pp. 953–958 [14.10]; Australian Government Department of Defence [Defence], 2022; United Kingdom Ministry of Defence, 2022; The French Ministry for the Armed Forces, 2019; New Zealand Ministry of Defence, 2022; High Representative of the Union for Foreign Affairs and Security Policy, 2023).[1] This is not surprising as military activities and space exploration have been connected from the outset. This connection has developed into a recognition of space as a dedicated military theatre of operations, and as an enabling domain for

The views of the authors are the authors' alone and are intended to provide commentary and general information, and do not represent the views of any organisation. This chapter should not be relied upon as a substitute for professional legal advice or for any other purpose. The authors would like to thank Ms. Joanna Jarose for her research assistance in the drafting of this chapter, noting that any errors in the chapter are solely the responsibility of the authors.

[1] For a detailed country-by-country assessment, see Weeden and Samson (2023).

D. Stephens (✉)
The University of Adelaide, Adelaide, SA, Australia
e-mail: dale.stephens@adelaide.edu.au

M. Giddings
LK Law, Adelaide, SA, Australia

J. A. Dennerley, M. A. Pozza (eds.), *The Business of Outer Space*, Space Law and Policy, https://doi.org/10.1007/978-981-95-2034-3_2

the integration of space assets and services into the conduct of all military operations whether they are occurring at sea, on land, in the air, or in cyberspace (United Nations General Assembly [UNGA], 2021, p. 5 [7]). As summarised by the United Kingdom (UK) Ministry of Defence:

> Space is a key enabler for Defence operations and is now an operational domain in its own right (alongside cyber, maritime, air and land). It is also fundamental to our aspiration to integrate across those five domains. Space enables our ability to command and control globally, provide surveillance, intelligence and missile warning, as well as support deployed Joint forces. (United Kingdom Ministry of Defence, 2022, p. 6)

Such reliance and integration require access to effective, resilient, and durable space services. In this context, commercial space services find an integral place within the framework of military operations. Capabilities critical to military operations include those relating to communications, navigation, optical and non-optical imaging, intelligence collection, and data transfer (New Zealand Ministry of Defence, 2022, p. 3). Commercial service providers are heavily relied on to provide these capabilities because of their cost effectiveness, widespread availability, and technical sophistication. Accessing a diversity of commercial vendors provides increased flexibility and redundancy, even to militaries with dedicated systems, such as the United States (US) (see National Reconnaissance Office [NRO], 2023). For militaries with more limited systems, such as Australia, reliance on commercial service providers, in conjunction with the military is unavoidable.

Such a close connection necessarily raises considerable legal and policy issues. These include legal challenges in safeguarding the transfer of space technology, ensuring the security and resilience of commercial assets servicing the military, managing the international legal responsibility of States for the conduct of private commercial entities in space, and dealing with issues of attribution concerning the use of force and the law of armed conflict. These issues are complicated by the unique legal regime that applies to space within international law. These rules require close assessment now and will only become more complex in the near future given plans by a number of commercial entities to engage in off-world mining and the establishment of semi-permanent settlements on the Moon and on other celestial bodies (Astroforge, 2023; Jamasmie, 2023; Fettes, 2023; SpaceX, 2023).

This chapter addresses these key issues and provides an outline and critique of the state of the law (both international and domestic law). It considers the policy choices that need to be carefully navigated by States seeking to leverage the commercial space sector in support of their sovereign space capability and in pursuit of projecting power in the space domain. The chapter considers developments in a range of jurisdictions but has a particular focus on the intersection of military and commercial space activities in Australia.

2 Commercialisation of Space and Connections with Defence

For many decades space exploration and use was the exclusive province of States, which were able to undertake the considerable investment of budget resources with accompanying technological capacity. The military saw the value in space capability from the very beginning of the space age (Harrison et al., 2017; Lambeth, 2004). Having the capacity (and legal ability) to observe and verify a potential adversary's military forces, weapons systems, and disposition provided a key strategic advantage (Bosker, 2003). This was recognised early by both the Soviet Union and the United States.

Space power as a concept has evolved considerably since the late 1950s and is now recognised as an important component of a State's military preparedness. Space is an independent operational environment (along with sea, land, air, and cyberspace) (see North Atlantic Treaty Organization [NATO], 2019; New Zealand Ministry of Defence, 2018, p. 7; Defence, 2020c, p. 96; Stokes et al., 2020, p. 9) and is a supported theatre of operations. Military space operations and space warfare also finds expression in State military law manuals and evolving doctrine (see United States Department of Defense, 2020; Office of General Counsel, 2023, pp. 953–958 [14.10]; Defence, 2022; United Kingdom Ministry of Defence, 2022; The French Ministry for the Armed Forces, 2019; New Zealand Ministry of Defence, 2022; High Representative of the Union for Foreign Affairs and Security Policy, 2023). The concept of space as an operational domain underpinned the work of the *Woomera Manual* project (The University of Adelaide, n.d.), which was an international academic exercise dedicated to developing a Manual dealing with the international law applicable to military space activities and operations and whose work has received considerable logistical support from a number of States.

In recent decades, commercial operators have readily entered the space field. Costs of launch have fallen considerably and the technology to undertake complex space operations has correspondingly advanced in tandem (Roberts, 2022). The global space economy was assessed to be worth approximately US$546 billion in 2023—representing a 91% increase in the past decade (Space Foundation Editorial Team, 2023). Indeed, Morgan Stanley projects that the industry will be worth over US$1 trillion by 2040 (Morgan Stanley, 2020). Commercial space activity presently accounts for almost 80% of the total space economy (Space Foundation Editorial Team, 2023).

Commercial space activity is well placed to provide space services relating to, inter alia, navigation, communications, intelligence gathering, data transfer, remote sensing, and imaging (Defence Space Command, 2022, p. 4; New Zealand Ministry of Defence, 2022, p. 3). Military forces have identified and integrated these services into their tactics, techniques, and procedures. The satellites and other space objects providing these services are thus 'dual use' as they are integral to the conduct of military operations (see generally UNGA, 2021; Ortega, 2023; Hitchens, 2022).

Given the emergence of space as an identified theatre of operations, it is not surprising that it has found focussed expression in numerous government white papers.

In particular, Japan and India have invested significantly in their space operations, and both stand as major actors in the Asian and Indo-Pacific region (Armstrong, 2023; Steer, 2021; Ireland-Piper, 2022). Australia's own intentions with regard to an increased focus on space were manifested in the 2020 Defence Strategic Update (Defence, 2020a, pp. 38–9), the 2020 Force Structure Plan (Defence, 2020b, pp. 61–3), and, more recently, the 2023 Defence Strategic Review (Defence, 2023, p. 62). Together, they confirm that Australia is moving towards acquiring assets and sovereign capability in space. Such capability is presently undefined but will almost certainly include reliance upon commercial providers and services.

Correlatively, in acquiring and bolstering this capability, there is also deep consideration given to their defence strategies that will deter attacks against Australian assets in space. In particular, Air Vice Marshal Cath Roberts highlighted in March 2023 that 'Australia is working on a plan to acquire "soft-kill" capabilities to take out enemy satellites without creating dangerous debris' (Greene, 2023b). Such terminology in the context of counterspace capability refers to the distinction between using non-kinetic means to degrade capability such as electromagnetic jamming[2] and spoofing[3] as 'soft kill' and actual physical attacks that are defined as 'hard kill'.

Given the increasingly central role that commercial satellites play within the conduct of military operations, it is no surprise that military forces are actively considering a broad range of 'destructive and non-destructive counterspace capabilities' (Weeden & Samson, 2023, p. xvi). The role that international law plays in the defence and attack of commercial satellites will be canvassed in Part 4 of this chapter. Such an international framework is also underpinned by an extensive domestic legal framework that outlines Australian governance and control of commercial space capability: this will be fully canvassed in the next Part. Commercial providers of space services to the military may be subject to additional compliance requirements and regulation to ensure national security priorities are maintained; it may be fairly asked whether such control can act as a disincentive to such providers (Kearney, 2023; Bernstein, 2023). Such an outcome is obviously concerning given the immense capacity of commercial services to facilitate the realisation of strategic goals.

Finally, an emerging future area where commercial activity may have a key impact upon national security and thus military actions is in relation to off-world mining. While such an endeavour is not yet possible, activity in the field is increasing as commercial start-ups seek to develop a viable process (David, 2023; Jamasmie, 2023). Resources in space are nearly infinite and if humanity is to be an

[2] Jamming is '[t]he deliberate radiation, reradiation, or reflection of electromagnetic energy for the purpose of preventing or reducing an enemy's effective use of the electromagnetic spectrum, with the intent of degrading or neutralizing the enemy's combat capability' (see Office of the Chairman of the Joint Chiefs of Staff, 2021, p. 70).

[3] Spoofing attacks 'deceive a [Global Navigation Satellite System ('GNSS')] receiver by broadcasting incorrect GNSS signals, structured to resemble a set of normal GNSS signals, or by rebroadcasting genuine signals captured elsewhere or at a different time' (see INTERTANKO, 2019, p. 5).

inter-planetary species, then feasible space mining processes are a necessary prerequisite. There is continuing controversy as to whether mining is a lawful activity under the *Treaty on Principles Governing the Activities of States in the Exploration and Use of Outer Space, including the Moon and Other Celestial Bodies*, referred to as the Outer Space Treaty (OST) (Outer Space Treaty [OST], 1967), where the question appears to be whether such mining constitutes a violation of the Article II non-appropriation prohibition (OST, 1967, Article II; Jakhu & Nyampong, 2016; Ganatra & Modi, 2015–2016, pp. 95–96; International Bar Association, 2023).

It would appear that States are undertaking both unilateral domestic actions as well as collective international actions to provide a legal foundation for such mining. The United States, United Arab Emirates, Japan, and Luxembourg all have passed domestic laws authorising their nationals to undertake mining activity (see Space Resource Exploration and Utilization Act of 2015; Luxembourg, 2017; Library of Congress, 2021; United Arab Emirates, 2019). In addition, the United States is leading the Artemis Accords (National Aeronautics and Space Administration [NASA], 2020) process that seeks to implement many of the provisions of the OST. Included within the Artemis Accords are provisions that expressly permit the conduct of off-world mining (by States and/or private companies) and provide for a basic structure for undertaking such activity (NASA, 2020, pp. 4–5 (Section 10)).

Should off-world mining occur, it will be against a background of Article II of the OST that does not countenance claims of sovereignty[4] and hence opens up the possibility of tension and clashes between private companies undertaking such activity. There will, therefore, need to be a security element that ensures that order is maintained, and incidents not escalate. This implicates Article IV of the OST which prohibits the establishment of military bases, fortifications, or installations on the Moon or on a celestial body.[5] Hence, if it is anticipated that military members will provide security oversight there would appear to be an obvious basis for protest by other States if the military contingent is housed in a habitat that could be construed as a base, fortification, or installation. The OST provides no definition of these terms, and hence until there is subsequent State agreement or practice (*Vienna Convention on the Law of Treaties* [VCLT], 1969, Articles 31(3), 32), it is unclear whether military members may provide such security. However, even the presence of private security personnel could have potential risks: as will be discussed in Part 5, the actions of companies and other non-State entities are the direct responsibility of the State under Article VI of the OST. Accordingly, there is an ever-present risk that a forceful action between private entities in space could be construed as a violation of the UN Charter (United Nations [UN], 1945) giving rise to a national right

[4] Article II reads, 'Outer space, including the moon and other celestial bodies, is not subject to national appropriation by claim of sovereignty, by means of use or occupation, or by any other means' (OST, 1967, Article II).

[5] Article IV reads, 'The establishment of military bases, installations and fortifications, the testing of any type of weapons and the conduct of military manoeuvres on celestial bodies shall be forbidden' (OST, 1967, Article IV).

to respond via countermeasures or even armed force. Hence, there may be serious consequences for not getting this right from the outset.

3 The Commercial Space Sector as an Enabler of Space Power and Sovereign Space Capability

From the early 2000s onwards, the commercial space sector had become an increasingly important enabler of national space power and capability. In the United States, since the retirement of NASA's space shuttle fleet in 2011, NASA has relied on commercial provider SpaceX to carry out launches to the International Space Station (ISS), while commercially operated launches have become the only means of launch for privately owned payloads (see Federal Aviation Administration [FAA], n.d.). More recently, SpaceX and Blue Origin were selected by NASA to provide human landing systems to transport astronauts to the surface of the Moon as part of the Artemis program (see O'Shea, 2023; NASA, 2021). These examples are illustrative of a shift in ways in which States develop and maintain space power.

During the Cold War, space power largely depended on national programs directed, funded, and carried out by States. Spaceports were State-operated facilities for the launching of government-owned launch vehicles. Research and development were directed in pursuit of national interests, with a strong focus on national security (see Handberg & Johnson-Freese, 1998, pp. 91–110). The indicators of relative space power included the number and size of launches, the achievement of various firsts (such as the first satellite placed in orbit or the first crewed mission), and the pace and scale of the deployment of military support technologies (Moltz, 2019, p. 69).

Describing the model of space power during this period, Moltz has characterised it as a 'technocracy' embodying the 'institutionalization of technological change for state purposes' (Moltz, 2019, p. 70 citing McDougall, 1985, p. 5). Space power was pursued through top-down military-led development, the maintenance of national independence and secrecy in relation to rival space programs, and a focus on the creation of relatively large space platforms. Private companies were subordinated within this technocratic ecosystem. This model of space power developed in circumstances where, throughout much of the 1960s, the United States and the USSR were the only spacefaring nations, and there was a direct rivalry between the two.

The launch of Australia's first satellite, WRESAT, typified this technocratic approach. The development of WRESAT was undertaken as a joint venture between a government agency, the Weapons Research Establishment, and the University of Adelaide, a publicly funded University. This project was also supported by the US Department of Defense, NASA, and the UK Ministry of Technology. In 1967, WRESAT was launched from the Commonwealth operated Woomera Rocket Range located in South Australia.

While the international framework of space treaties concluded between 1963 and 1979 did not prohibit the involvement of private enterprise, it established the principle that States were responsible for national space activities, including the acts of individuals and private companies (see Isnardi, 2020, pp. 489–530). This reinforced the role of States as the primary actors in relation to space. The proper role and scope for private commercial actors was left largely undefined, except by reference to a number of broad statements regarding permitted activities (such as exploration and scientific investigation) and a small number of specific prohibitions (such as prohibitions on placing nuclear weapons in orbit or subjecting celestial bodies to claims of national appropriation).

Domestic legislation reflected this approach. Australia was the sixth nation to enact legislation regulating space activities. The *Space Activities Act 1998* (Cth) (*Space Activities Act*) gave effect to obligations under the five space treaties, which were incorporated as schedules to that Act. The focus of the Act was on ensuring Australia's compliance with its international obligations to authorise and supervise activities of non-governmental entities.

Although the *Space Activities Act* was partly a response to proposals from private industry to establish commercial space launch facilities at Christmas Island, Woomera, and Cape York, the Act was not commercially encouraging (see generally Freeland, 2017, pp. 507–533). It prohibited the operation of launch facilities, and the carrying out of launches and returns, without a licence, and it imposed a minimum insurance requirement of $750 million on entities conducting launches from Australia. This made participation in the space sector out of reach for all but the most well-funded private entities.

Following that enactment, the anticipated establishment of commercial launch facilities failed to occur, and there was limited progress towards the establishment of Australian commercial space industry. As recently as 2013, the policy of the Australian government assumed the inevitability of Australia's reliance on international support for access to space, stating that 'the Australian Government does not see an Australian satellite manufacturing or launch capability as an essential element of its approach to assured access to critical space-enabled services' (Australian Government, 2013, p. 11).

However, rapid commercialisation in the space industry has led to a marked shift in policy. Six years later in 2019, the far more ambitious *Australian Civil Space Strategy 2019–2028* identified the need to '[d]evelop a world-class regulatory system that enables entrepreneurship while ensuring national safety and security, including cyber security, and meeting international and national obligations' (Australian Space Agency [ASA], 2019). The strategy called for 'a timetable for regulatory reform to enable launch to space from Australia and the foundations for human space flight from Australia' (ASA, 2019, p. iv) and expressly recognised that 'Australia's civil space businesses can provide capability to support our national defence capability' (ASA, 2019, p. 6). This was followed by *Australia's Defence Space Strategy* in 2022, which identified that a line of effort is to 'advance sovereign space capability to support the development of a sustainable national space enterprise' (Defence, 2022).

As evident from these policy developments, the commercial space sector is now seen as integral to national space capability. Other countries have been even more explicit in recognising and developing this connection. The new model of space power emerging from the intersection of commercial and governmental activities has been charactered as a 'netocracy' based on 'public-private partnerships, distributed architectures, rapid innovation, and the use of multiple commercial and allied partnerships' (Moltz, 2019, p. 78). The defining features of the space-related 'netocracy' are rapid bottom-up innovation, a focus on international cooperation with increased transparency, and the creation of many smaller platforms leading to increased resilience (Moltz, 2019).

The challenge for States, such as Australia, that seek to promote and grow their domestic space industry is to find a regulatory balance between encouraging enterprise while also ensuring responsible behaviour by private actors and complying with obligations imposed on States by international law. Where the regulatory burden and the associated compliance costs imposed by domestic legislation are excessive, States risk stifling entrepreneurship and losing out to more commercially attractive jurisdictions.

To this end, in 2018 the Australian government amended the *Space Activities Act* to open up access to small and medium enterprises. The renamed *Space (Launches and Returns) Act 2018 (Cth)* (*Space (Launches and Returns) Act* [SLAR Act], 2018) lowered the insurance requirements for launch licences and removed other monetary barriers to participation in the space industry. It also established the Australian Space Agency and sought to accommodate technological developments in the way payloads are launched. These amendments were broadly seen as positive developments by relevant stakeholders.

There are now a number of Australian companies seeking to establish a sovereign launch capability, including Equatorial Launch Australia, Gilmour Space Technologies, and Southern Launch. In 2022, three suborbital NASA rockets were launched from Equatorial Launch Australia's site in the Northern Territory. There are also a number of Australian companies operating constellations of small satellites including Skykraft, Fleet Space Technologies, and Myriota.

The *Defence Strategic Review 2023* identified that '[a]s Australia's civil and military space capabilities progress, Defence must consider the level of sovereign capability needs' (Defence, 2023, p. 62 [8.49]). The caveat to this is stated to be that the desirability for developing sovereign capability 'must be offset by the cost requirements of such capabilities against opportunities to collaborate with the United States and other partners' (Defence, 2023, p. 62 [8.49]). In this regard, *Australia's Defence Space Strategy* (2022) acknowledges that in light of Australia's limited sovereign space capability it is necessary to leverage agreements with international partners (Defence, 2022, p. 12).

While international collaboration is of great importance, Australia's access to space will remain vulnerable to the extent that it depends on international partners.

Unpredictable factors such as geopolitical instability, armed conflict, and market disruptions can restrict access to launch facilities and heighten competition for remaining launch capacities, such that Australia could find itself unable to launch its payloads into orbit. For example, the fallout from Russia's invasion of the Ukraine in 2022 included Russian authorities denying foreign access to Russian-controlled launch facilities in Kazakhstan. This led to a reduction of 15–20% in large payload launch capacity globally (Organisation for Economic Co-operation and Development [OECD], 2022).

The United States has sought to address its need for continuity of access to space services under a program called the Commercial Augmentation Space Reserve (CASR) (Erwin, 2023). This will entail a series of agreements with private companies to ensure that services such as satellite communications and remote sensing are prioritised for use by the US government during national security emergencies. The CASR makes strategic sense for the United States, but has negative implications for States such as Australia, which could see Australian space missions being de-prioritised during a time of critical need.

Establishing a sovereign space industry with the ability to design, construct, launch, and operate satellites would ensure that Australia has access to space, even in the face of disruptions in the global market or other unforeseen circumstances beyond Australia's control. If Australia is to do this effectively, it will need to keep its regulation under review in order to remain competitive and to encourage entrepreneurship. At the same time, government and defence will need to provide meaningful opportunities for Australian companies to supply space services and to thereby grow the domestic commercial space sector.

4 Export Controls, Technology Transfer, and the Security of Critical Infrastructure

As participation in the space sector by private commercial companies grows, and the space enterprise becomes increasingly decentralised, States are faced with the challenge of maintaining security over space technology and space systems. Particular risks include the open and networked commercial ecosystem, the cross-border nature of supply chains and markets, and the uneven levels of security awareness and maturity among commercial providers. Legal and policy responses have taken a number of forms, including controls over the export of space technology, international partnership arrangements regulating technology transfer, and critical infrastructure legislation imposing security obligations on private companies.

The purpose of export controls is to ensure that the export of defence and dual-use goods, software, and technologies aligns with States' national interests, international obligations, and efforts to maintain peace and stability. Just how proscriptive a particular jurisdiction's export control regime is will depend on a wide range of factors, resulting in considerable variation among different jurisdictions. While the avowed focus of such regimes is on protecting security interests, there are often politico-economic factors at play, with States using export controls as a form of protectionism. However, onerous export controls can be a double-edged sword, protecting and preferencing domestic companies in some instances, but also potentially preventing those same companies from competing in foreign markets (see Center for International and Security Studies at Maryland, 2023).

Many activities undertaken by the Australian space industry require an export authorisation of some form, whether from Australia or another jurisdiction. The export of space technology from Australia is controlled under the Defence and Strategic Goods List (2021) (Cth). In particular, many items of space technology are listed on the dual use goods list.[6] Accordingly, an Australian company must obtain a permit from Defence Export Controls before engaging in a range of activities, such as sending space technology overseas, using overseas launch facilities, or collaborating with foreign partners on space-related research.

The Australian space sector is highly dependent on space technology produced by international partners, including the United States. The export of US space technology is controlled under the *US International Traffic in Arms Regulations* (ITAR) and the *Export Administration Regulations* (EAR) (U.S. Department of State, n.d.; Bureau of Industry and Security (BIS), U.S. Department of Commerce, n.d.). As such, a US licence is often required from the US Department of State before companies in the Australian space industry can receive, access, or use US space technology. There are a number of features of the US regime that make it particularly onerous. For example, unlike Australian export controls that only regulate exports from Australia, the US regime regulates re-exports extraterritorially.

A number of international arrangements between States seek to ensure that the transfer of space technology does not lead to the development or enhancement of adverse military capabilities that could undermine national security. These include the *Wassenaar Arrangement on Export Controls for Conventional Arms and Dual-Use Goods and Technologies* (The Wassenar Arrangement, 2023) and the *Missile Technology Control Regime* (Missile Technology Control Regime, 2023). Australia is a participant in both regimes, which are aimed at fostering a level of harmonisation in the approaches to export controls among members.

While export controls serve the security interests of exporting States, such interests need to be balanced against the business interests of private enterprise. In particular, the commercial space industry has been critical of export controls imposing burdensome impediments on the sharing of technology (Aerospace Industries Association [AIA], 2023; Citowicki, 2022). This is not surprising given that the modern space industry is inherently cross-border, relying on international supply chains for specialised parts and components, access to foreign governments for

[6] See in particular Division 5, Part 2, Category 9 of the Defence and Strategic Goods List (2021). See also the military end-use provisions in Section 112BA of the Customs Act (1901), Weapons of Mass Destruction (Prevention of Proliferation) Act (1995), Defence Trade Controls Act (2012).

lucrative defence contracts, and reliance on international providers for launch and operations.

Australia has entered various international arrangements to facilitate technology transfer in the space sector. In 2021, Australia, the UK, and the United States announced a trilateral AUKUS security partnership (Greene et al., 2021). While Pillar I of AUKUS is focussed on the transfer of nuclear submarine technology, Pillar II is focussed on developing joint advanced military capabilities, including in relation to space. In 2023, it was announced that this would include the establishment in Australia of a Deep Space Advanced Radar Capability (DARC) to strengthen space domain awareness. Later that same year, the United States and Australia also concluded a Technology Safeguards Agreement (TSA), which will streamline compliance with US export controls and allow US companies to carry out space launch activities in Australia.

The TSA is directed at the establishment of a licence-free export environment that will lessen the regulatory burden for industry in sharing defence and dual use technology, including space technology. However, the cost of this is that the Australian government will have to adopt some of the more onerous and restrictive elements of the US export control regime. This could have a detrimental impact on the international competitiveness of Australia's space industry, potentially hindering Australian companies from selling into markets with non-AUKUS States.

In addition to controlling the transfer of space technology, States have sought to ensure that they retain control over the operation of such technology within their jurisdictions. In Australia, for example, under the SLAR Act the minister has the power not to grant, or to suspend, a licence, permit, or authorisation for reasons relevant to the 'security, defence or international relations of Australia' (SLAR Act 2018, section 10).

Where there are incidents involving domestic and foreign-controlled satellites, States will monitor these closely and intervene if necessary. In 2023, a Chinese military satellite engaged in proximity operations to come within hundreds of metres of a commercially owned and operated Australian satellite. The satellite operator, Skykraft Pty Ltd., was provided assistance and guidance from Australian Defence Space Command as well as the US Air Force in responding to these events (Greene, 2023a).

States also impose security obligations on commercial operators to ensure that they are sufficiently hardened against cyberattacks by malicious actors. In Australia, rules made under the SLAR Act require that applicants for most licensees prepare a technology security plan as part of the application process (Space (Launches and Returns) (General) Rules, 2019). The plan must identify procedures to prevent unauthorised access to technology, a proposed cybersecurity strategy, and measures to ensure that Australia gives effect to any agreement in place between Australia and another country that relates to safeguarding of the technology (see Space (Launches and Returns) (General) Rules, 2019, section 22). This latter requirement would require Australian space companies to address requirements arising under the AUKUS and TSA arrangements, once they take effect.

While the need to protect against cyber security attacks has recently been more acute, it has been a long-standing concern. For example, NewSat Limited was at one time Australia's largest specialist satellite company, carrying communications for resources companies as well as defence. NewSat had plans to build and launch satellites to provide communication services in Australia and the Asia-Pacific. In 2011, NewSat contracted with Lockheed Martin for the design and manufacture of a communications satellite, which made NewSat a target (see Lockheed Martin, 2011).

Shortly after entering into the contract, NewSat was the victim of a sophisticated attack by hackers apparently supported by the Chinese government. NewSat was unaware that its systems had been infiltrated for almost 2 years until it was contacted by the Australian Signals Directorate in 2013. Its systems were so compromised that NewSat was told they were not allowed to launch until their systems were rebuilt (The Australian, 2016). Ultimately, NewSat ran into financial difficulties and went into liquidation in 2017.

In response to such attacks, governments have looked to uplift the security capabilities of commercial companies with control of critical assets. One of the earliest and most notable examples is the United States. In 1996, Presidential Decision Directive 63 (PDD-63) established a policy for critical infrastructure protection and created mechanisms for identifying and prioritising critical assets. It also emphasised the need for a public-private partnership to enhance the security of critical systems. Other countries have followed suit in recognising the importance of protecting critical infrastructure (see generally Hesse & Hornung, 2015, pp. 187–201).

In Australia, the *Security of Critical Infrastructure Act* (2018) (Cth) (SOCI Act) introduced a legislative framework for the management of national security risks associated with critical infrastructure. The SOCI Act regulates both critical industry sectors, including the space technology sector, as well as critical infrastructure assets. It imposes positive security obligations on companies and establishes mechanisms for government assistance in responding to security incidents.

Under the SOCI Act, the space technology sector is defined as encompassing the commercial provision of space-related services, including position, navigation, and timing services in relation to space objects, space situational awareness services, space weather monitoring and forecasting, communications, tracking, telemetry, and control in relation to space objects, remote sensing Earth observations from space, and facilitating access to space (Security of Critical Infrastructure Act, 2018, section 5).

While the SOCI Act does not currently define any categories of critical space technology assets, certain assets will be caught under other assets categories. For instance, telecommunications networks and facilities will be caught under the SOCI Act as 'critical telecommunications assets' (Security of Critical Infrastructure Act, 2018, section 5). The entities responsible for such assets will also be caught as carriers or carriage service providers under the *Telecommunications Act 1997* (Cth), which also contains a range of obligations in relation to critical infrastructure security.

The overarching trend is that as commercial entities have become more integral to the space enterprise, States have taken steps to ensure that they can protect their national interests by regulating the export and transfer of space technologies, as well as by requiring that commercial entities uplift their capabilities to promote cyber security and resilience along the supply chain.

5 The Interplay Between Commercial Space Operations and Use of Force/Armed Conflict

5.1 Use of Force and Jus Ad Bellum

5.1.1 Use of Force and Article VI Attribution

Article VI of the OST creates a unique and strict relationship between non-government entities and the State in the context of space activities. In relevant part, Article VI provides:

> States Parties to the Treaty shall bear international responsibility for national activities in outer space, including the moon and other celestial bodies, whether such activities are carried on by governmental agencies or by non-governmental entities, and for assuring that national activities are carried out in conformity with the provisions set forth in the present Treaty. The activities of non-governmental entities in outer space, including the moon and other celestial bodies, shall require authorization and continuing supervision by the appropriate State Party to the Treaty (OST, 1967, Article VI).

The effect of this provision is to directly impose State responsibility whenever a non-government entity undertakes a 'national space activity'. This provision reflects a compromise position between the USSR and the United States taken during the OST negotiations (United Nations Digital Library System, 1966; United Nations Committee on the Peaceful Uses of Outer Space [UNCOPUOS] Legal Subcommittee, 1966; Cheng, 1998, p. 14).[7] At that time, the USSR insisted that only States would be permitted to undertake space activities, whereas the United States anticipated that private companies would one day be involved in space activities and sought their express inclusion. The compromise position was reflected in Article VI that permitted private entities to participate in space activities but ensured that States would remain strictly responsible for their actions.

The term 'national activities' might be understood as wording that limits State responsibility, and academics have come to varying interpretation about the correct interpretation (see Hobe et al., 2009, pp. 112–114; von der Dunk, 2011, pp. 3, 5–7). However, State practice and the UN General Assembly have generally supported an expansive interpretation of what a 'national space activity' is (UNGA, 2013, p. 2 [2]; Hobe et al., 2009, p. 114). In effect, it broadly includes a State where space activities are 'carried out from territory under its jurisdiction or control' or 'by its

[7] The original Soviet position was that 'all activities... shall be carried out solely and exclusively by States' (UNCOPUOS Legal Subcommittee, 1962, [7]).

citizens and/or legal persons established, registered or seated in territory under its jurisdiction and/or control' (UNGA, 2013, p. 2 [2]).

The imposition of State responsibility in such a direct manner is an exceptional manifestation of attribution. Under general principles of international law, State responsibility is generally imposed in very restrictive circumstances, normally where: (1) the State itself acts through its organs or public agencies (International Law Commission [ILC], 2002, p. 2 Article 4), or (2) a private entity is expressly authorised in law to undertake a public function (ILC, 2002, p. 3 Article 5), or (3) a State expressly adopts the behaviour of a non-State entity (ILC, 2002, p. 4 Article 11), or (4) a State exercises a high level of effective control over a non-State entity (ILC, 2002, p. 3 Article 8). In the context of a national space activity under Article VI, State responsibility is imposed at a radically lower level of engagement. Such a position is understandable in terms of ensuring that safety is maintained within space and that space development occurs in an orderly and regulated manner. Space is both an inherently dangerous environment and an area that is beyond territorial jurisdiction. Hence, it requires particular vigilance and oversight to ensure that activities are de-conflicted. States have that capacity to oversee and regulate wide ranging activities where connected to a national, or originating from their territory.

Within this legal framework, however, are implications that are potentially troubling when dealing with reconciliation of other areas of international law. One key area of law that has direct military significance is that relating to the Use of Force under the UN Charter. International law sets many legal boundaries relating to State-on-State interaction along the Use of Force continuum. Hence, there exist prohibitions relating to violating sovereignty (see Schmitt, 2017, pp. 17–27), to intervening in another State's internal matters (Nicaragua v United States of America, Merits, 1986, pp. 106–108 [202]–[205], 128 [251]; UNGA, 1970; UNGA, 1949, Article 3), to using force against another State (UN, 1945, Article 2(4)) and most egregiously, prohibiting armed attacks by one State against another (UN, 1945, Article 51; Nicaragua v United States of America, Merits, 1986, pp. 94 [176], 101 [191]). Given the seriousness of this body of law (as well as the consequences following violation) it is both reasonable and understandable that international law imposes a high threshold for attribution of the actions of a non-State entity to a State to ensure that actions do not unnecessarily escalate. Except, however, where it comes to space.

A literal reading of Article VI allows for the actions of non-State entities in outer space, such as those of commercial companies, to attract State responsibility. This, in turn, allows for the possibility that a commercial company undertaking a 'national activity' in space can violate international law on behalf of a State. Situations in the context of the Use of Force continuum are not hard to imagine. Hence, commercial satellites manoeuvring so as to cause a conjunction with another space object; private company miners on the Moon or an asteroid who in competition for resources resort to force between themselves; industrial espionage that causes damage (or otherwise) are all examples that come to mind. That such actions can implicate a State as a use of force or in an armed attack thus giving rise to countermeasures and even the use of reactive force by a victim State in self-defence are deeply concerning. That a commercial action would have this consequence is unique within contemporary international law.

Fortunately, to date, such outcomes have not occurred. Hence, States (so far) have not expressly tied Article VI State responsibility to commercial space companies in the context of use of force. Such a conclusion would be fully justified on policy grounds given the goal of the OST is to promote peaceful cooperation. It would seem a very counterproductive interpretation that positively facilitated the capacity of commercial space companies to plunge States into war, or even authorised the use of countermeasures between States. The position taken in the *Woomera Manual* is that such an interpretation would not be supportable under international law. Accordingly, conduct by a commercial actor must be attributable to a State under traditional rules of State responsibility for any action taken to be a use of force or armed attack by the State. It may be noted that this position is met with no objection by those States attending The Hague State consultation on the draft manual that occurred in June 2022. However, there is no positive public statement made by a State to this effect that can be located at present.

5.1.2 State Interests in a Satellite

A further area of intersection between commercial space operations and the Use of Force lies in the very characterisation of a space object. Unlike ships and aircraft that carry with them flag State nationality (United Nations Convention on the Law of Sea, 1982, Article 91; Convention Relating to the Regulation of Aerial Navigation, 1919, Article 6), there is no equivalent provision under international law for a satellite. Hence there is no one nationality of a space object. In fact, the applicable law sets up a myriad of State legal interests over a space object and this becomes a critical matter when construing the circumstances of a use of force or other violation of international law against a space object.

In summary, a space object such as a satellite can have up to four separate States acting as a 'launching State' (OST, 1967, Article VII; Convention on International Liability for Damage Caused by Space Objects (Liability Convention), 1972, Article I(c); Convention on Registration of Objects Launched into Outer Space (Registration Convention), 1975, Article I(a)), though one of those States must also be the State of Registration for the space object (OST, 1967, Article VIII; Registration Convention, Article II). Unlike the situation under international maritime law where a flag State must have a genuine connection with a ship, the same does not apply for space. If there are multiple launching States, they must simply 'jointly determine which one of them shall register the object' (Registration Convention, Article II(2)). Hence, a State of registration can merely be the State from which the space object was launched, with another State or States having a much greater connection with that space object. Similarly, outside of these legal relationships as established under international law, a company that is registered in yet another State may have actual ownership of the space object. Additionally, it may also be the case that the transponders and associated services of a space object are leased to yet another company or State.

With such a composite array of States who may directly, or indirectly (through the actions of companies who are engaging in 'national space activities' as described above) participate in the launching and operation of a space object, it is often unclear just who is the State that is 'really' most connected to a space object. This collection of multiple State legal interests may become a pressing issue when force or other negative actions are directed at a space object. Many States could be potentially implicated, but it may be unclear who was the intended target of such an action.

As will be discussed in the next section, this raises issues concerning compensation for damage should a satellite be directly targeted by another State.[8] Legitimate actions of military necessity undertaken in accordance with the law of armed conflict are not compensable under that body of law (Protocol Additional to the Geneva Conventions, 1977, Article 91). This would include collateral damage undertaken to a dual use space object where a third-party State has a legal interest. Hence, it is entirely possible that a major capital investment made by a commercial company in a space object can be lawfully destroyed without compensation as a manifestation of national self-defence/law of armed conflict application. This is the case, notwithstanding that the company is associated with a third State that has no direct involvement in the forceful actions between the two protagonist States.

5.1.3 Jamming, Spoofing, and Dazzling

Understanding the limits of what an application of force is has taken on a nuanced application as a result of State practice in space. Clearly, any kinetic action resulting in physical damage squarely comes within a use of force paradigm. However, when moving beyond that modality and focussing on non-kinetic interference that disrupts satellite functionality, then characterisation becomes more difficult. It is evident that States do engage in electronic interference with foreign satellites, such as jamming (see Weeden & Samson, 2023, 01-01, 02-01, 02-23, 02-25–6, 03-17–19, 08-04, 10-04). The effect of such actions, at least where there is no damage and the results are temporary, has never resulted in claims that they constitute a use of force.

Of course, such actions may offend other rules of international law, especially those relating to International Telecommunications Union (ITU) instruments (International Telecommunication Union [ITU], 2020, Articles 15.1, 15.2), but they have not been construed as falling within the use of force spectrum. When in 2008, China and Russia sought to introduce a new treaty proposal that would define such temporary actions as a use of force (Conference on Disarmament, 2008, Article I(a)), the initiative found significant opposition. Although a further 2014 draft of the treaty modified the definition of 'use of force' (Conference on Disarmament, 2014a, Article I(d)), the United States again criticised the definition for being ambiguous

[8] See 'Effects of Armed Conflicts on Treaties' in UN (2011, pp. 173, 181–182 [4]).

about whether it still sought to prohibit 'temporary and reversible effects' (Conference on Disarmament, 2014b, pp. 4–5 [13]). In the face of such opposition, the combined Chinese and Russian initiative has not progressed any further.

Given this background, it is evident that commercial satellite operators could be subject to jamming, spoofing, and/or dazzling actions by an opposing State, and that such actions do not cross a serious line within the use of force spectrum. Where such action is justified as being based upon countermeasures they are excused (ILC, 2002, p. 6 Article 22). Moreover, where they are based upon Article 51 of the UN Charter (national self-defence) then they take precedence and can displace any contrary legal regime (such as that contained within the ITU framework) (UN, 2011, p. 177, Article 14). As a consequence, there may be real financial cost and loss that is experienced by such commercial operators without any ready recourse for compensation or reparation.

5.2 *Law of Armed Conflict and Commercial Satellite Providers*

As mentioned earlier, in recent years outer space has been formally designated by many States, including Australia and New Zealand (Defence, 2020c, p. 96; New Zealand Ministry of Defence, 2018, p. 7), as an operational military area. For many decades, space was a supporting element of terrestrial warfare in that it provided communications and intelligence capability to inform war fighting on the Earth. This was largely due to the fact that satellites and other space objects were somewhat practically immune from attack given their distance and far-ranging orbits. However, advances in recent years have rendered satellites potentially vulnerable (see Secure World Foundation, 2022). This has necessarily required careful consideration of the manner in which the Law of Armed Conflict applies to warfighting in space.

The Gulf War of 1991 is often considered the first space war (see generally Anson & Cummings, 2008, Lambakis, 1995). This was not because fighting occurred in space itself, but rather it was universally realised that modern military fighting capacity relied heavily upon space-based assets to conduct warfare on the Earth. This was in the form of, inter alia, position, navigation, and timing capabilities as well as communications and intelligence gathering. The more recent Ukraine-Russia war has been termed the first commercial space war (Erwin, 2022). This is because of the unprecedented reliance by Ukraine upon commercial space systems to undertake their military operations in response to the Russian invasion (Erwin, 2022; Beale, 2022).

Prior to August 2022, Ukraine did not have any dedicated military satellites (Iceye, 2022; Beale, 2022). Ukrainian government officials put out an appeal for commercial satellite intelligence in late February 2022 and many private companies responded favourably (Erwin, 2022; Beale, 2022). The services provided by these commercial satellite providers have included tracking troop movements, exposing issues with Russian logistics, and detecting both military infrastructure and strategic objectives (Morris, 2023).

One of the first actions undertaken by Russia was to undertake widespread cyberattacks to bring down Viasat's KA-SAT network, which provided most internet services to Ukraine (including to its government and military) (Manson, 2023, p. 45; Brumfield, 2023). In late February 2022, Starlink (a private US company owned by Elon Musk) stepped in to provide internet resources to Ukraine at no cost (Miller et al., 2022). The Starlink system comprises over 4500 small communications satellites in Lower Earth Orbit (LEO), which when combined provide global high-speed internet and communications coverage for the civilian population (Satariano et al., 2023; Pultarova & Howell, 2023).

To the extent that these, and other commercial satellites, are providing the Ukrainian military with capability to attack Russian soldiers, they become 'military objectives' under the law of armed conflict and may be lawfully attacked. Article 52(2) of Additional Protocol I provides that 'military objectives' are those 'objects which due to their nature, location, purpose or *use* make an effective military contribution to military action and whose total or partial destruction, capture or neutralization in the circumstances ruling at the time, offers a definitive military advantage' (emphasis added) (Protocol Additional to the Geneva Conventions, 1977, Article 52(2)). Hence to this end, commercial satellites that are being used by the Ukrainian military lose their civilian protection and may be lawfully attacked.

Moreover, as such attacks would be lawful, Article 91 of Additional Protocol I provides that no compensation is payable to the private interests who are allowing such satellites to be used in this manner (Protocol Additional to the Geneva Conventions, 1977, Article 91). Indeed, Russian statements have readily emphasised that point about the lawful targeting of commercial satellites that are supporting the Ukrainian military effort (Reuters, 2022). It is telling that Elon Musk, the CEO of Starlink, has more recently taken steps to reduce use of the Starlink system for military purposes (Roulette, 2023).

The Ukraine-Russia war is in fact very revealing about the manner in which belligerent States are conditioning their responses to commercial satellites that have become military objectives. Hence, despite the possibility of launching anti-satellite kinetic attacks against Starlink satellites, this has not been undertaken. Instead, it is evident that Russia is relying upon electronic warfare means (jamming, spoofing, and dazzling) to respond to commercial satellites supporting Ukraine. As Brian Weeden of the Secure World Foundation notes, '[t]hey are not blowing up satellites. They're going after the interference and denial of service' (Erwin, 2022).

There are several explanations as to why this type of response is preferred. In the case of Starlink, the answer is likely pragmatic: kinetically targeting thousands of satellites would be unrealistically expensive and complex, while attacking only a few would have no impact on the ability of the system to function. Hence using a broader 'area' type weapon such as those employed in electronic warfare can have more decisive effect. But even for satellite systems with fewer space objects, such as imaging satellites, there are clear reasons not to pursue a kinetic attack. This would result in considerable debris that would likely impact many third-party States' space objects. Hence, rules regarding precautions (Protocol Additional to the Geneva Conventions, 1977, Article 57) and proportionality (Protocol Additional to the Geneva Conventions, 1977, Article 51(4)–(5)) apply to potentially render such attacks unlawful. Finally, there is also the very real possibility of escalation. As discussed above, Article VI of the OST creates a direct link between the commercial space object and a State. In undertaking a hypothetical kinetic attack against a system such as Starlink, Russia would risk drawing the United States into the conflict (as Starlink is a US company and the launch of the satellites a 'national activity'). Whereas, as discussed above, activities such as jamming do not even constitute a use of force, thus allowing for a desired effect without crossing a major legal line concerning a use of force or armed attack. It is likely that this may be establishing a precedent concerning the manner of responding to commercial satellite operations in armed conflict.

It is clear that commercial space operators are exposed to considerably more legal control than what occurs in the terrestrial environment. This is a result of the unique legal regime that applies to space and to space operations. Hence, while future space activity is all but assured to be led by commercial entities, there are new and unforeseen dangers relating to the intersection with military operations. This provides a level of explanation as to why the domestic regulation of space activities is so focussed on commercial actors. Unwittingly committing a use of force and perhaps leading a State into armed conflict are ever-present hazards that require commercial actors to be ever vigilant to the heightened risks that follow their actions in space. Moreover, the dedication of commercial satellite services to one side in an armed conflict renders such satellites susceptible to lawful attack by the other belligerent side. To date, however, any interference with such commercial providers appears to be undertaken through non-kinetic means, hence denying capability without causing physical destruction, though without any requirement for providing compensation for loss of functionality.

6 Emerging Issues and Conclusion

Modern military activities draw extensively on the services of commercial space providers. This is a function of technical advancement, lower costs to launch and operate in space, and the opportunities that the free market provides. This relationship is, however, regulated by the space law regime in a manner that imposes unique and specific requirements on both commercial space providers and State militaries which seek to rely on them. Such requirements directly link the activities of commercial companies to that of States. Hence States must exercise a high level of control and oversight to ensure that they are not left exposed to unanticipated risk. Moreover, under the existing legal regime, the close connection between State military forces and private companies in the space field raises specific issues under the use of force and law of armed conflict regimes that impose substantial risks upon commercial operators. Not least of these is the capacity for opposing/belligerent States to lawfully degrade or destroy privately owned satellites, in circumstances where they are military objectives, without any need to provide compensation.

As space becomes more fully established as a military operational area, it is likely that some of the ambiguities surrounding the application of international legal principles discussed in this chapter will become more firmly resolved. Manuals such as the *Woomera Manual on the International Law of Military Space Activities and Operations* provide a useful starting point to navigating these uncertain legal issues. However, it will be the role of States to finally articulate their views on the nature of the law and the manner of the intersection between military activities and commercial space providers. When States do assert their positions publicly then such subsequent State practice can inform treaty interpretation and the development of customary international law. It is likely, but by no means assured, that questions of attribution in space will resolve themselves in accordance with normal rules of State responsibility. Such an outcome will be a welcome clarification as it will reduce the likelihood of strategic uncertainty and miscalculation. Given the beginnings of State practice regarding the modalities of targeting commercial satellites that are providing services in the Ukraine-Russia war, it is hoped that non-kinetic means of targeting will become the accepted manner of response in armed conflict in space.

The future will doubtlessly also bring other challenges. Off-world commercial mining, greater use of autonomous systems, and the potential of human settlement in space could create further uncertainties with the existing international space law regime. These, in turn, would raise further questions about the intersection between military and commercial space activities that will need to be answered to provide a level of confidence that peaceful and co-operative activities can be sustained in space.

The growth of the commercial space sector represents an opportunity for States to leverage the flexibility and innovation of private enterprise as an integral component of an overall national space enterprise. A self-sustaining commercial space sector can facilitate the establishment of sovereign space capability, lessening reliance on international partners, as well as allowing States to make greater contributions to such partnerships. States that effectively facilitate private commercial activity will enhance their capacity to project space power. This requires States to find a balance between, on the one hand, the domestic regulation necessary to ensure the fulfilment of international obligations and the management of the risk posed by State responsibility for the conduct of private actors in space, and on the other hand, a legal and policy framework that promotes entrepreneurship and allows for private actors to readily engage in space activities.

An ongoing challenge for States is how to ensure that the space technology and systems that they rely upon are kept secure. In contrast to the Cold War era when space exploration began, the modern space ecosystems are more networked, decentralised, and diverse. There is greater reliance on partnerships between government entities and private companies, which brings with it the challenge of ensuring that there is security and resilience along supply chains. Again, there is a balance to be struck between legal and policy settings that seek to limit and control the exchange of space technology and to impose security obligations on private companies, and settings that allow sufficient freedom for commercial entities to innovate and grow. This highlights that a successful and secure commercial space sector requires ongoing monitoring and regular regulatory reform if it is to effectively support military activities in the space domain.

References

Aerospace Industries Association (AIA). (2023, 1 September). *Statement of industry consensus on AUKUS, selected defense trade provisions, and other policy matters*. https://www.aia-aerospace.org/wp-content/uploads/AIA Statement-of-Consensus.pdf.

Anson, P., & Cummings, D. (2008). The first space war: The contribution of satellites to the Gulf war. *RUSI Journal, 136*(4), 45.

Armstrong, M. (2023, 7 March). The governments with the largest space budgets. Statista. https://www.statista.com/chart/29454/governments-with-the-largest-space-budgets/.

Astroforge. (2023). https://www.astroforge.io/.

Australian Government Department of Defence. (2020a). *2020 Defence strategic update*. Commonwealth of Australia.

Australian Government Department of Defence. (2020b). *Force structure plan*. Commonwealth of Australia.

Australian Government Department of Defence. (2020c, 21 September). *Defence Annual Report 2019–20*. Commonwealth of Australia.

Australian Government Department of Defence. (2022). *Australia's defence space strategy*. Commonwealth of Australia.

Australian Government Department of Defence. (2023). *National Defence: Defence strategic review*. Commonwealth of Australia.

Australian Government Department of Defence. (n.d.). *WRESAT—weapons research establishment satellite*. https://www.dst.defence.gov.au/innovation/wresat-%E2%80%94-weapons-research-establishment-satellite.

Australian Government. (2013). *Australia's satellite utilisation policy*. https://www.kiwispace.org.nz/download/attachments/33161354/Australias-satellite-utilisation-policy.pdf?version=1&modificationDate=1365693512000&api=v2.

Australian Space Agency. (2019). *Advancing space, Australian civil space strategy 2019-2028*. https://www.space.gov.au/Advancing%20Space%20Australian%20Civil%20Space%20Strategy%202019%20%E2%80%93%202028.

Beale, J. (2022). Space, the unseen frontier in the war in Ukraine. *BBC News*. https://www.bbc.com/news/technology-63109532.

Bernstein, L. (2023, 1 May). DoD's commercial space domain awareness Dilemma. Constellations. https://www.kratosdefense.com/constellations/articles/dod-commercial-space-domain-awareness-dilemma.

Bosker, A. J. (2003, 27 May). Space is ultimate high ground. air force. https://www.af.mil/News/Article-Display/Article/139149/space-is-ultimate-high-ground/.

Brumfield, C. (2023, 16 August). Incident response lessons learned from the Russian attack on Viasat. CSO. https://www.csoonline.com/article/649714/incident-response-lessons-learned-from-the-russian-attack-on-viasat.html.

Brunner, K. H. (2021, 10 October). Science and Technology Committee, Space and Security: *NATO's role*. Special Report to NATO Parliamentary Assembly.

Bureau of Industry and Security (BIS), U.S. Department of Commerce. (n.d.). Export Administration regulations (EAR). Title 15, Parts 730-780.

Case Concerning Military and Paramilitary Activities in and against Nicaragua (Nicaragua v United States of America) Merits. (1986). Judgment, 27 June 1986, ICJ Reports 14.

Center for International and Security Studies at Maryland. (2023, June). The desirability and feasibility of strategic trade controls on emerging technologies. https://www.cissm.umd.edu/sites/default/files/2023-06/Strategic%20Trade%20Controls%20and%20Emerging%20Tech_CISSM_Final.pdf.

Cheng, B. (1998). Article VI of the 1967 space treaty revisited: "International Responsibility", "National Activities", and "The Appropriate State". *Journal of Space Law, 26*(1), 7.

Citowicki, P. (2022, 28 September). Triple constellation: AUKUS in space. Policy options paper. The Australian National University.

Conference on Disarmament. (2008, 29 February). Draft treaty on the prevention of the placement of weapons in outer space, the threat or use of force against outer space objects. UN Doc CD/1839.

Conference on Disarmament. (2014a, 12 June). Draft treaty on the prevention of the placement of weapons in outer space, the threat or use of force against outer space objects. UN Doc CD/1985.

Conference on Disarmament. (2014b, 3 September). *Note Verbale dated 2 September 2014 from the Delegation of the United States of America to the Conference on Disarmament addressed to the Acting Secretary-General of the Conference Transmitting the United States of America Analysis of the 2014 Russian-Chinese Draft Treaty on the Prevention of the Placement of Weapons in Outer Space, the Threat or Use of Force against Outer Space Objects*. UN Doc CD/1998.

Convention on International Liability for Damage Caused by Space Objects (Liability Convention). (1972). 961 UNTS 187.

Convention on Registration of Objects Launched into Outer Space (Registration Convention). (1975). 1023 UNTS 15.

Convention Relating to the Regulation of Aerial Navigation. (1919).

Customs Act. (1901). (Cth).

David, L. (2023, 7 January). Space mining startups see a rich future on asteroids and the moon. *Space Insider*. https://www.space.com/space-mining-grinding-into-reality.

Defence and Strategic Goods List. (2021). (Cth).

Defence Space Command. (2022). *Space power eManual: Light Speed Edition*. Commonwealth of Australia.

Defence Trade Controls Act. (2012). (Cth).

Erwin, S. (2022, 20 May). On National Security: Drawing lessons from the first "Commercial Space War". *SpaceNews*. https://spacenews.com/on-national-security-drawing-lessons-from-the-first-commercial-space-war/.

Erwin, S. (2023, 18 October). Space force finalising roadmap for partnering with commercial companies. *SpaceNews*. https://spacenews.com/space-force-finalizing-roadmap-for-partnering-with-commercialcompanies.

Fallon, S. (2022, June). The ongoing militarisation of space. Parliamentary library briefing book: Key issues for the 47th parliament. Commonwealth of Australia.

Federal Aviation Administration. (n.d.). *Frequently asked questions (FAQs)*. https://www.faa.gov/space/additional_information/faq

Fettes, J. (2023, 21 September). Room on the moon: Building our future in space. CSIRO. https://www.csiro.au/en/news/all/articles/2023/september/mining-moon-famelab.

Freeland, S. R. (2017). Australia and international space law. In D. R. Rothwell & E. Crawford (Eds.), *International law in Australia* (pp. 507–533). Thomson Reuters.

Ganatra, D. & Modi, N. (2015–2016). Asteroid mining and its legal implications. *Journal of Space Law*, 40(1), 81.

Greene, A. (2023a, 18 October). Details emerge of near collision between Australian and Chinese Satellites. *ABC News*. https://www.abc.net.au/news/2023-10-18/space-incident-australia-china-satellite-conjunction/102988030.

Greene, A. (2023b, 3 March). Australia's space command pushes for 'soft kill' capability to take out enemy satellites. *ABC News*. https://www.abc.net.au/news/2023-03-03/adf-space-command-pushes-for-soft-kill-capability-for-satellites/102045496.

Greene, A., Probyn, A., & Dziedzic, S. (2021, 16 September). Australia to get nuclear-powered submarines, will scrap $90b program to build French-designed subs. *ABC News*. https://www.abc.net.au/news/2021-09-15/allied-naval-united-states-biden-australia-nuclear-submarines/100465628.

Handberg, R., & Johnson-Freese, J. (1998). State spaceport initiatives: Economic and political innovation in an intergovernmental context. *Publius: The Journal of Federalism, 28*(1), 91–110.

Harrison, T., Cooper, Z., Kaitlyn, J., & Roberts, T. (2017, 9 October). The evolution of space as a contested domain. *SpaceNews*.

Hesse, M., & Hornung, M. (2015). Space as a critical infrastructure. In K.-U. Schrogl, P. L. Hays, J. Robinson, D. Moura, & C. Giannopapa (Eds.), *Handbook of space security. Policies, applications and programs* (pp. 187–201). Springer Reference.

High Representative of the Union for Foreign Affairs and Security Policy. (2023, 10 March). Joint Communication to the European Parliament and to the Council: European Space Strategy for Security and Defence. Joint Communication, European Commission.

Hitchens, T. (2022, 1 September). To protect and maybe defend: NRO, SPACECOM ponder commercial satellite defense options. Breaking Defense. https://breakingdefense.com/2022/09/to-protect-and-maybe-defend-nro-spacecom-ponder-commercial-satellite-defense-options/.

Hobe, S., Schmidt-Tedd, B., & Schrogl, K.-U. (Eds.). (2009). *Cologne commentary on space law, vol. 1: Outer Space Treaty*. Carl Heymanns Verlag.

Iceye. (2022, 18 August). ICEYE Signs Contract to Provide Government of Ukraine with Access to its SAR Satellite Constellation. Press Release. https://www.iceye.com/press/press-releases/iceye-signs-contract-to-provide-government-of-ukraine-with-access-to-its-sar-satellite-constellation.

International Bar Association. (2023, 18 January). *Disputes over space mining on the horizon?*. https://www.ibanet.org/disputes-over-space-mining-on-the-horizon.

International Law Commission (ILC). (2002, 28 January). Articles on Responsibility of States for Internationally Wrongful Acts. UN Doc. A/RES/56/83.

International Telecommunication Union (ITU). (2020). *Radio regulations*.

INTERTANKO. (2019). Jamming and spoofing of global navigation satellite systems (GNSS).

Ireland-Piper, D. (2022, 30 July). Developing Australia's Role in Space is Vital for National Security. *The Strategist*. https://www.aspistrategist.org.au/developing-australias-role-in-space-is-vital-for-national-security/.

Isnardi, C. (2020). Problems with enforcing international space law on private actors. *Columbia Journal of Transnational Law, 58*(2), 489–530.

Jakhu, R. S., & Nyampong, Y. O. M. (2016). Some legal aspects of space natural resources. *European Journal of Law Reform, 18*(1), 86.

Jamasmie, C. (2023, 13 April). Asteroid Mining Startup AstroForge Readies First Mission. Mining.com. https://www.mining.com/asteroid-mining-startup-astroforge-readies-first-mission/.

Kearney. (2023, 12 April). *Navigating the transition from space systems to commercial services*. https://www.kearney.com/industry/aerospace-defense/article/-/insights/navigating-the-transition-from-space-systems-to-commercial-services.

Lambakis, S. (1995). Space control in desert storm and beyond. (Summer) *Orbis* 417.

Lambeth, B. S. (2004, 1 December). A short history of military space. *Air & Space Forces Magazine*. https://www.airandspaceforces.com/article/1204space/.

Library of Congress. (2021, 15 September). Japan: Space resources act enacted. https://www.loc.gov/item/global-legal-monitor/2021-09-15/japan-space-resources-act-enacted/ (Japan).

Lockheed Martin. (2011, 12 December). Lockheed Martin awarded contract to deliver Jabiru-1 for NewSat limited of Australia. Media Release.

Loi du 20 juillet 2017 sur l'exploration et l'utilisation des ressources de l'espace. https://legilux.public.lu/eli/etat/leg/loi/2017/07/20/a674/jo (Luxembourg).

Lopez, C. T. (2019, 29 March). DOD official: Maintaining space dominance 'Pivotal' for US Warfighters. US Department of Defense. https://www.defense.gov/News/News-Stories/Article/Article/1800891/dod-official-maintaining-space-dominance-pivotal-for-us-warfighters/.

Manson, K. (2023, 6 March). The Russian Hack Everyone is Finally Talking About. *Bloomberg Businessweek* 42.

Matthews, J. (n.d.). The decline of commercial space launch costs. Deloitte. https://www2.deloitte.com/us/en/pages/public-sector/articles/commercial-space-launch-cost.html.

McDougall, W. A. (1985). *The heavens and the earth: A political history of the space age*. Basic Books.

Miller, C., Scott, M., & Bender, B. (2022, 8 June). UkraineX: How Elon Musk's space satellites changed the war on the ground. *Politico*. https://www.politico.eu/article/elon-musk-ukraine-starlink/.

Missile Technology Control Regime. (2023). https://www.mtcr.info/en.

Moltz, J. C. (2019). The changing dynamics of twenty-first-century space power. (Spring) *Strategic Studies Quarterly* 66.

Morgan Stanley. (2020, 24 July). Space: Investing in the Final Frontier. https://www.morganstanley.com/ideas/investing-in-space.

Morris, C. (2023, 16 June). Ukraine war: Offensive use of satellite tech a sign of how conflict is increasingly moving into space. *The Conversation*. https://theconversation.com/ukraine-war-offensive-use-of-satellite-tech-a-sign-of-how-conflict-is-increasingly-moving-into-space-207641.

National Aeronautics and Space Administration. (2020, 13 October). The Artemis Accords: Principles for Cooperation in the civil exploration and use of the moon, mars, comets, and asteroids for peaceful purposes. https://www.nasa.gov/specials/artemis-accords/img/Artemis-Accords-signed-13Oct2020.pdf.

National Aeronautics and Space Administration. (2021, 16 April). As Artemis Moves Forward, NASA Picks SpaceX to Land Next Americans on Moon. https://www.nasa.gov/news-release/as-artemis-moves-forward-nasa-picks-spacex-to-land-next-americans-on-moon/.

National Reconnaissance Office. (2023, 31 August). Trial-Seal Commercial Space Protection Framework. https://www.nro.gov/news-media-featured-stories/news-media-archive/News-Article/Article/3512203/tri-seal-commercial-space-protection-framework/.

New Zealand Ministry of Defence. (2018). *Strategic defence policy statement*. www.defence.govt.nz/assets/Uploads/8958486b29/Strategic-Defence-Policy-Statement-2018.pdf.

New Zealand Ministry of Defence. (2022). *Overview: Defence's interests and engagement in space*. https://www.nzdf.mil.nz/assets/Uploads/DocumentLibrary/NZDF-Overview-of-Defences-interests-and-engagements-in-space.pdf.

North Atlantic Treaty Organization. (2019, 4 December). *London declaration — issued by the heads of state and government participating in the meeting of the North Atlantic Council in London 3–4* December 2019. Press Release. www.nato.int/cps/en/natohq/official_texts_171584.htm.

O'Shea, C. A. (2023, 19 May). NASA Selects Blue Origin as Second Artemis Lunar Lander Provider. https://www.nasa.gov/news-release/nasa-selects-blue-origin-as-second-artemis-lunar-lander-provider/.

Office of General Counsel. (2023). *Department of Defense law of war manual* (rev ed). Department of Defense.

Office of the Chairman of the Joint Chiefs of Staff. (2021, November). *DOD Dictionary of Military and Associated Terms*. (Washington DC: The Joint Staff, As of November 2021).

Organisation for Economic Co-operation and Development. (2022, 15 November). How the war in Ukraine is affecting space activities: New challenges and opportunities. https://www.oecd.org/ukraine-hub/policy-responses/how-the-war-in-ukraine-is-affecting-space-activities-ab27ba94/.
Ortega, A. A. (2023, 5 June). Not a rose by any other name: Dual-use and dual-purpose space systems. *Lawfare*. https://www.lawfaremedia.org/article/not-a-rose-by-any-other-name-dual-use-and-dual-purpose-space-systems.
Protocol Additional to the Geneva Conventions of 12 August 1949, and relating to the Protection of Victims of International Armed Conflicts. (1977). 1125 UNTS 3.
Pultarova, T., & Howell, E. (2023, 3 August). Starlink Satellites: Everything You Need to Know About the Controversial Internet Megaconstellation. Space.com. https://www.space.com/spacex-starlink-satellites.html.
Reuters. (2022, 27 October). Russia Warns West: We Can Target Your Commercial Satellites. *Reuters*. https://www.reuters.com/world/russia-says-wests-commercial-satellites-could-be-targets-2022-10-27/.
Roberts, T.G. (2022, 1 September). Space launch to low earth orbit: How much does it cost?. Aerospace Security. https://aerospace.csis.org/data/space-launch-to-low-earth-orbit-how-much-does-it-cost/.
Roulette, J. (2023, 10 February). SpaceX Curbed Ukraine's Use of Starlink Internet for Drones—Company President. *Reuters*. https://www.reuters.com/business/aerospace-defense/spacex-curbed-ukraines-use-starlink-internet-drones-company-president-2023-02-09/.
Satariano, A., Reinhard, S., Metz, C., Frenkel, S., & Khurana, M. (2023, 28 July). Elon Musk's unmatched power in the stars. *New York Times*. https://www.nytimes.com/interactive/2023/07/28/business/starlink.html.
Schmitt, M. N. (Ed.). (2017). *Tallinn manual 2.0 on the international law applicable to cyber operations* (2nd ed.). Cambridge University Press.
Secure World Foundation. (2022, May). Anti-satellite weapons: Threatening the sustainability of space activities. https://swfound.org/media/207392/swf-asat-testing-infographic-may2022.pdf.
Security of Critical Infrastructure Act. (2018). (Cth).
Space (Launches and Returns) (General) Rules. (2019). (Cth).
Space (Launches and Returns) Act. (2018). (Cth).
Space Foundation Editorial Team. (2023, 25 July). *Space foundation releases the space report 2023* Q2, showing annual growth of global space economy to $546B. Press Release. https://www.spacefoundation.org/2023/07/25/the-space-report-2023-q2/.
Space Resource Exploration and Utilization Act of 2015, 51 USC 513 (US). (n.d.)
SpaceX. (2023). Mars & beyond. https://www.spacex.com/human-spaceflight/mars/.
Steer, C. (2021, May). Australia as a space power: Combining civil, defence and diplomatic efforts. National Security College Policy Options Paper no 19. Australian National University.
Stokes, M., Alvarado, G., Weinstein, E., & Easton, I. (2020, 30 March). China's space and Counterspace capabilities and activities. Research Report, US–China Economic and Security Review Commission.
The Australian. (2016, 30 August). Hackers Corrupt Newsat Systems. *The Australian*.
The French Ministry for the Armed Forces. (2019). *Space Defence Strategy: Report of the 'Space' Working Group*.
The University of Adelaide. (n.d.) The Woomera manual. https://law.adelaide.edu.au/woomera/; https://academic.oup.com/oxford-law-pro/book/57847
The Wassenar Arrangement. (2023). https://www.wassenaar.org/.
Treaty on Principles Governing the Activities of States in the Exploration and Use of Outer Space, Including the Moon and Other Celestial Bodies (Outer Space Treaty). (1967). 610 UNTS 205.
U.S. Department of State. (n.d.). International traffic in arms regulations (ITAR). Title 22, Parts 120–130.
United Kingdom Ministry of Defence. (2022, February). *Defence space strategy: Operationalising the space domain*. Crown.

United Nations Committee on the Peaceful Uses of Outer Space Legal Subcommittee. (1962, 6 June). *USSR proposal: Declaration of the basic principles governing the activities of states pertaining to the exploration and use of outer space*. UN Doc A/AC.105/C.2/L.1.

United Nations Committee on the Peaceful Uses of Outer Space Legal Subcommittee. (1966, 11 July). *Letter Dated 11 July 1966 to the Chairman of the Legal Subcommittee by the Representative of the USSR*. UN Doc A/AC.105/C.2/L.13.

United Nations Convention on the Law of Sea. (1982). 1833 UNTS 397.

United Nations Digital Library System. (1966, 16 June). *Letter Dated 16 June 1966 From the Permanent Representative of the Union of Soviet Socialist Republic to the United Nations Addressed to the Secretary-General*. UN Doc A/6352.

United Nations General Assembly. (1949, 6 December). *Draft declaration on rights and duties of states*. GA Res A/375(IV). UN Doc A/RES/375(IV). Annex 66.

United Nations General Assembly. (1970, 24 October). *Declaration on principles of international law concerning friendly relations and co-operation among states in accordance with the charter of the United Nations*. GA Res 2625(XXV). UN Doc A/RES/2625(XXV). Annex 123.

United Nations General Assembly. (2013, December). *Recommendations on National Legislation Relevant to the peaceful exploration and use of outer space*. GA Res 68/74. UN Doc A/RES/68/74.

United Nations General Assembly. (2021, 13 July). *Reducing space threats through norms, rules and principles of responsible behaviours: Report of the secretary general*. UN Doc A/76/77.

United Nations. (1945). Charter of the United Nations and Statute of the International Court of Justice.

United Nations. (2011). *Report of the international law commission: Sixty-third session (26 April–3 June and 4 July–12 August 2011)*. UN Doc No A/66/10.

United States Department of Defense. (2020, June). *Defense space strategy summary*.

Vienna Convention on the Law of Treaties (VCLT). (1969). 1155 UNTS 331.

von der Dunk, F. G. (2011). The origins of authorisation: Article VI of the outer space treaty and international space law. In F. G. von der Dunk (Ed.), *National Space Legislation in Europe: Issues of authorisation of private space activities in the light of developments in European space cooperation. Studies in space law* (Vol. 6). Martinus Nijhoff.

Weapons of Mass Destruction (Prevention of Proliferation) Act. (1995). (Cth).

Weeden, B., & Samson, V. (Eds). (2023). *Global counterspace capabilities: An open source assessment*. Secure World Foundation.

Dr. Dale Stephens CSM FAAL (B.A. (Flin), LL.B(Hons) (Adel), LL.M (Harv), SJD (Harv)), is Professor of Law at The University of Adelaide. He is Director of the Adelaide University Research Unit on Military Law and Ethics. He was an editor of *The Woomera Manual on the International Law of Military Space Activities and Operations* (OUP, 2024).

Mark Giddings is the Principal at LK Law.

Artificial Intelligence, Risk Management, and the Space Industry

Thomas Graham

1 Introduction

Space activities form a lucrative commercial industry, currently valued at approximately USD 384 billion (BryceTech, 2023). Projections suggest this figure may increase to between USD 1 and 3 trillion annually by the year 2040 (Higginbotham, 2018). Similarly, and in parallel, the artificial intelligence (AI) industry is experiencing its own rapid expansion throughout government and the business world. Currently valued at around USD 136.6 billion the AI industry is expected to grow to approximately USD 1.8 trillion by the year 2030 (Grand View Research, 2022). Both the space sector and AI sectors are catalysts for economic development, pushing the envelope of humanity's technological capabilities while providing a multitude of potential benefits to society. Despite the opportunities created by both sectors, the rapid pace at which space and AI technologies are advancing causes a tension with the regulatory frameworks that govern them as the emergent uses of novel technologies outpace the ability of regulation to mitigate the associated emergent risks. This tension between innovation and regulation, while not unique to the space and AI sectors, highlights the importance of developing regulatory frameworks that can remain flexible and adaptive to novel uses of cutting-edge technologies and the harms that may arise from them.

The views of the author are the authors' alone and are intended to provide commentary and general information, and do not represent the views of any organisation. This chapter should not be relied upon as a substitute for professional legal advice or for any other purpose. Some sections of this chapter have been reproduced from the author's forthcoming doctoral thesis.

T. Graham (✉)
Swinburne University of Technology, Melbourne, VIC, Australia
e-mail: thomasgraham@swin.edu.au

J. A. Dennerley, M. A. Pozza (eds.), *The Business of Outer Space*, Space Law and Policy, https://doi.org/10.1007/978-981-95-2034-3_3

AI systems are increasingly being integrated into upstream and downstream operations within the space industry and its associated supply chains. The upstream segment is typically associated with activities directly related to getting to space—such as the launch segment, satellite manufacturing, rocket development, and rover missions—and it stands as the public face of the space sector. These high-visibility elements represent not only the 'hardware' of space exploration but also the initial touchpoints where AI integration is beginning to reshape processes and enhance capabilities. Downstream activities, in contrast, consist of applications and services that are derived from operations in space, and which benefit from the outputs generated upstream. The downstream segment focuses on making use of information gathered in space, such as Earth observation (EO) and remote sensing data. This information is valuable and can be used for a multitude of purposes such as climate science analysis. Artificial intelligence technologies and methods can be employed to analyse space data in a multitude of ways. AI's role in the space sector is extensive and multifaceted, and ranges from the enhancement of predictive analytics in satellite operations to the automation of rovers on extraterrestrial surfaces to the analysis of EO data for a variety of purposes both scientific and commercial. It aids in the efficient processing of complex datasets and supports decision-making processes essential to both the exploration and commercial exploitation of space-based resources and information. This extends to use cases such as precision agriculture, weather forecasting, minerals exploration, oceanography, disaster management, and many more (Russo & Lax, 2022). AI is emerging as a cornerstone technology in the space industry, innovatively applied in the upstream segment, and providing critical analytical capabilities in the downstream segment.

Whilst AI enables a multitude of new industrial and business activities and forges new business and operational capabilities, it is a tool, and like all tools it can cause harm even if it is wielded without ill intent. While public conceptions of harmful AI are shaped by depictions in science fiction—epitomised by malevolent robots or ominous entities like Skynet from the 'Terminator' series—the true risks of current AI systems are less dramatic but still demand our attention. Although AI often appears in pop-culture as some form of existential threat, AI systems as they currently exist do not operate in this way or present this level of risk. The actual risks posed are nevertheless still of consequence and have the capacity to significantly negatively impact people's lives if risks are not managed appropriately. For instance, the notorious COMPAS AI system in America, designed to assess the probability of reoffending for individuals undergoing parole hearings, was shown to contain biases against people of colour, overestimating the probability of reoffending for individuals from minority backgrounds, conversely underestimating the probability for white individuals (Angwin et al., 2016). Furthermore, AI-driven biometric surveillance, implemented by governments and police forces via CCTV, has the potential to impinge on personal freedoms, infringing upon individual rights. These risks are not solely tied to what might be conventionally considered artificial intelligence; instances of automation, even without sophisticated AI or machine learning technologies underlying them, can have severe consequences. In Australia, the 'Robodebt' program automated decisions related to welfare debt calculations and recovery employing contentious calculation methods which resulted in the creation of inaccurate debt notices being sent to welfare recipients. Many of these notices were inaccurate and stated that recipients owed money to the government when in reality (and according to more accepted accounting methods) they did not. This resulted in considerable distress for those receiving the notices, as well as hardship due to their inability to pay the claimed debt. In some tragic cases, recipients even died by suicide due to the stress and perceived hopelessness of their financial situation. The scandal prompted a Royal Commission and will likely prompt significant changes to government procedures, including the use of automated software affecting individuals' rights (see Royal Commission into the Robodebt Scheme, 2023; Australian Government Department of Prime Minister and Cabinet, 2023). In this way, AI (and other automated systems) can potentially cause harm to individuals in a variety of different ways.

It can be easy to perceive the space industry as operating in a domain completely separate from 'the real world'. For the public, the space industry evokes rockets and astronauts, far from the Earth itself. For the industry, it may evoke hardware and software, assets both tangible and intangible. Between both groups, it is unlikely that there is a perception that the space industry directly touches the lives of individuals and affects their wellbeing (Moss et al., 2023). The perception that the space industry operates in a distinct realm, divorced from the concerns of individual rights and the pitfalls associated with AI encountered in other economic sectors, is misleading. Although AI applications within the space sector are often not public facing, they still carry risks. These risks may encompass financial, safety, regulatory, and reputational dimensions. It is imperative for organisations leveraging AI in space operations to address these risk areas comprehensively in order to ensure safe and sustainable operations both internally, within organisations, and externally, between different entities in the broader space sector. Another potential issue is the unfortunately popular belief that because space is beyond the jurisdictions of Earth's nation States, it is a 'Wild West' devoid of rules. In reality, there are both international and national legal frameworks in place governing the activities of governments and private organisations (Steer, 2022, p. 173). This misconception may be extended to the intersection of AI and the space sector, as AI is a new set of technologies that are as yet largely unregulated. The current lack of significant regulation for AI in space implies that most risk management practices in this area are, at this stage, voluntary for organisations engaged in these activities. (Schaefer, 2017). That notwithstanding, the technology underpinning AI systems and the regulatory environment governing them is developing rapidly, with the ongoing development of regulatory frameworks continues to proceed at pace. Previously it has been suggested that a move towards structure oversight of AI is emerging across sectors and jurisdictions, though recent policy statements from the new US administration may undermine this trend (LiveNOW from FOX, 2025).

To summarise, although AI has the potential to enable many new capabilities and push forward innovation in a multitude of fields, it also comes with risks that must be managed carefully throughout the lifecycle of AI systems. These risks are not merely theoretical, and can affect individuals, society as a whole, and the environment. As such, these risks necessitate informed and conscientious implementation of controls and oversight to prevent adverse outcomes for all stakeholders in the AI development lifecycle.

2 AI Risk in the Space Industry

In exploring the risks associated with AI in the space industry, it is essential to understand what risk is, and to place AI risks into their appropriate risk contexts. Knowing a risk's context allows for effective analysis of that risk's causes, consequences, controls, and if required, its treatments. A useful starting point is the definition of risk as articulated by Douglas Hubbard, who characterises risk as 'A potential loss, disaster, or other undesirable event, quantified by the probabilities assigned to losses of various magnitudes' (Hubbard, 2020, p. 9). Alternatively, and more simply, risk can be understood simply as "The possibility that something bad [or adverse] could happen" (see Hubbard, 2020, p. 9; Dennerley et al., 2022, p. 3). While standard risk management principles and practices remain applicable to AI in the space sector, this chapter will not delve into the concept of risk management exhaustively. Instead, this chapter is directed towards highlighting specific aspects of AI design and management that warrant attention from organisations striving to effectively mitigate AI-related risks in the space sector, while remaining cognisant of the ever evolving technological and regulatory landscapes in the space and AI sectors. When examining AI risk management, the American National Institute of Standards and Technology's (NIST) AI Risk Management Framework (AI RMF) provides a useful reference point (National Institute of Standards and Technology [NIST], 2023b). It conceives of AI risk management as the process of reducing the negative impacts, and augmenting the positive effects, of AI systems, thereby leading to more trustworthy AI, while also referring to established International Organization for Standardization (ISO) standards on risk management (see International Organization for Standardization [ISO], 2021; NIST, 2023b, pp. 1–4). The NIST AI RMF is noteworthy in that it adopts an expansive perspective on risk management, postulating that effective risk management not only benefits the organisation employing or utilising AI but also positively affects various stakeholders across the value chain, including individuals, communities, organisations, and ecosystems (NIST, 2023b, p. 4). Having established this, it is time to explore some possible risks AI may pose related to the space sector.

Firstly, it is important to establish a clear definition of 'artificial intelligence' as this central term determines the scope of potential use cases to be discussed and also the scope of any regulations relevant to this discussion. As mentioned above, it isn't useful to focus on pop-culture representations of AI, as contemporary AI lacks the capabilities often depicted in fiction and is inherently more constrained. Currently, there is no universally accepted definition of artificial intelligence.[1] This poses a challenge for risk management approaches whereby nuances in terminology can result in the inclusion or exclusion of AI systems within the purview of risk activities. This challenge is compounded by the necessity for harmonisation between the various emerging regulatory frameworks which may be enlivened if AI risks eventuate. For the purposes of this chapter, we draw upon the definition provided by the European Union's (EU) artificial intelligence legislation, which in turn draws upon the Organisation for Economic Co-operation and Development's (OECD) established AI definition (Hersey, 2023). Notably, the OECD's AI definition, along with the OECD's principles for AI, is about as close to country consensus as has been found to date (Bianzino et al., 2023, p. 5). In its draft regulation, the EU Artificial Intelligence Act offers a broad definition of an 'AI system' as:

> a machine-based system that is designed to operate with varying levels of autonomy and that may exhibit adaptiveness after deployment, and that, for explicit or implicit objectives, infers, from the input it receives, how to generate outputs such as predictions, content, recommendations, or decisions that can influence physical or virtual environments. (European Union, 2024, Article 3)

The AI Act definition encompasses a broad range of possible use cases, including those that may not be considered 'true' artificial intelligence but rather are systems that mimic human intelligence through pattern-seeking processes. This would include technologies such as machine learning, neural networks, deep learning, and other technologies and methods. This inclusive definition is apt for most, if not all, artificial intelligence systems currently employed in commercial and scientific operations, making it a good basis from which to begin any risk management activities in the space industry context.

Given this definition, it is possible to envision a multitude of AI systems applicable within the space industry and the risks that may accompany them. Fortunately (though unfortunately for the purposes of this discussion), there are to date only limited examples of AI risks in the space sector causing harm, leaving many potential risks in the realm of pure speculation. As such, much of the following paragraph is informed speculation on possible AI risk in the space industry. Considering privacy issues, AI systems could pose risks within the space industry due to their potential scope of operation. While terrestrial systems ingest various datasets, they are typically limited by locality (i.e., sensors located in one geographic location) or limited by the scope of what they are trying to achieve (i.e., a business or government system processing data for a very particular purpose such as service provision). Conversely, activities such as EO and remote sensing operate on a much larger scale in terms of geography, with EO satellites surveying large swaths of territory often at very high resolutions. Such space systems could, directly or indirectly, infringe upon privacy by surveilling private spaces where individuals expect privacy (Dennerley et al., 2022, pp. 12–13). Although conventional high-resolution satellite imagery could accomplish this without utilising AI, the issue becomes

[1] This stems from the fact that there is no universally agreed upon definition for intelligence.

more complex when AI is involved. EO imagery has limits regarding resolution, making it difficult to see or infer meaningful information at times. However, through the use of AI one may be able to determine or infer further details (White et al., 2024) or easily track objects between images taken at different times. When an AI-enabled system is directed at an improper subject (such as an individual), whether intentionally or otherwise, it could facilitate harmful outcomes. As a hypothetical example, an AI-enabled system processing satellite imagery could be used to track maritime activity. Such a system could be modified to detect and track personal vehicles, tracking peoples' movements throughout their daily lives. This is concerning since such data would not only violate an individual's reasonable expectation of privacy, but it could also capture more than the individual of interest—it could track numerous vehicles, objects, or even large portions of national populations (Cho, 2013). Such uses of AI systems could enable authoritarian governments to track and control their citizens, preventing gatherings or protests, representing a serious tool of oppression.

In this hypothetical example, the AI system itself is not necessarily unfairly biased or systematically discriminatory against particular groups of individuals. Rather, there may be a lack of transparency or beneficence on the part of the developers and users of the system. Misuse of such systems could not only result in harm for those that are targeted by the system, but also the subsequent reputational damage to the organisations making and utilising such systems. A more exotic form of risk emerges from the domain of space traffic management. Some satellites have already begun to use AI to some extent for deconflicting their orbits and avoiding collisions in the course of managing their orbits. However, if these systems are not accurate enough to sufficiently ensure the proper deconfliction of orbits, this could lead to the possible destruction of satellites through conjunction events, and the subsequent generation of space debris that could cause harm to additional space objects. In this scenario, the risks are more tangible and easily understood by the actors within the space industry due to the prominence of the ongoing discussions surrounding space debris and space traffic management. The risks in this context are multifaceted and include: financial risks, in terms of lost assets; safety-related, due to the potential damage from falling and colliding debris; legal, in light of liabilities arising from international law and State liability for space object collisions (Dennerley, 2018); and reputational, given the current emphasis on responsible and safe conduct in space activities and the potential for public backlash. Overall, the potential applications and corresponding risks of AI in the space sector are varied and, in some instances, profound. Given the scarcity of real-world examples of such risks eventuating into harms, much of the discourse remains theoretical. However, the potential for issues related to privacy infringements, misuses of AI systems, space traffic management, and more still necessitate consideration.

More broadly, the space industry epitomises a sector where high risks are commonplace, yet the tolerance of risks is low and the margin for error is extraordinarily slim. Because of this, it is extremely important that the robustness of AI systems being deployed in the space sector is ensured. The possibility of errors in the underlying data science models causing catastrophic outcomes underpins the necessity of safe and reliable AI systems for the space sector. Particularly crucial are rigorous design verification and validation standards, which must be subject to regular review (Richards et al., 2023, pp. 4–5). Furthermore, the attributes of explainability and transparency found in 'Responsible AI' literature, while always significant, may be of limited utility when examined against the constraints placed on human oversight and control within the vast space environment (Graham & Thangavel, 2023, pp. 4–5). These facets of explainability and transparency should not eclipse the fundamental elements of safety and reliability where there may be a conflict between them. Indeed, when conflicts arise, it is the latter attributes that must take precedence to safeguard against the inherent risks associated with operations in the space domain. Beyond the technical challenges, the space industry has a high degree of interconnectedness with defence applications due to the potential for space assets to be 'dual use', acting as both civilian and military assets (Hesterman-Crane, 2022). This integration between domains necessitates a prioritisation of security (particularly cybersecurity) as these systems possess high-value or sensitive information that must be shielded from potential adversaries. These peculiarities of the space industry influence the way AI risks must be addressed and mitigated within the sector.

The emergence of AI and the risks it may entail have pre-empted the development of a new interdisciplinary domain often referred to as 'Responsible AI' (or 'RAI'). RAI is a multifaceted concept that, although challenging to define comprehensively, aims to establish a broadly accepted framework for the responsible development and deployment of AI systems that mitigates the array of harms AI may pose on individuals, groups, and the environment. RAI essentially functions as a starting point when discussing risk management for AI. It provides some of the languages and concepts necessary to approach the broader task of risk management. At this stage, the various approaches to implementing RAI and AI assurance can be described as a 'disorganised toolbox', with no cohesive approach or methods emerging between organisations (Burr & Leslie, 2023, p. 76). Despite this disorganisation, a variety of guidelines, frameworks, principles, and other instruments designed to evaluate and mitigate the risks associated with AI systems may be useful. These tools framed the discourse on AI risks and how organisations might manage them—in a time before the inception of the now maturing regulatory frameworks governing AI around the world. Many RAI strategies are structured around so-called Responsible AI Principles (RAI Principles) which are worth discussing here as they will have a bearing on how governments and corporations utilise AI. RAI Principles serve to categorise and address the unique risks posed by AI systems. Many organisations, including governments, non-profits, and private businesses, have each introduced their own sets of RAI Principles. While there is no singular, authoritative set of RAI principles, those prescribed by entities with political, legal, or financial clout tend to be more influential. In a particular country, any set of principles published or endorsed by the national government will hold significant sway within that country. Entities operating within countries where this is the case would find such sets of principles a key source of guidance. However, the lack of broad agreement and a consistent set of principle, terminology, and definitions between jurisdictions makes core concepts such as trust, responsibility, and the nature of AI itself unclear and inconsistent between groups. Such inconsistency makes it difficult to consolidate an end goal for RAI without shared definitions to serve as a foundational starting point (Slingerland et al., 2022, p. 2).

Many RAI frameworks emerging from both public and private organisations have garnered substantial attention (Ezeani et al., 2022). A number of meta-analyses of such frameworks have been conducted to determine which are the most effective in enabling RAI practices (see Jobin et al., 2019; Narayanan & Schoeberl, 2023; Lee et al., 2023). In Australia, the Commonwealth Scientific and Industrial Research Organisation (CSIRO) Data 61 group's systematic mapping study evaluated a variety of frameworks to gauge their utility, noting alignment with the Australian AI ethics principles (Lu et al., 2022). Data 61 discovered that of the 16 principle sets they reviewed in-depth, 11 encompassed principles such as human-centred values, fairness, reliability, safety, transparency, explainability, privacy protection, security, and accountability, while only a select few included contestability. Some sets of principles extend to include notions of beneficence or the 'do no harm' precept, gaining popularity despite their implementation being less clear and more challenging to interpret than other principles (Department of Industry, Science and Resources, 2019; van Maanen, 2022). Additionally, although some frameworks were found to be applicable at all stages of AI development, others were limited in their applicability. They also noted the lack of guidance on implementing principles from the various frameworks across different contexts and settings. This lack of specific guidance may reduce the efficacy of the frameworks in question as the risks and relevant mitigating actions relevant to each context may vary significantly (e.g., military uses of AI compared to commercial contexts). The unique environment in which the space sector operates makes this specificity particularly important.

The RAI Principles listed above are broad and could be interpreted and implemented differently depending on the context and use case of the AI in question. Different industries may need to implement these ideas in different ways to achieve the underlying goal of RAI (creating safe and responsible AI). Within the space sector, the implementation of RAI, the regulation of AI systems, and the implications for the sector are beginning to be considered (Martin & Freeland, 2021). Central to the discourse on RAI is the mitigation of bias and the promotion of fairness. But bias and fairness may not already be relevant in the space sector because the exact use cases in which AI or automated decision-making (ADM) may be deployed often do not directly impact individuals. Where the system is not 'individual facing', social discrimination may be less relevant than data integrity issues which may affect the robustness, accuracy, and predictability of the outputs of AI models and systems as a whole. Within the space sector, reliability (epitomised by accuracy and robustness) emerges as the most significant facet of RAI (Graham & Thangavel, 2023, p. 9). This has been recognised by organisations such as the National Aeronautics and Space Administration's (NASA) Jet Propulsion Laboratory (JPL) and the Aerospace Corporation which have worked to create guidance regarding assurance for autonomy in space missions (Slingerland et al., 2022). Their guidance focuses primarily on AI designed for deep space missions, requiring a high degree of autonomy from operators on Earth. It outlines the importance of trust for autonomy, and the means for cultivating trust among stakeholders through demonstrable reliability, testing, and risk mitigation in a way that is relevant to any groups developing or operating AI systems in the space sector, regardless of the particular use case (Slingerland et al., 2022). Also, given the heavy connections between the defence sector and the space sector (such as the possibility of adversarial attacks targeting platforms in the space domain), the security of AI platforms is highlighted. The protection of valuable data and assets is notably important, regardless of whether personal data is captured by the system. Furthermore, the principle of accountability is underscored by the primary rules and obligations arising from international space law, namely the Treaty on Principles Governing the Activities of States in the Exploration and Use of Outer Space, including the Moon and Other Celestial Bodies, referred to as the Outer Space Treaty (OST) (Outer Space Treaty [OST], 1967), and the Convention on International Liability for Damage Caused by Space Objects, referred to as the Liability Convention (Liability Convention, 1972). Importantly, the concept of RAI is merely a starting point in the realm of AI risk management. Other sources of guidance are required to flesh out the practices required of those working with AI to properly mitigate AI-related risks and ensure compliance with forthcoming regulatory regimes.

3 Applicable Regulatory Regimes

Although RAI frameworks are useful to consult at a conceptual level, binding laws and regulations are arguably more important in the field of risk management for AI. This is because although the specific legal documents or frameworks may not be targeted towards the regulation of AI in the space sector, they nevertheless cover some aspect of its development or use, and are binding and enforceable, making them impossible to ignore. Consequently, the international space law framework as established under the United Nation's (UN) space treaty regime and the nascent AI regulation frameworks from jurisdictions around the world are important sources of guidance to consult for those wishing to understand AI risk mitigation in the space sector. This chapter will now examine several select regulatory regimes.

3.1 The United Nations Space Treaty Framework

The international legal framework that governs activities in outer space comprises a series of treaties, resolutions, and agreements between States and international organisations that is supported by the United Nations Office for Outer Space Affairs (UNOOSA) and the United Nations Committee on the Peaceful Uses of Outer Space (UNCOPUOS). These foundational legal instruments are certainly pertinent when considering the use of AI in the space domain. Although the Outer Space

Treaty does not explicitly account for AI—no surprise given this treaty was drafted during the 1960s—it remains a fundamental element in the development of regulatory approaches on an international level (see generally OST, 1967). Within this established international treaty regime, issues of liability are of particular importance when considering the operation of AI in the space sector. The Liability Convention prescribes a bifurcated approach: an absolute liability regime for damage occurring on the Earth's surface, and a fault-based liability regime for damage taking place in all other locations such as in outer space (Liability Convention, 1972, Articles II, III). These binding international treaties make States responsible for national space activities undertaken by governmental and non-governmental entities such as corporations (OST, 1967, Articles VI, VII). The advent of AI introduces nuances to this already complex arena. Determining fault for an accident is notoriously challenging in the outer space context, not least because the precise definition of the term 'fault' under the Liability Convention is not agreed upon (see Dennerley, 2018), coupled with the complexity that is exacerbated when AI is involved. AI's inherent opacity complicates the task due to the 'black-box' nature of such systems which often precludes human comprehension of their inner workings, rendering an intelligible understanding of their logic and operations virtually impossible (Pasquale, 2015). This opacity will likely directly affect any examination of fault in the context of interpreting the Liability Convention, with implications for the enforcement of the international space law regime. However, the lack of space sector-specific guidance does not negate sector agnostic guidance relevant to risk management in this context. Financial, safety, reputational, and compliance risks, along with their associated mitigation measures, remain relevant in the context of the space sector. Thus, even as the dynamics of regulatory enforcement may shift owing to AI's unique characteristics, the central principles of risk assessment and risk management in space ventures remain constant.

3.2 The European Union

The frontrunner in AI regulation, as highlighted earlier, is the European Union with its AI Act (European Union, 2024). Although some details of implementation are still being debated, the regulation was passed, with provisions of the framework becoming enlivened in stages over the years following its ascension into law. This legal framework is informed by the European Commission's independent High-Level Expert Group on Artificial Intelligence. A core reference in this regard is the High-Level Expert Group's 'Ethics Guidelines for Trustworthy AI', which, since its release in 2019, has significantly influenced global AI regulatory initiatives (European Commission, 2019). The EU's AI regulation shares common ground with its General Data Protection Regulation (GDPR) in terms of extraterritorial scope (European Union, 2016). The AI Act applies to any AI systems that have an impact on individuals 'irrespective of whether those [systems and their] providers are established or located within the [European] Union or in a third country'

(European Union, 2024, Article 2), a stipulation of particular importance to the global space sector given its inherently cross-jurisdictional nature. Cross-border collaborations and the potential use of data from one jurisdiction in the jurisdiction of another signify that space sector activities, such as Earth observation imagery processed by AI, could enliven the AI Act's provisions. The AI Act's risk-based approach to regulation outlines a method for categorising AI systems as 'high-risk' (European Union, 2024, Article 6). Systems identified as presenting 'unacceptable risk' will be outright prohibited, whereas 'high-risk' systems will be subject to stringent compliance obligations throughout their lifecycle (European Union, 2024, Articles 5, 6). High risk systems are required to meet a plethora of requirements including having effective risk management systems, data governance mechanisms, technical documentation, record keeping systems, transparency, and provision of information to users, effective human oversights, accuracy, robustness, cybersecurity, quality management systems, technical documentation, conformity assessments, automatically generated logs, post-market monitoring, and information-sharing mechanisms (among other requirements) (see European Union, 2024, Articles 9–20).

These stringent requirements for 'high risk' systems are akin to those in place for new pharmaceutical products that could impact the health of those taking them, with rigorous testing, applications, reviews, post-market monitoring, and risk management plans occurring throughout the 'lifecycle' of the product to minimise the risk of harm occurring (U.S. Food and Drug Administration [FDA], 2020). While this may seem overly cautious, when considering examples such as self-driving cars and the impacts they could have on humans were the autonomous systems powering them to malfunction, the need for such controls becomes clear. Likewise, while the physical impact of an AI malfunction in the space domain may be less likely to physically impact humans and their bodies, they nevertheless may be considered 'high risk' for the purpose of the AI Act as they could significantly impact their rights and the way they live their lives were an AI-enabled system to invade their privacy using Earth observation imagery, or cause a collision between satellites, or even disrupt the myriad of systems and critical infrastructures around the world that rely on satellite technology to function (as discussed above) (Graham et al., 2024, p. 202).

To avoid significant penalties for non-compliance, organisations must comply with the above obligations, where failure to do so can result in penalties that reach up to 7% of annual turnover[2] (European Union, 2024, Article 99). Furthermore, the AI Act's implications may be magnified when considered alongside the GDPR. The GDPR's remit, particularly concerning the collection and use of personal information, may affect remote sensing data that is determined to contain personal information of EU residents (Graham et al., 2024, p. 202). Organisations dealing with space-based activities should be aware that non-compliance with the GDPR carries substantial financial, legal, and reputational risks, as it is an established regime with

[2] Accurate at the time of writing.

a history of enforcement actions against major corporations (see Freeland & Ireland-Piper, 2022, pp. 16–17). Because of this, the EU AI Act is expected to generate a 'Brussels Effect', prompting other jurisdictions to either emulate its regulatory model, or for organisations outside of the EU jurisdiction to nevertheless follow its regulation for the sake of maintaining a unified set of business operations globally, similar to the influence of the GDPR (Bradford, 2020).

3.3 The United States of America

The United States (US) dominates the tech sector, AI included, and so any analysis discussion of artificial intelligence and the regulatory frameworks governing it must consider the US approach to AI regulation. Because Silicon Valley is the home of many of the world's biggest organisations developing and implementing AI systems, the US market and its stance on AI regulation is relevant to every organisation working with AI around the world. Contrary to the European Union's approach, the US does not have any overarching or cohesive policy or regulatory approach to the governance of AI. The US is generally reluctant to enact legislation which would limit the technology sector, and thus far this trend seems to be holding in relation to AI. Notwithstanding the absence of a unified regulatory framework, it is incorrect to assume that the US is completely devoid of initiatives in this domain. Indeed, the US Government has been proactive in certain respects, as evidenced by the relevant executive orders issued across multiple administrations (Executive Office of the President, 2020; Executive Office of the President, 2023). The executive orders covered a variety of issues related to the use of AI, emphasising the need for trust in AI system design and the protection of individual rights. These orders also furthered a concerted effort to ensure that the US Government and public agencies fostered responsible AI development as a part of their ongoing operations. These orders represent a desire of US authorities to set an example as a market that promotes responsible AI practices. However, the Biden era executive order on AI safety was repealed by another executive order on day one of the second Trump administration (Executive Office of the President, 2025). Furthermore, JD Vance in his capacity as Vice President of the US bemoaned European overregulation in relation to AI and stated that the US would not follow the EU, opting instead for a free-market approach to regulation. These new developments effectively set the US regulatory efforts back to square one, with little guidance coming directly from the government (LiveNOW from FOX, 2025).

3.4 Australia

Artificial intelligence, although a new technological advent for many nations, is not yet the focus of regulators worldwide. Many countries, preoccupied with other issues, have not placed AI regulation high on their agendas (though this may be beginning to change). Because of this, many jurisdictions are monitoring Europe and the US for evolving market trends and regulatory developments. When choosing how to react to these developments, these jurisdictions face a choice between being proactive (forming their own regulations) or reactive (mimicking regulatory frameworks in those jurisdictions). It could be argued that Australia is a prime example of one such jurisdiction. Australia is a developed nation with skilled workers but limited economic and regulatory influence when compared with larger markets (such as the EU and US). Consequently, Australia tends to take a more reactive approach to new areas of regulation, reacting to developments from other jurisdictions rather than leading the way itself. To date, Australian Government engagement in AI regulation has been modest, focusing primarily on the development and endorsement of the Australian AI Ethics Principles (Department of Industry, Science and Resources, 2019). This initiative provides a framework of RAI practices similar to other sets of principles but is endorsed by the Australian Government. Alongside these principles, guidance documents and case studies regarding their application are provided to assist organisations in employing the principles as a part of their operations (Department of Industry, Science and Resources, 2019). Notably, these principles acknowledge the need for contextual adaptation. As such, principles such as 'fairness' may be interpreted differently according to specific use cases.[3] Although the Australian Government has provided some guidance to the Australian market regarding AI ethics, more concrete regulatory initiatives are yet to be confirmed.

Recently, the advent of mass-market generative AI platforms such as ChatGPT has prompted the Australian Government to actively consider the appropriate approach to regulate AI systems. The Australian Government has subsequently sought input on potential regulatory strategies by releasing a consultation paper, which solicits industry and academic perspectives on various matters, including the suitability of adopting a risk-based regulatory approach analogous to that of the European Union (Department of Industry, Science and Resources, 2023, p. 31). Australia has been influenced previously by European regulations, exemplified by recent proposed reforms to its Privacy Act aiming to align more closely with Europe's GDPR (Attorney General's Department, 2023). Balancing itself culturally and jurisprudentially between Europe and the US, Australia is attempting to

[3] For example, in the context of the space sector, the concept of fairness may be interpreted in the context of broader policy objectives rather than individual rights, and so fairness may take on a more collective connotation, instead referring to outcomes related to climate change, scientific research, national security, and defence capabilities. The broad scope of such concerns may cause those considering 'fairness' to consider collective or national benefits to outweigh the privacy concerns of individuals, though this would be context dependent and within the limits of existing laws.

navigate the tension between the potential extremes of an overregulated environment on one hand, and a laissez-faire, free-market approach on the other. Overall, the approach appears to want to balance the mitigation of potential harms associated with AI with the need to allow Australian businesses to grow and not unduly stifle innovation and economic growth through overregulation of a nascent field. There are varied approaches regarding the appropriateness of adopting an EU-style regulatory model for AI in Australia. Critics of the EU approach suggest it may not suit Australia's unique legal and cultural context (Fraser et al., 2023, pp. 10–16). In spite of the ongoing academic discussions regarding regulation in Australia, the government's response to its aforementioned consultation paper was, while still important, largely vague and non-committal about the direction the Australian Government plans to take (Department of Industry, Science and Resources, 2024). Recent developments further undermined this, with the ruling Labor party (prompted by a report from the productivity commission) to reneg on its previous plan and instead commit to further rounds of regulatory consultations and pursue light touch AI regulation. This leaves Australia in a passive and a reactionary stance to AI regulation, keeping its options open while providing non-binding advice and guidance to organisations within its AI ecosystem (Reid et al., 2023).

The international nature of AI development and space operations makes collaboration between jurisdictions and markets a necessity. Ensuring safe and coordinated operations requires that regardless of the strategic direction pursued by the US or Europe, a concerted effort must be made towards the alignment of practices. The purpose of such alignment is to establish normative industry practices that are interoperable across jurisdictions and reduce regulatory friction. Ensuring interoperable regulatory and risk management practices in both industries is crucial to their continued sustainable operation. Any misalignment between different frameworks regulating AI creates a stronger need for a cohesive set of voluntary regulatory and risk management practices to facilitate operations and collaboration between jurisdictions.

Although many smaller players in the global AI industry are in similar positions to Australia, the adoption of risk-based approaches to AI regulation is gaining traction globally (Bianzino et al., 2023). Such frameworks are becoming popular for ensuring that regulations across jurisdictions remain interoperable, alongside other compelling reasons for their widespread adoption.

4 Standards and Other Risk Management Strategies

The above discussion encompasses legally binding instruments at the international, regional, and national levels. This stands in contrast to so-called soft law, which are non-binding instruments intended to guide behaviour through the creation of norms and standards of behaviour (Dennerley, 2018, p. 299). Standards usually refers to technical standards, often created by well-known organisations such as the ISO, and the Institute of Electrical and Electronics Engineers (IEEE). Such standards do not legally bind those that follow them and are not directly connected to legislative processes or law-making by national government. However, standards can be integrated into legislation, which provides a mechanism to enforce and ensure compliance with standards as a matter of law. This looks to be the case with the forthcoming EU AI Act requiring standards to be complied with to fulfil the requirements of the regulations (European Union, 2024, Articles 40–43). This incorporation gives standards a form of authoritative weight, despite their design as non-legal guidelines (see Soucek & Tapio, 2023, pp. 219–221). In the space industry, standards could also be enforced by proxy if insurers were to require compliance with standards before granting insurance (or discounted premiums) to AI-enabled payloads or launch vehicles[4] (McNamara, 2022, pp. 86–91). Regardless of their potential enforceability, standards are important for risk management in other ways. Their primary utility is in providing clear and detailed technical documentation that can be followed and reproduced by organisations to ensure the quality of a product or process is acceptable and can be assumed to be free of certain faults. In this sense, standards provide a roadmap for organisations to follow and consequently mitigate the risks that are addressed by the standards to which they are conforming. Standards effectively set the 'rules of the game', which enables organisations to claim that their products and services are high quality, safe, and efficient, thereby becoming a key selling point. Especially useful is the fact that these standards can be updated to reflect new developments (such as new technologies like AI) and so they can be more easily updated compared to traditional legislation and regulation which struggles to keep pace with evolving circumstances. This mitigates the risk of standards becoming outdated and irrelevant as technology advances.

The adoption of (and certification against) standards already forms a key part of the space sector's operations. The international nature of the space sector necessitates cooperation and interoperability of systems and processes between jurisdictions and economies, seemingly a perfect context to which standards could be applied. For instance, the International Space Station stands as a prime example of how standards encourage cooperation (Soucek & Tapio, 2023, p. 213). Given the paramount importance of safety and reliability to protect humans and space assets as a part of missions in the space sector, standards are a cornerstone of the space industry's operations (Soucek & Tapio, 2023, p. 214). Moreover, in market terms, if a normative behaviour is established from the following of particular standards, it becomes expected that all organisations operating within a specific sector comply with these norms. Products and services aligned with high-quality and low-risk standards are inherently more attractive to prospective clients and customers

[4] The issue of AI opaqueness is noteworthy here as it pertains to insurance practices, particularly the principles of utmost good faith and the duty of disclosure. Future deliberations may need to consider whether the lack of transparency in AI operations presents new challenges for insurance validity and what additional measures might be required to uphold the integrity of insurance agreements concerning AI systems.

(Soucek & Tapio, 2023, p. 217). Failure to be certified against relevant standards could be seen as a mark of low-quality products or services when compared to competing organisations. This pressure could make organisations adopt and maintain certification against standards in order to keep a competitive advantage in their market. Adherence to standards can also ensure alignment with regulatory requirements if they exist, or, importantly, non-binding standards documents can nevertheless take on a binding quasi-legal form when adherence to them is mandated under regulation (Soucek & Tapio, 2023, pp. 217, 219). In risk management terms, although standards are 'optional' in the sense that they are non-binding, they represent an effective means of ensuring their risk management strategies remain appropriate, relevant, and compatible with the regulatory environments they operate within. In summary, the global space industry aims to leverage standards to establish norms of industry practices through technical, non-political means of self-regulation, as opposed to the traditional treaty-based international law approach.

The implementation of international standards often presents significant challenges, regardless of the applicable domain. One issue is the accessibility of these standards, as they typically require the payment of substantial fees to obtain complete document sets. The cost of accessing standards and contributing to standard development can affect smaller organisations disproportionately when compared to larger organisations. This could create issues with certain groups lacking proper representation in the standards creation process and the ability of smaller organisations to enter markets where larger organisations have the heritage and resources to maintain standards compliance (see Fraser et al., 2023, p. 14; Soucek & Tapio, 2023, p. 224). Other critiques of standards stem from the fact that the bodies that create and disseminate them are not elected, hence, they lack a democratic mandate akin to traditional legislation. Standards bodies also tend to be wholly technical in nature, lacking sufficient input from those with expertise in non-technical fields (such as ethics, law, and the humanities more generally). This raises concerns regarding their ability to create standards that adequately handle potential moral or cultural issues arising from the technologies they seek to regulate (Fraser et al., 2023, p. 12). Moreover, the AI-focused standards that are being developed by various organisations are for the most part industry agnostic and overlook the distinct factors influencing their application across different industries. While standards should ideally be neutral and transferable across sectors, it is important to acknowledge that mindful application is necessary in particular instances. This is not to suggest that the use of AI within the space domain is particularly special, especially considering that most down-stream space data is processed on Earth: the space-derived aspect of the data being the sole distinction. Nevertheless, the space domain does present unique challenges that could affect the adoption of such standards, or more broadly, the principles of 'Responsible AI'. For example, 'human in the loop' or 'human on the loop' is often used to describe a practice where human operators were integrated into the system to review (and potentially override) decisions made by AI-enabled systems in order to mitigate the risks posed by poor decisions and ensure legal and moral accountability. This arrangement could be practical and effective depending on the use case in question. However, in the space sector, circumstances may arise where this human oversight is not viable—for instance, when the communication latency caused by the distance between Earth and an automated platform (that may be orbiting Mars or the Moon for instance) introduces unacceptable delays. Any delays in communications could compromise the safety and accountability benefits accrued from having a human on the loop because of additional time required for processing information and sending command signals by humans on Earth. Therefore, the autonomy of a system may need to take priority over accountability concerns where necessary for the sustainable operation of a system. In the context of the extreme operating conditions found in outer space, this could mean that rigorous testing and validation of a space system's accuracy, reliability, and safety in unexpected situations may be prioritised over the implementation of human oversight measures. It is important to note, however, that striking the balance between factors affecting the control and autonomy of AI systems can be complicated and may depend on several factors including social acceptability, the principles of RAI being considered, and legal and technical considerations (Pagallo et al., 2023, p. 8). These points underscore the complexity and necessity of adapting AI standards to the unique context of space technology and the space sector thoughtfully.

Notwithstanding the points of policy and nascent nature of some standards that may be applicable to AI in the space industry, standards remain an important source of guidance and so some specific examples of standards relating to AI should be examined. The ISO and the IEEE have played a significant role in establishing guidelines for the management of risks associated with AI. The creation of ISO Subcommittee 42, dedicated to standards related to AI systems, stands as a testament to the ISO's commitment to creating standards pertaining to AI systems as the associated technologies continue to evolve and mature. Standard '23894 Information Technology – Artificial Intelligence – Guidance on Risk Management' (ISO 23894) has emerged as a foundational document with regard to AI risk management (ISO, 2023a). Along with '42001 Information Technology – Artificial Intelligence – Management System' (ISO 42001), (ISO, 2023b), these standards form a critical resource that organisations should consult irrespective of the industry that they operate in, their need for tailoring, or jurisdictional considerations when working to address AI risks.

Beyond international standards organisations, many national- and regional-level organisations are also beginning to either create or adapt standards related to AI for adoption within their national economies. Given one purpose of standards is to create internationally interoperable processes and methods, these national and regional bodies tend to work with the ISO and IEEE wherever possible to mirror the international standards within their jurisdictions. To this end, a number of standards organisations relevant to major markets in the space industry have begun implementing and promoting AI-related standards. Standards Australia and the CSIRO's National Artificial Intelligence Centre have jointly published their 'Introduction to Standards for Artificial Intelligence' (Standards Australia & Commonwealth Scientific and Industrial Research Organisation, 2023) aimed at educating Australian organisations on the role of standards and which standards may be useful in the context of their organisation's work, as well as adopting the standard 'Introduction to Standards for Artificial Intelligence' (Standards Australia, 2024), which is a mirror of the ISO's 42001:2023 (ISO, 2023b). The European Committee for Electrotechnical Standardization (CENELEC) also adopts and creates standards, having its own Joint Technical Committee 21 focusing on AI, and working to implement standards for the EU to support its soon-to-be enacted AI Act (CENELEC, 2024). It has also been noted by the European Space Agency (ESA) that AI models must be improved before being used extensively in space, and so the development of new standards for AI use in outer space is likely to become an increasingly significant topic of discussion within the legal and policy fields (Pagallo et al., 2023, pp. 13–14). Across the Atlantic, in the US, the NIST previously released a special publication setting forth policy standards for the US focused on the identification and management of biases in AI and addressing discrimination against populations such as minorities or those with disabilities (Schwartz et al., 2022). As noted earlier, such concerns may differ from those generally prioritised in the space sector where data inaccuracies could compromise the reliability and safety of systems (instead of concerns relating to ethical or moral shortcomings of a system). More recently in January 2023, the NIST published its AI Risk Management Framework aimed at providing a resource to aid organisations in managing AI risks in a holistic sense. These risks are multifaceted, stemming from a variety of sources including third-party software, hardware, and data. The NIST AI RMF delineates four key categories of action for organisations to effectively manage AI-related risks which include: govern, map, measure, and manage, with guidance for each of those four categories (NIST, 2023b, p. 20). Notably, the document acknowledges the swift pace of innovation in AI and other software technologies, advocating for adaptive and routinely revised governance frameworks to tackle emergent risks (NIST, 2023b, p. 2). Importantly, the AI RMF is publicly available, unlike ISO standards (and their national mirrors), making it an accessible risk management resource. The AI RMF notes that completely eradicating all negative risks related to an AI system is not practical and could potentially lead to suboptimal resource allocation (NIST, 2023b, p. 7). Instead, cultivating a culture of risk management that duly recognises the inherent nature of AI risks and allocates resources in a considered manner is recommended. This involves setting precise guidelines for evaluating AI system trustworthiness and prioritising policies and resources based on assessed risk levels and potential impacts. The NIST document underscores that risk prioritisation will inherently differ between AI systems that interact directly with humans versus those that do not, with systems directly interacting with humans possibly requiring higher initial prioritisation (NIST, 2023b, p. 8). This is particularly pertinent to the space industry, where many AI systems may not have direct human contact. Nevertheless, for those that do, prudent caution and deliberate care are imperative in their development and implementation. The AI RMF also notes that the various characteristics of RAI that may go through trade-offs depending on contextual factors, and that the participation and input of subject matter experts across diverse sectors throughout the AI lifecycle are essential to navigate these tensions and achieve well-rounded, trustworthy AI systems (NIST, 2023b, pp. 12–13). An example of such a tension could be seen in the balance between the multitude of benefits derived from remote sensing (such as in coordinating humanitarian aid, climate monitoring, and scientific research) and the potential for individual's right to privacy being eroded (Freeland & Ireland-Piper, 2022, pp. 14–16). Although this example does not explicitly involve AI, it is germane, given that AI could analyse the data from remote sensing for various purposes. Further, although the NIST AI RMF is an industry-agnostic framework that does not have space sector-specific guidance, it nevertheless contains useful guidance that could benefit those working with AI in the space sector and aiming to create responsible AI systems. The AI RMF is itself relatively concise. However, the NIST complemented it with a thorough 'playbook' which explores various scenarios that AI systems could encounter during development and deployment and outlines potential responses and actions that could be taken to mitigate the risks presented by said scenarios (NIST, 2023a). The NIST AI RMF represents a significant source of guidance for organisations working with AI specifically because it is accessible and doesn't require large fees to be paid, making it likely that the AI RMF will become a leading source of guidance around the world provided it remains largely compatible with other regulation, standards, and sources of guidance.

Another consideration related to the use of AI-enabled systems in the space sector is the interconnectedness of the space industry with the defence sector. This often dual-use nature of space payloads and various partnerships or funding arrangements for space organisations from military sources means that guidance aimed at defence would be relevant for those in the space sector. As such, developers of AI systems within the space industry should strive to adhere to, and be guided by, defence sector standards in addition to other standards to ensure compatibility with the requirements of the sector. The North Atlantic Treaty Organization (NATO) has published its AI strategy, outlining key aims, principles, and obligations of NATO members when utilising AI systems, though these are high level and light on the detail (North Atlantic Treaty Organization [NATO], 2021). Separately, the Innovation Unit of the Department of Defence in the US has released guidelines pertaining to RAI practices, drawing upon learnings from RAI implementation activities conducted by the Department of Defence in the past (U.S. Department of Defence, 2020). The guidelines states that AI systems must minimise bias and be equitable in their operation. They should also be traceable, ensuring clear identification of the developers and deployers, prioritising transparency and auditability, alongside reliability—concepts which are congruent with pre-existing sets of RAI principles. Moreover, AI systems must be governable, implying they must be capable of being controlled and that unintended consequences can be pre-empted and mitigated. By implementing RAI principles, practices, and associated risk mitigation measures that are interoperable with defence sector guidance makes it more likely that systems operating at the intersection of the space and defence sectors will enjoy greater interoperability and collaborative opportunities in the future.

More directly relevant than the defence sector is the space sector itself. NASA represents a source of expertise and practice that can positively influence the practices of other organisations in the space industry. A key resource for risk management from NASA is its Risk Management Handbook which encompasses broader risk management practices integral to space systems engineering and space project management (NASA, 2011). Adoption of these practices is especially relevant for individuals aiming to achieve a high standard of work or to ensure interoperability with NASA and its supply chain. Of note however, it does not currently provide informative guidance tailored to AI and other automation-related risks. Separately, NASA's own ethical AI principles emerge as a useful resource for those incorporating AI systems into their space operations (NASA, 2022; see also Richards et al., 2023), though these standards are relatively light on detail in terms of their application (NASA, 2022). Regardless, the Handbook could be updated in the future to explicitly include NASA's AI ethics framework and any risk management strategies employed by NASA in the course of working with AI systems. Given NASA is an American entity, and sits within the American AI ecosystem, it is possible that any such updates to the Handbook in the future would align with other American AI risk management frameworks such as the NIST AI RMF. This would result in guidance that is tailored to the space sector while remaining harmonised with better established industry agnostic sources of risk management guidance.

5 Key Takeaways

The discourse surrounding AI and the potential risks it could pose in the context of the space sector is by no means clear and organised. It comes from many sources, and lacks a singular message, making it difficult to understand both the risks and proper mitigation measures relevant to AI in the space sector. The EU's AI Act is the most comprehensive and important legislative development that should be taken into consideration at this stage, and complying with its requirements will not only be a good starting point but will put an organisation in a good place in terms of integrating AI into space operations and activities and managing any associated risks. However, different organisations have different risk appetites and so the baseline of regulatory compliance may not suffice for their risk management needs (Dennerley et al., 2022, p. 4; NIST, 2023, p. 7). For those aiming to get ahead of the curve, rather than simply keeping up with it, the following suggested organisation-level practices may be of use.

The CSIRO's Data 61 group has published multiple works aimed at providing practical guidance to organisations on implementing RAI practices (Lu et al., 2022, 2023; Narayanan & Schoeberl, 2023). These works describe industry-wide sources of governance (law and regulations, standards and certification, independent oversight, etc.) akin to those discussed above, and organisation-level governance activities that can be adopted voluntarily by individual organisations, and processes that can be undertaken by individual teams. The organisation-level practices include leadership commitments to RAI (active commitments from management to RAI going forward), RAI risk committees (groups dedicated to reviewing and approving proposals of AI projects), Codes of RAI (an organisation-wide set of guidelines for employees working with AI), RAI risk assessments (systematic assessment of risks related to an AI project), RAI training (employee training for awareness and skills related to AI), role-level accountability contracts (documents describing the roles and responsibilities of individuals related to AI), RAI bills of materials (a list of components used to create an AI system for transparency purposes), and standardised reporting (standardised processes and templates for informing different stakeholders about the development process) (Lu et al., 2023, pp. 100–118). An important non-technical practice that occurs at the team level is ensuring that teams working on the development and deployment of AI are diverse, with their members being from a range of gender, ethnic, religious, sexual, and socio-economic backgrounds where possible to provide viewpoints that may otherwise be overlooked (Lu et al., 2023, pp. 123–125; NIST, 2023, pp. 9–10). Importantly, the NIST's AI RMF covers many of the same concepts, practices, and processes (though the terminology and the level of depth may vary) creating a degree of interoperability between leading AI risk management resources in the US and Australia that will be of value to both markets.

Beyond these public sphere publications, Reid Blackman's 'Ethical Machines' provides clear, concise, and accessible guidance from a corporate management (and non-technical) standpoint (Blackman, 2022). It provides straightforward explanations as to the importance of bias mitigation strategies, diverse engineering teams, and stakeholder consultations. Additionally, Blackman covers the tension between explainability and the precision of AI systems, including exploring how explainability can be crucial in ensuring the reliability and accuracy of the underlying data model. This is in contrast to the example discussed above regarding Earth to Mars communication delays and so can provide food for thought for those operating in the space domain. Among many other topics it also covers the need to appropriately distribute the ethical responsibility for AI systems beyond just engineers and data scientists to others such as managers and company boards through the use of ethics committees, and to highlight the potential pitfalls that can come with such bodies. For a more technical perspective, the paper 'Ethical assurance: a practical approach to the responsible design, development, and deployment of data-driven technologies' should also be consulted (Burr & Leslie, 2023). Importantly, these also align and mirror the advice given by the CSIRO and the NIST and create an entry point for those seeking to explore the topic and allow for a degree of cross referencing between the different sources of guidance. As with many of the documents discussed, these too are industry agnostic, and so special care must be taken to consider the characteristics of the space industry and the use case of AI in the space domain that may require departure from the general guidance (though this will likely be unnecessary in most cases).

6 Conclusion

As AI and related automation technologies continue to develop, AI will become increasingly embedded throughout the space industry—for both systems on Earth and in situ in the space domain. The benefits AI can bring must be balanced against the possible risks that emerge through its use. Responsible AI has emerged as a concept to be engaged with thoughtfully and provides a basis for AI risk identification and management, though it tends to fall short of providing sufficiently actionable guidance for those engaging in AI assurance. Although the international space law regime lacks specific rules related to AI systems, other regulatory frameworks are emerging which will direct the development and deployment of AI systems across all domains, beyond just the space industry. The EU, US, Australia, and other jurisdictions are creating regulations and non-binding guidance to shape the future of AI. Beyond this though, standards are emerging as a key tool to foster uniformity and interoperability at both the international and national levels. Although many of these sources of guidance are still nascent, the field of AI risk management is developing quickly, with both public and private sector organisations publishing guidance on the topic. Going forward, it is possible that sources of guidance regarding the regulation of AI systems and associated risk mitigation measures will harmonise further, though this depends on the political will displayed by politicians and business leaders. If regulatory alignment does emerge, this may allow for a unified and consistent AI risk management framework to form. Even if such a framework were not tailored in any way to the space sector, organisations in the space sector could use it to mitigate the risks associated with AI in their operations while space sector-specific guidance is formulated. Although guidance specific to the space domain will take some time to be articulated, the frameworks, concepts, and practices referenced in this chapter provide a foundational starting point for those proactively addressing AI risk in their organisation, regardless of their industry.

References

Angwin, J., Larson, J., Mattu, S., & Kirchner, L. (2016). Machine bias. *ProPublica*. https://www.propublica.org/article/machine-bias-risk-assessments-in-criminal-sentencing?token=l0i8JndZRzf9U7hmG1DlFV6RjLJo1zYf

AttorneyGeneral'sDepartment.(2023).*Governmentresponsetotheprivacyactreviewreport*.https://www.ag.gov.au/rights-and-protections/publications/government-response-privacy-act-review-report.

Bianzino, N. M., Delarue, M.-L., Maher, S., Koene, A., Kummer, K., & Hassan-Szlamka, F. (2023). The artificial intelligence (AI) global regulatory landscape. EY. https://assets.ey.com/content/dam/ey-sites/ey-com/en_gl/topics/ai/ey-the-artificial-intelligence-ai-global-regulatory-landscape-v7.pdf?download.

Blackman, R. (2022). *Ethical machines: Your concise guide to totally unbiased, transparent, and respectful AI*. Harvard Business Press.

Bradford, A. (2020). *The Brussels effect: How the European Union Rules the World*. Oxford University Press. https://doi.org/10.1093/oso/9780190088583.001.0001

BryceTech. (2023). *The 2022 global space economy at a glance*. https://brycetech.com/reports.

Burr, C., & Leslie, D. (2023). Ethical assurance: A practical approach to the responsible design, development, and deployment of data-driven technologies. *AI and Ethics, 3*(1), 73–98. https://doi.org/10.1007/s43681-022-00178-0

CENELEC. (2024). *CEN/CLC/JTC 21—artificial intelligence*. https://standards.cencenelec.eu/dyn/www/f?p=205:22:0::::FSP_ORG_ID,FSP_LANG_ID:2916257,25&cs=1827B89DA69577BF3631EE2B6070F207D.

Cho, G. (2013). Privacy and EO: An overview of legal issues. In R. Purdy & D. Leung (Eds.), *Evidence from earth observation satellites* (Vol. 7, pp. 259–292). Brill.

Convention on International Liability for Damage Caused by Space Objects (Liability Convention). (1972). 961 UNTS 187.

Dennerley, J. A., Young, A., & Pozza, M. A. (2022). An introduction to risk management in outer space activities. In M. A. Pozza & J. A. Dennerley (Eds.), *Risk management in outer space activities: An Australian and New Zealand perspective* (pp. 1–17). Springer Nature. https://doi.org/10.1007/978-981-16-4756-7_1

Dennerley, J. A. (2018). State liability for space object collisions: The proper interpretation of 'fault' for the purposes of international space law. *The European Journal of International Law, 29*(1), 281–301. https://doi.org/10.1093/ejil/chy003

Department of Industry, Science and Resources. (2019). *Australia's AI ethics principles*. https://www.industry.gov.au/publications/australias-artificial-intelligence-ethics-framework/australias-ai-ethics-principles.

Department of Industry, Science and Resources. (2023). *Safe and responsible AI in Australia: Discussion paper.* https://consult.industry.gov.au/supporting-responsible-ai.

Department of Industry, Science and Resources. (2024). *Safe and responsible AI in Australia consultation: Australian government's interim response*. https://consult.industry.gov.au/supporting-responsible-ai.

Department of Prime Minister and Cabinet. (2023). *Government Response | Royal Commission into the Robodebt Scheme*. https://www.pmc.gov.au/resources/government-response-royal-commission-robodebt-scheme.

European Commission. (2019). Ethics guidelines for trustworthy AI. https://digital-strategy.ec.europa.eu/en/library/ethics-guidelines-trustworthy-ai.

European Union. (2016). Regulation (EU) 2016/679 of the European Parliament and of the Council of 27 April 2016 on the protection of natural persons with regard to the processing of personal data and on the free movement of such data, and repealing Directive 95/46/EC (General Data Protection Regulation). OJ L 119, 4.5.2016.

European Union. (2024). EU Artificial Intelligence Act. https://artificialintelligenceact.eu/article/3/.

Executive Office of the President. (2020, 3 December). *Promoting the use of trustworthy artificial intelligence in the Federal Government*. E.O. 13960 of Dec 3, 2020. 85 FR 78939. https://www.federalregister.gov/documents/2020/12/08/2020-27065/promoting-the-use-of-trustworthy-artificial-intelligence-in-the-federal-government.

Executive Office of the President. (2023, 30 October). *Safe, secure, and trustworthy development and use of artificial intelligence*. E.O. 14110 of Oct 30, 2023. 88 FR 75191. https://www.federalregister.gov/documents/2023/11/01/2023-24283/safe-secure-and-trustworthy-development-and-use-of-artificial-intelligence.

Executive Office of the President. (2025, January 20). *Initial rescissions of harmful Executive Orders and Actions*. Executive Order 14148. https://www.federalregister.gov/documents/2025/01/28/2025-01901/initial-rescissions-of-harmful-executive-orders-and-actions.

Ezeani, G., Koene, A., Kumar, R., Santiago, N., & Wright, D. (2022). A survey of artificial intelligence risk assessment methodologies. EY, Trilateral Research. https://www.trilateralresearch.com/wp-content/uploads/2022/01/A-survey-of-AI-Risk-Assessment-Methodologies-full-report.pdf.

Fraser, H., Haines, F., Villarino, J.-M. B. Y., Weatherall, K., & Parker, C. (2023). What role for standards and Assurance in Regulating Artificial Intelligence in Australia? *ADM+S working paper series 2023*, 8. https://apo.org.au/node/326309.

Freeland, S., & Ireland-Piper, D. (2022). Space law, human rights and corporate accountability. *UCLA Journal of International Law and Foreign Affairs, 26*(1) https://escholarship.org/uc/item/3636p0sp

Graham, T., & Thangavel, K. (2023, 2 October). Artificial intelligence in space: An analysis of responsible AI principles for the space domain. [Paper Presentation] International Astronautical Congress, Baku, Azerbaijan. https://www.researchgate.net/publication/374419104_Artificial_Intelligence_in_Space_An_Analysis_of_Responsible_AI_Principles_for_the_Space_Domain.

Graham, T., Thangavel, K., & Martin, A.-S. (2024). Navigating AI-lien terrain: Legal liability for artificial intelligence in outer space. *Acta Astronautica, 217*, 197–207. https://doi.org/10.1016/j.actaastro.2024.01.039

Grand View Research. (2022). Artificial intelligence market size report, 2022-2030. https://www.grandviewresearch.com/industry-analysis/artificial-intelligence-ai-market.

Hersey, F. (2023, March 8). *EU AI Act definition of AI aligns with OECD definition, biometric risk updated | Biometric Update.* https://www.biometricupdate.com/202303/eu-ai-act-definition-of-ai-aligns-with-oecd-definition-biometric-risk-updated.

Hesterman-Crane, A. (2022). Ethical considerations on the challenges of the dual-use satellite problem. In N. Coleman (Ed.), *Military space ethics* (pp. 95–114). Howgate Publishing Limited.

Higginbotham, B. (2018, October 11). The space economy: An industry takes off. U.S. Chamber of Commerce. https://www.uschamber.com/series/above-the-fold/the-space-economy-industry-takes.

Hubbard, D. W. (2020). *The failure of risk management: Why it's broken and how to fix it* (2nd ed.). Wiley. https://doi.org/10.1002/9781119198536

International Organization for Standardization. (2021). *ISO 31000:2018—risk management. A practical guide*. https://www.iso.org/publication/PUB100464.html.

International Organization for Standardization. (2023a). *Information technology—artificial intelligence—guidance on risk management* (ISO/IEC Standard No. 23894:2023). https://www.iso.org/standard/77304.html.

International Organization for Standardization. (2023b). *Information technology—artificial intelligence—management system* (ISO/IEC Standard No.42001). https://www.iso.org/standard/81230.html.

Jobin, A., Ienca, M., & Vayena, E. (2019). The global landscape of AI ethics guidelines. *Nature Machine Intelligence, 1*(9) Article 9. https://doi.org/10.1038/s42256-019-0088-2

Lee, S. U., Perera, H., Xia, B., Liu, Y., Lu, Q., Zhu, L., Salvado, O., & Whittle, J. (2023). *QB4AIRA: A question Bank for AI risk assessment.* arXiv. https://doi.org/10.48550/arXiv.2305.09300.

LiveNOW from FOX. (2025, February 11). VP JD Vance on the future of artificial intelligence. YouTube. https://www.youtube.com/watch?v=64E9O1Gv99o.

Lu, Q., Zhu, L., Whittle, J., & Xu, X. (2023). *Responsible AI: Best practices for creating trustworthy AI systems* (1st ed.). Addison-Wesley Professional.

Lu, Q., Zhu, L., Xu, X., Whittle, J., Zowghi, D., & Jacquet, A. (2022). *Responsible AI pattern catalogue: A multivocal literature review* (arXiv:2209.04963). arXiv. https://doi.org/10.48550/arXiv.2209.04963.

Martin, A.-S., & Freeland, S. (2021). The advent of artificial intelligence in space activities: New legal challenges. *Space Policy, 55*. https://doi.org/10.1016/j.spacepol.2020.101408

McNamara, B. (2022). Transferring risk through insurance law: Insuring space activities in Australia and New Zealand. In M. A. Pozza & J. A. Dennerley (Eds.), *Risk Management in Outer Space Activities: An Australian and New Zealand perspective* (pp. 85–106). Springer Nature. https://doi.org/10.1007/978-981-16-4756-7_4

Moss, T., Robison Hasani, K., & Deejay, A. (2023). *Looking up from down under: Australian attitudes to national space activities*. Australian Centre for Space Governance. https://www.spacegovcentre.org/_files/ugd/ff2a5a_76d6c587c5444703acc72faffa81c492.pdf.
Narayanan, M., & Schoeberl, C. (2023). A matrix for selecting responsible AI frameworks. Center for Security and Emerging Technology. https://cset.georgetown.edu/publication/a-matrix-for-selecting-responsible-ai-frameworks/.
National Aeronautics and Space Administration. (2011). NASA risk management handbook. https://www.nasa.gov/wp-content/uploads/2023/08/nasa-risk-mgmt-handbook.pdf.
National Aeronautics and Space Administration. (2022). NASA's responsible AI plan. https://ntrs.nasa.gov/api/citations/20220013471/downloads/RAI%20Plan%20Sept%201%202022.pdf.
National Institute of Standards and Technology. (2023a). AI RMF playbook. U.S. Department of Commerce. https://airc.nist.gov/AI_RMF_Knowledge_Base/Playbook.
National Institute of Standards and Technology. (2023b). *Artificial intelligence risk management framework (AI RMF 1.0)*. U.S. Department of Commerce. https://doi.org/10.6028/NIST.AI.100-1.
North Atlantic Treaty Organization (NATO). (2021, 22 October). *Summary of the NATO artificial intelligence strategy*. http://www.nato.int/cps/en/natohq/official_texts_187617.htm.
Pagallo, U., Bassi, E., & Durante, M. (2023). The normative challenges of AI in outer space: Law, ethics, and the realignment of terrestrial standards. *Philosophy & Technology, 36*(2), 23. https://doi.org/10.1007/s13347-023-00626-7
Pasquale, F. (2015). *The black box society: The secret algorithms that control money and information*. Harvard University Press.
Reid, A., O'Callaghan, S., & Lu, Y. (2023). Implementing Australia's AI ethics principles: A selection of responsible AI practices and resources. Gradient Institute and CSIRO. https://www.csiro.au/en/work-with-us/industries/technology/national-ai-centre/implementing-australias-ai-ethics-principles-report.
Richards, C. E., Cernev, T., Tzachor, A., Zilgalvis, G., & Kaleagasi, B. (2023). Safely advancing a spacefaring humanity with artificial intelligence. *Frontiers in Space Technologies, 4*. https://www.frontiersin.org. https://doi.org/10.3389/frspt.2023.1199547
Royal Commission into the Robodebt Scheme. (2023). *Report: Royal Commission into the Robodebt Scheme*. https://robodebt.royalcommission.gov.au/publications/report.
Russo, A., & Lax, G. (2022). Using artificial intelligence for space challenges: A survey. *Applied Sciences, 12*(10), 5106. https://doi.org/10.3390/app12105106
Schaefer, M. (2017). The contours of Permissionless innovation in the outer space domain. *University of Pennsylvania Journal of International Law, 39*(103), 82. https://papers.ssrn.com/sol3/Delivery.cfm/SSRN_ID2942526_code158168.pdf?abstractid=2942526&mirid=1
Schwartz, R., Vassilev, A., Greene, K., Perine, L., Burt, A., & Hall, P. (2022). Towards a standard for identifying and managing bias in artificial intelligence. *National Institute of Standards and Technology*. https://doi.org/10.6028/NIST.SP.1270
Slingerland, P., Perry, L., Kaufman, J., Bycroft, B., Linstead, E., Mandrake, L., Doran, G., Goel, A., Feather, M. S., Fesq, L., Ono, H., & Amini, R. (2022). Adapting a trusted AI framework to space mission autonomy. *IEEE Aerospace Conference (AERO), 2022*, 1–20. https://doi.org/10.1109/AERO53065.2022.9843376
Soucek, A., & Tapio, J. (2023). Standardization in the space sector and its role in the long-term sustainability of space activities: Regulation by stealth or a function creep? *Air and Space Law*, 48 (special). https://kluwerlawonline.com/api/Product/CitationPDFURL?file=Journals\AILA\AILA2023039.pdf.
Standards Australia & Commonwealth Scientific and Industrial Research Organisation. (2023) *Introduction to standards for artificial intelligence*. https://www.standards.org.au/documents/introduction-to-standards-for-artificial-intelligence.
Standards Australia. (2024). *Information technology—artificial intelligence—management system* (AS ISO/IEC 42001:2023). https://www.standards.org.au/standards-catalogue/standard-details?designation=as-iso-iec-42001-2023.

Steer, C. (2022). Star laws: The role of international law in regulating civil and military space activities. In N. Coleman (Ed.), *Military space ethics* (pp. 159–177). Howgate Publishing Limited.

Treaty on Principles Governing the Activities of States in the Exploration and Use of Outer Space, Including the Moon and Other Celestial Bodies (Outer Space Treaty). (1967). 610 UNTS 205.

U.S. Department of Defense. (2020). *DOD adopts ethical principles for artificial intelligence.* https://www.defense.gov/Newsroom/Releases/Release/Article/2091996/dod-adopts-ethical-principles-for-artificial-intelligence/.

U.S. Food and Drug Administration (FDA). (2020, February 21). Learn about drug and device approvals. FDA. https://www.fda.gov/patients/learn-about-drug-and-device-approvals.

van Maanen, G. (2022). AI ethics, ethics washing, and the need to politicize data ethics. *Digital Society, 1*(2), 9. https://doi.org/10.1007/s44206-022-00013-3

White, J., Codoreanu, A., Zuleta, I., Lynch, C., Marchisio, G., Qin, K., Petrie, S. M., & Duffy, A. R. (2024). Quantifying trade-offs in satellite hardware configurations using a super-resolution framework with realistic image degradation. *Remote Sensing Letters, 15*(3), 291–301. https://doi.org/10.1080/2150704X.2024.2318756

Thomas Graham, BSci, JD, GDLP. Graham is a PhD candidate researching the application of responsible AI development practices and artificial intelligence regulation within the space sector.

Regulating Satellite Constellations

Christopher J. Newman and J. Lauren Napier

1 Introduction

Human space activities in the twenty-first century have undergone a series of significant and fundamental changes. Advances in the use of novel materials, miniaturisation of key technology, and a concomitant development of computing power has seen a revolution in the application of small satellites. This in turn has led to their increased ubiquity in Low Earth Orbit (LEO), and the use of a large number of satellites operating synchronously in satellite constellations. The idea to use groups of connected satellites acting as part of a collective network is not new, and dates to the middle of the twentieth century (Lüders, 1961). This idea failed to materialise, and even in the 1990s, telecoms companies such as Iridium developed 'impressive' plans for global connectivity via satellite constellations, but which were unsuccessful due to high costs and limited demand (Daehnick et al., 2020, p.2).

It is only now in the 2020s that commercial providers of high-speed internet from space, such as OneWeb, Starlink, and Telesat (Henry, 2018), have fully embraced the potential of constellations by harnessing the benefits of low-cost production and cheap access to LEO. Whereas the weak demand in the 1990s reflected a time of much less connectivity, limited technology, and an expensive 'per kg to LEO' launch market, these twenty-first-century telecommunications firms have a ready-made market, and recognise the attraction of global, high-speed internet access to customers. The new satellite constellations are comprised of hundreds—and in

The views of the authors are the authors' alone and are intended to provide commentary and general information, and do not represent the views of any organisation. This chapter should not be relied upon as a substitute for professional legal advice or for any other purpose.

C. J. Newman · J. L. Napier (✉)
Northumbria University, Newcastle, UK
e-mail: l.napier@northumbria.ac.uk

J. A. Dennerley, M. A. Pozza (eds.), *The Business of Outer Space*, Space Law and Policy, https://doi.org/10.1007/978-981-95-2034-3_4

some cases thousands—of small satellites that are cheap to manufacture. The promise of launch, priced at a point that is cheap enough to sustain deployment and renewal of a large-scale constellation, a production line of cheap satellites, and a market hungry for connectivity looks set to herald a revolution in the telecommunications industry.

Nonetheless, despite the potential of unparalleled connectivity facilitated by these constellations, there are a host of associated legal, environmental, and organisational difficulties. This chapter will examine these issues, because the contemporary space sector has moved on significantly from the era of signing international space treaties. Indeed, the concept of networked satellites was not explicitly dealt with in the original tranche of international treaties that form the core principles of space law. Yet the launch industry has evolved to provide cheap and easy access to LEO, and there is now a significant strain placed on the radio frequency (RF) spectrum, due in part to the unprecedented numbers of satellites in these constellations which heightens the need for increased coordination between States and operators in respect of both orbital operations and end-of-life protocols.

2 Methodology and Context: Constellations and Space Law

As pointed out by McConville and Chui (2017, p. 1), legal scholarship has traditionally followed two broad methods of analysis: the first is a doctrinal examination of law as an internal, self-sustaining set of principles accessible through statutes and case law and requiring no reference to the world outside of the law. Given the unique nature of the space environment and the need to incorporate technical, geopolitical, and increasingly environmental considerations, it is argued that a doctrinal exploration of the space law as it applies to constellations would be unnecessarily limiting. This discussion will, therefore, adopt the second method of analysis, that of looking at the law in the context of other factors, as part of a broader search for solutions and explanations (McConville & Chui, 2017, p. 1).

This chapter will engage in an original, rigorous exploration of the current contours of the law focusing on the idiosyncrasies of regulating constellations of networked satellites that work synchronously and in large numbers. Such a discussion will involve discussing what is understood by the term ‘constellation’. Indeed, there have been numerous attempts, outside of the international treaties, to define a satellite constellation. Wood (2003, p.13) provides that it is ‘a number of similar satellites, of a similar type and function, designed to be in similar, complementary, orbits for a shared purpose, under shared control’. This definition has been developed upon to include, as a fundamental feature of satellites flying within a constellation, ‘autonomous navigation of separate spacecraft as part of a group and control of their mutual but relative position in the group’ (Abashidze et al., 2022, p. 177).

This ability to determine and control the relative positions of satellites means that the formation of the group can be reconfigured depending on the needs of the system and will be able to adapt to losses or outages of individual satellites

(Abashidze et al., 2022, p. 177). Importantly, when defining constellations, the size of the individual satellites, the location of the constellation in space, or its purpose are significant but not determinative in the context of developing a precise definition. Rather, 'the question arises whether there should be a certain minimum number of satellites in order to call a group of satellites a constellation' (Bielicki, 2020, p. 246). The United States' Orbital Debris Mitigation Standard Practices (ODMSP) (National Aeronautics and Space Administration [NASA], 2019, p. 7) holds that a large constellation is 'a constellation consisting of 100 or more operational spacecraft cumulative'. Numerous academic definitions have been proposed (for instance see Abashidze et al., 2022, p. 179), but for the purposes of this chapter, the term 'constellation' will be taken to be the definition offered above by Wood, with the ODMSP definition holding for a large constellation.

As can be seen from the definitional discussion, any analysis of space systems will involve consideration of technical and engineering aspects. This is a legal inquiry and does not propose to intrude on the realm of those trained as scientists and engineers. Nonetheless, advances in connective technology cannot be overlooked. There are some pioneering changes, in terms of the creation of low-latency robust downlinks to ground stations (Vasisht et al., 2021), the need to improve the (often AI-enabled) processing loads to move data analysis into space (Fernholz, 2024), and—perhaps most intriguingly—the use of off-the-shelf laser crosslinks (so-called lasercom) to allow satellites to connect directly to commercial networks such as Starlink and Telesat (Doumitt & Speckman, 2023, p. 3). These developments will serve only to enhance the functionality and utility of constellations and make them more attractive to commercial operators.

The advances are, however, not free from consequences. There is a significant legal dimension that needs to be addressed in respect of the spectrum usage of large constellations. The allocation of radio frequency spectrum for satellite communication is a critical issue. With numerous constellations vying for bandwidth, ensuring equitable access while minimising interference is paramount. The law must navigate competing commercial and political interests and this discussion will evaluate whether there are clear rules for spectrum allocation that prevent conflict in this area. Indeed, this discussion will engage in a systemic analysis of the role of the International Telecommunications Union (ITU) in coordinating and managing key aspects of the satellite constellation revolution.

The discussion will examine the law determining liability and responsibility for satellite collisions or environmental damage. The difficulty of attributing responsibility in the event of accidents or malfunctions will be examined in the context of the unique challenges posed by the dramatic increase in orbiting satellites. The focus of the chapter will then move to institutions, such as the United Nations Committee on the Peaceful Uses of Outer Space (UNCOPUOS) and the ITU, and how they are managing to keep up with the developments in constellation technology, and how, in turn those advances have impacted upon the licensing process in the United States (US) and the United Kingdom (UK). The discussion will then focus on the environmental impact of constellations and how the law, regulation, and political agreements combine to deal with the challenges posed by the emergence of constellations. Nonetheless, as with any inquiry into the legality of activity in outer space, the first recourse is to the *Treaty on Principles Governing the Activities of States in the Exploration and Use of Outer Space, including the Moon and Other Celestial Bodies*, referred to as the Outer Space Treaty (OST) (Outer Space Treaty [OST], 1967). This, along with the other international space treaties, will be critically evaluated to establish how constellations fit into the international legal order.

3 International Law and the Governance of Satellite Constellations

The Outer Space Treaty forms the foundation of the international space legal order. Article I of the Treaty holds that the use and exploration of outer space 'shall be carried out for the benefit and in the interests of all countries [...] and shall be the province of all mankind' (OST, 1967, Article I). The Treaty goes on to provide that all States shall be free to use and engage in the exploration of outer space 'without discrimination of any kind, on a basis of equality and in accordance with international law' (OST, 1967, Article I). As the development of satellite technology is second only to that of rocketry in the history of space technology, it is well established that the use of satellites falls within the ambit of the *use* of space as defined under Article I. Therefore, the existence and deployment of, for instance, the Starlink constellation highlights the positive international law position on constellations, and the use of multiple satellites acting in a coordinated fashion is a legitimate use of space.

Important to this discussion is the fact that there is no definition within the five international space treaties for a satellite constellation. The only mention made in respect of artificial satellites is the term 'space object' or 'object launched into outer space'. This is found throughout Articles VII, VIII, and X of the Outer Space Treaty and the term 'space object' is defined in the *Convention on International Liability for Damage Caused by Space Objects* referred to as the Liability Convention which specifies that it 'includes component parts of a space object as well as its launch vehicle and parts thereof' (Liability Convention, 1972, Article I(d)). Any satellite irrespective of whether it is launched as or intended to operate within a constellation of satellites would then be classed as a space object under international space law. In terms of international law, a constellation is a collection of space objects. The fact that they are connected and work together, does not—of itself—convey any special duties on States.

Article I of the Outer Space Treaty provides for the scope of human activity covered. The rest of the Outer Space Treaty goes on to outline the conditions under which the exploration and use of outer space can be undertaken by States, some of which is relevant to the deployment of large constellations of satellites. The Treaty circumscribes certain activities, such as in Article II, which forbids the appropriation of space 'by claim of sovereignty, by means of use or occupation, or by any other means' (OST, 1967, Article II). Article IV prohibits the placement in orbit of any objects carrying nuclear weapons or weapons of mass destruction. As well as prohibitions, the Treaty also imposes behavioural requirements on States. Article III explicitly requires that the activities in the use and exploration of space are carried out in accordance with international law, and Article V puts in place requirements for the rapid safe return of space objects and astronauts of signatory States.

4 Responsibility and National Authorisation for Constellations

It is Article VI of the Outer Space Treaty that points towards the duties of States in respect of their own space activities, and it is here that an analysis of the use of constellations can start. Article VI is broken down into three sentences. The first sentence provides that signatory States 'shall bear international responsibility for national activities [...] carried out' in outer space (OST, 1967, Article VI). The second sentence goes on specifically to deal with national space activities by stating that where the activities are carried out by 'non-governmental entities [...] authorization and continuing supervision' is required by the appropriate State (OST, 1967, Article VI). The Treaty does not specify the 'activities' for which the State is responsible, nor is there any restrictions or limitations on the operation and control of space objects. It is also clear from this, that all activities, whether carried out by the State or not, shall be the responsibility of the 'appropriate' State.

When trying to identify which would be the 'appropriate' State, the normal principles of public international law are applicable. This means that a State has jurisdiction over any activity that is carried on from its territory as well as over any activities carried on by its nationals as 'natural or judicial persons' (see, OST, 1967, Articles VII-VIII). Even if the drafters of the Treaty did not have direct contemplation of large numbers of satellites working as a constellation, it is quite clear that the treaty intended to ensure that all non-governmental space activities were ultimately assigned to a State. Even where the non-governmental entity is a powerful, high-profile corporation, international responsibility for the activity conducted in outer space rests with the 'appropriate State'.

The position within the Outer Space Treaty is that satellite constellations come within the prescribed activity, as they are groups of space objects which utilise the space domain. Similarly, so long as States have authorised the group(s) of space objects, any non-governmental entity can have a satellite constellation in Low Earth Orbit. The one caveat is that LEO is becoming increasingly congested (Snyder, 2024). Accordingly, there is a danger that increasing numbers of satellites could both hinder access to specific orbits for other space actors and increase the potential risk of collision with other space objects. As of April 2024, Starlink is the largest constellation in LEO with 5800 active satellites (Howell & Pultarova, 2024). Other companies have plans for similar numbers, with Amazon Leo (formerly Project Kuiper) having filed to launch 3236 satellites in its constellation (Daehnick et al., 2020). It is not just companies within the US that are looking to put large constellations in LEO. The China Satellite Network Group is preparing to acquire licensing and filings for a large constellation of 13,000 satellites for the creation of a high-speed internet network, and the private company GalaxySpace has plans to send 1000 'low orbit' satellites (Tabeta, 2024).

Given the preponderance of LEO constellations, consideration should also be given to the principles of due regard and the importance of preventing harmful interference. Article IX of the Outer Space Treaty declares that States shall 'conduct all their activities in outer space [...] with due regard to the corresponding interests of all other States Parties to the Treaty' (OST, 1967, Article IX). Article IX, 'refers to the performance of an act with a certain standard of care, attention or observance' (Marchisio, 2009, p. 175). The corollary of this is that, in using and exploring space, States must ensure that the exercise of their rights under the Outer Space Treaty does not interfere with, or compromise the safety of, space operations of other State parties or their non-governmental entities. Indeed, 'States should avoid any measures aimed at hampering the space activities of other States' (Marchisio, 2009, p. 175). This standard of care or due regard for other actors' activities is in line with the ITU Constitution and Convention (International Telecommunication Union [ITU Constitution], 2022), and the ITU Radio Regulations (ITU Radio Regulations, 2020), regarding harmful interference.

Article IX of the Outer Space Treaty refers to 'harmful interference' as a trigger for international consultation if one State believes there is potential for an activity to cause harmful interference with other space activities (OST, 1967, Article IX). The Treaty does not provide details as to what constitutes harmful interference. There is further mention in the ITU Constitution and the ITU Radio Regulations on the notion of what may constitute harmful interference. Article 45 of the ITU Constitution stipulates that States must 'not [...] cause harmful interference' and should also prevent causing harmful interference (ITU Constitution, 2022, Article 45). Article 45 is supported by ITU Radio Regulations Article 15 which outlines detailed rules on interference such as how to avoid harmful interference or what procedures are in place if harmful interference does occur (ITU Radio Regulations, 2020, Article 15). Whilst this does not specifically apply to constellations, States could have recourse to the provisions of Article IX of the Outer Space Treaty and refer to the ITU if constellation activity could demonstrably be proven to cause interference with the space activities of another State Parties (Carpanelli, 2024). Whilst there is a duty on States to consult in the context of harmful interference, it should be noted that harmful interference differs from liability for damage.

5 Registration Requirements for Constellations

The requirement related to the registration of space objects can be found in the Outer Space Treaty under Article VIII where States Parties to the Treaty 'on whose registry an object launched into outer space is carried shall retain jurisdiction and control over such object' (OST, 1967, Article VIII). This general principle was extended in the *Convention on Registration of Objects Launched into Outer Space*, referred to as the Registration Convention (Convention on Registration of Objects Launched into Outer Space (Registration Convention) 1976). Like the other international space treaties, the Registration Convention does not use the term 'satellite' or 'constellation' (but it too does speak of a space object) and, as mentioned above, a space object can be a satellite and therefore it also applies to constellations (Newman & Napier, 2020).

The Registration Convention dictates that each space object shall be registered to the 'Secretary-General of the United Nations' which is available with 'full and open access' (Registration Convention, 1976, Article III). Each State registering a space object (either for themselves or on behalf of a non-State actor) 'shall furnish [...] as soon as practicable' (Registration Convention, 1976, Article IV) a collection of information about the space object(s) including things such as the name of the 'launching State or States', date of launch, orbital parameters, registration number, or other appropriate designator(s), and the general functions of the object (see Registration Convention, 1976, Article IV).

Within the United Nations Committee on the Peaceful Uses of Outer Space and its Legal Subcommittee, registration has been a reenergised topic of concern especially around satellite and megaconstellations. While the same registration requirement applies to single satellites as it does to constellations, 'when registering relevant space objects, States of registry often do not indicate that an object is part of a large constellation or mega constellation' (United Nations Committee on the Peaceful Uses of Outer Space Legal Subcommittee [UNCOPUOS LSC], 2022a, p. 4). This largely comes down to fragmentation amongst States regarding registration and licensing mechanisms at the national level. It is recognised that 'the registration practices of States do not change when they register single satellites or multiple satellites that form large constellations and megaconstellations' (UNCOPUOS LSC, 2022a, p. 6). While some States have 'taken steps to accommodate the increased number of registrations' (UNCOPUOS LSC, 2022a, p. 6) some States have not registered space objects with the UN (UNCOPUOS LSC, 2022a, p. 6). This lack of compliance with the need to register space objects, however, is not a problem exclusive to constellations.

6 Liability for Damage Caused by Constellations

There has been much written about the current state of the regime which ascribes liability for damage caused by space objects of one State to another (see Dennerley, 2018). When considering the issues that apply to satellites working as part of large constellations the problem of the current, ill-defined regime is magnified. A constellation will potentially include thousands of satellites, all working as a collective and almost certainly with some element of autonomous navigation. When considering the contours of liability for damage caused by constellations, as with other areas of space law, one must first look to the international treaties.

Liability for damage caused by space objects is found in Article VII of the Outer Space Treaty which imposes liability upon the State 'that launches or procures the launching of an object into outer space' for damage caused by its space objects (OST, 1967, Article VII). This has a twofold consequence for the operation of constellations. First, liability rests with States, not 'non-governmental entities' such as private commercial operators. Should the operator of a constellation either suffer damage, or have damage inflicted upon it by the space object of another State, then the private operator cannot seek a remedy directly, and it must instead be undertaken at the State-to-State level. Second, there is no provision within Article VII for damage caused by space objects of the same State. It is assumed that the normal channels of dispute resolution would be explored in this instance.

The Outer Space Treaty has created a subset of States who are assigned liability based on their status as a launching State (confirmed by Article I of the Liability Convention). This reflects the view of those drafting the Treaty that liability for damage caused by the launching of an object into outer space should be borne by those States who are active in the launch business (Kerrest & Smith, 2009, p. 136). A State will be a launching State if it launches, procures a launch, or if a space object is launched using its territory or facilities. As a launching State, it will be 'internationally liable for damage to another State Party to the Treaty or its natural or juridical person by such object or its component parts on the Earth, in air space or in outer space' (OST, 1967, Article VII).

Article VII of the Outer Space Treaty provides only the core principles as to how liability for damage caused by a space activity is assigned to States. The Liability Convention is the international treaty which expands upon the general principle of international State liability for damage resulting from a space object (Kerrest & Smith, 2009, p. 129). Article III of the Liability Convention provides the conditions for liability for States as regards damage occurring on-orbit. Article III holds that 'in the event of damage being caused elsewhere than on the surface of the earth to a space object of one launching State or to persons or property on board such a space object by a space object of another launching State, the latter shall be liable only if the damage is due to its fault or the fault of persons for whom it is responsible' (Liability Convention, 1972, Article III).

The Liability Convention specifies damage caused by space objects rather than by *satellites* and none of the criteria for liability specifies that the damage is caused to, or by, a space object working as part of a constellation. Importantly, 'if damage is caused by the space object of "State A" to the space object of "State B", then "State A" will be liable only if the State or persons for whom the State is responsible is at fault' (Newman & Napier, 2020, p. 295).

There are both conceptual and practical difficulties associated with this formulation of liability, a problem that is exacerbated by the number of satellites that work as part of a constellation(s). The principle conceptual issue is that the notion of 'fault' is unclear within Article III, specifically whether it is fault in the sense of a breach of a duty of care within a liability regime or whether it falls within the regime of State responsibility for wrongful acts (see Dennerley, 2018, p. 301). States have been reluctant to test the parameters of fault through litigation, and notably there was no litigation in respect of the collision in 2009 between the Cosmos 2251 and Iridium 33 satellites (von der Dunk, 2010, p. 199). Equally, just as there is no explicit way to interpret fault as enshrined in the international space treaties, there are no softer, political agreements to indicate emerging consensus as regards fault in the context of orbital operations (Newman et al., 2021, p. 3867).

This ambiguity leads to two key issues in relation to the operation of constellations. The first is that the deployment of satellites in a constellation will depend heavily on the use of autonomous systems for keeping track of onboard sensors and equipment in real time, which in turn is used to 'identify collision risks and, when needed, implement an optimal manoeuvre for collision avoidance' (Thangavel et al., 2024, p. 19). This could, of itself lead to questions of fault becoming convoluted, with non-governmental entities retaining proprietary details about 'black box' algorithms and disputes about decisions made by non-human decision-makers. When two competing algorithmic collision avoidance systems make decisions that lead to damage to one or more space objects, unpicking where the liability rests may fall short of proving fault. The question arises as to 'whether and how the system of liability as foreseen in the UN Space Treaties, is suitable in the context of AI components in space programmes' (Martin & Freeland, 2021, p. 6).

Another practical area of concern in respect of liability is the current 'data deficit' regarding the independent provision of information regarding the position of objects in LEO (Newman & Cheney, 2023, p. 130). The information that is provided in respect of Space Situational Awareness (SSA) comes largely from the US military (Weeden, 2019). Should there be a collision on-orbit, when presented with SSA data to investigate the possibility of fault, there may be States who are geopolitical adversaries who would dispute the veracity of the information as the SSA information is coming from a military source. Obversely, the military provision of SSA data may also mean that should it be strategically necessary, a State in possession of SSA capability could close the pipeline of information to its adversaries, meaning that a State may not have the capability to prove fault.

In addition to the probity of SSA data, there is also a question about the capacity and coverage of space tracking capability, which is especially problematic in LEO (Peldszus & Faucher, 2019). This will only become more pronounced given the number of satellites that are already in orbit and the vast increase that have been proposed in various filings (Daehnick et al., 2020, p. 2). Given the current state of

SSA capability, the question must also be asked whether not only fault, but also causation can be independently verified, as 'the limitations of the existing data [...] mean(s) that the ultimate SSA goal of having knowledge of the position and orbit of every object in space is far from a reality' (Newman & Cheney, 2023, p. 18). Returning to the question of fault, upgrading the capacity of space object tracking systems and the provision of data about the orbital environment is of paramount importance. After all, SSA data will be the crucial piece of evidence in any complaint involving State fault.

In summary, the five international space treaties remain central to the law regarding the regulation of satellite constellations. States can use LEO for the purpose of situating constellations to provide high-speed global internet coverage. States are, however, responsible for their own national activities and that responsibility starts with an obligation on States to authorise non-governmental activity. Even if the drafters of the Outer Space Treaty did not have direct contemplation of large numbers of satellites working as a constellation, it is quite clear that the Treaty intended to ensure that all non-governmental space activities were ultimately assigned to a State. Even where the non-governmental entity is a powerful, high-profile corporation, international responsibility for the activity conducted in outer space rests with the 'appropriate State'. Finally, when considering the sheer size of the proposed, future constellations for LEO, the issues concerning liability, which affect the wider space sector, become even more pronounced for constellations. The challenges posed by increasingly autonomous decision-making systems, coupled with the paucity of data at an evidential standard level and the general ambiguity over the requirements of fault will all come to the fore as ever larger constellations begin to occupy LEO.

7 National Licensing and Constellations

The Outer Space Treaty embeds agreed principles into State behaviour when exploring outer space. States are responsible at the international level, under Article VI of the Outer Space Treaty, for any non-State actors. Similarly, under Article VII, States are liable for damage caused by their space objects if they launched, procured a launch, or allowed their territory or facilities to be used for a launch. The final element of these components of accountability comes in Article VIII with the recognition of States having 'jurisdiction and control' of all space objects that carry their registry (OST, 1967, Article VIII). Registration does not guarantee liability but places jurisdiction and control—as key elements of responsibility—in the hands of a single launching State.

To ensure that space objects, and indeed overarching mission concepts, are suitable to bear the load of this responsibility, States will require all constellations to go through national approval processes. National approval processes for space activities are not prescribed within the Outer Space Treaty and their content and administration varies between States. This discussion will now examine the approach to licensing for the US, the country responsible for the largest current satellite constellations in LEO. This will not be a granular examination of *how* to apply for a constellation licence. Rather, the focus will be on the underlying principles informing national regulation and compliance and will demonstrate the potential reach that national regulators have and how they are seizing the initiative in respect of managing the LEO environment.

A private (non-governmental) operator looking to launch a constellation must seek approval from their national regulator. In the US, there is a tripartite arrangement established by the Commercial Space Launch Act 1984. This establishes a regulatory framework for commercial space transportation activities in the US (Commercial Space Launch Act 1984). It grants the Federal Aviation Administration (FAA) authority to license commercial space launches and re-entries, ensuring compliance with safety standards and environmental regulations. Similarly, the Department of Commerce, through the National Oceanic and Atmospheric Administration (NOAA), is responsible for the licensing of private remote sensing space systems through the Land Remote Sensing Policy Act 1992. Where there exists a satellite providing Earth Observation (EO) data, and the operator is either based in the US or a US person (including a legal person) operating an EO system outside of the US, then the entity must apply for a licence as laid down in the regulations.

The third government agency involved in regulating space, and the most crucial for private operators of constellations, is the Federal Communications Commission (FCC). Under the Communications Act 1934, the FCC has oversight of all aspects of satellite communications, is the domestic regulator of telecommunications which is responsible for liaison with the ITU, and has fundamental responsibility for all activities that involve the transmission of radio frequencies (see generally Communications Act 1934). Additionally, the FCC is also responsible for regulating the services of companies like Starlink and other satellite constellation operators—namely the regulation of satellite mobile and broadband internet, and the use of ground equipment and other aspects of operation which are crucial for the delivery of these satellite services (for example, see Code of Federal Regulations, n.d.-a, 47 CFR 25.143).

In 2023 the creation of the Space Bureau as a separate unit within the FCC was announced (Federal Communications Commission [FCC], 2023). This body was created to handle the licensing of satellite systems and more generally consolidate the FCC's role in leading the regulation of commercial space operations. The Space Bureau will also coordinate with the Office of International Affairs to broadly consult with other States on the development of space policy and the management of satellites and novel space applications, especially in respect of the challenges posed by such constellations (Shepardson, 2022). Having already amended the post mission disposal requirements for the de-orbiting of satellites which have reached the end of their life from 25 years down to 5 years (FCC, 2024), the Space Bureau has taken steps to try and augment and update the FCC regulatory toolkit to reflect the changes in the satellite industry (Shepardson, 2022).

Perhaps most fundamentally, in response to the increasing numbers of satellites now being placed in orbit, the Space Bureau is putting in place regulatory standards for the mitigation of orbital debris for new missions. These form part of the licensing requirements (Code of Federal Regulations, n.d.-b, 47 CFR 5.64) and, where the system has not already been approved by the FCC, must include an explicit statement that an operator 'has assessed and limited the amount of [space] debris' that will arise, either in normal operations, through an isolated accident, or should a collision occur (Code of Federal Regulations, n.d.-b, 47 CFR 5.64 (b)). Where the application is for a non-geostationary orbit (NGSO) system, an assessment of the risk of collision across the operational phase of the mission and deorbiting, together with the accuracy with which the orbital parameters will be maintained, must be supplied (Code of Federal Regulations, n.d.-b, 47 CFR 5.64(b)(4)(i)(A-D). The operators must also commit to deal with any SSA conjunction warnings by reviewing and taking all possible steps to assess the collision risk and mitigate that risk. This includes contacting and sharing data with other operators and modifying their satellite operation if needed.

The FCC debris mitigation provisions go further. As well as requiring disclosure of any planned proximity operations (Code of Federal Regulations, n.d.-b, 47 CFR 5.64(b)(6)) and details of disposal plans specific to NGSO (Code of Federal Regulations, n.d.-b, 47 CFR 5.64(b)(7)), the FCC requires a statement addressing the trackability of the satellites and the extent to which the space object will be registered with the 18th Space Control Squadron (or its successor) and any other entities that engage in SSA or space traffic management functions as well as any other operators. The provisions found throughout 47 CFR 5.64 stop short of mandating the disclosure of such information. This emphasises that the FCC are mindful of treating each licence on a case-by-case basis. Recent applications by industry stakeholders to reconsider disclosure requirements on manoeuvrability and other technical information were dismissed by the FCC as 'speculative' and affirmed that the rules 'reinforced [the FCCs] commitment to space sustainability' (Foust, 2024).

The evolution of the FCC rules over the course of recent times has reflected the increasing significance of the role of constellations in contemporary space activities. A request made in 2024 for comments on refreshing the rules pertaining to orbital debris mitigation (FCC, 2024) made a specific request for stakeholder input on the rules governing orbital debris mitigation for satellite constellations. Specifically, the consultation asks whether the FCC should evaluate collision risk presented by multi-satellite NGSO constellations on the aggregate of the entire system or on a 'per satellite' basis. When looking across the system, the question then arises as to the appropriate metric by which an operator can demonstrate compliance. Determination and evaluation of the risk could then be identified by examining the manoeuvring capabilities and reliability of the satellite, the orbital lifetime, the number of satellites in the system, including the constellation replenishment rate and replacement of satellites over a specified time period and the size of individual satellites. The FCC also inquired whether there should be a distinction between large constellations and smaller systems in respect of the metrics used or whether there should be a 'scalable metric for both types of systems' (FCC, 2024, p. 3).

The questions asked in the FCC consultation are perhaps indicative of the direction of travel that regulators will take when assessing the implications of constellations. Perhaps of even greater significance is that these questions are being asked on a national rather than an international level. The US and the FCC are not the only regulators of space activities to be engaged in widespread consultations about the form and content of regulations, given the contemporary rise in constellations. Within the UK, the regulator for space activities is the Civil Aviation Authority (CAA) and there has been several externally facing, cross-government consultations on regulatory matters (see for example, UK Space Agency, 2024). Elsewhere, the recent promulgation of Indian Space Policy looks to develop a 'flourishing commercial presence in space' (ISRO, 2023, p. 5) by creating 'a stable and predictable regulatory framework to provide a level playing field to Non-Government Entities' through the creation of IN-SPACE (the Indian National Space Promotion and Authorisation Centre) (ISRO, 2023).

In seeking normative standards for the development of regulations, national regulators can also look to established industry best practices. There are standards from the International Organization for Standardization (ISO) specific to space systems that are technical standards for use in design and operations of space systems. Currently under development is an ISO standard which will apply specifically to constellations (see International Organization for Standardization [ISO], 2024). There are other ISO standards published that can and should be applied to constellations such as ISO 24113:2023 Space Systems—Space Debris Mitigation Requirements (see, ISO, 2023) which works in conjunction with the United Nation's Space Debris Mitigation Guidelines (SDMG) (see United Nations Office for Outer Space Affairs [UNOOSA], 2010; Dennerley, 2022). This is not an exhaustive list and there are other industry and standards setting bodies, such as CONFERS which are developing standardised practices on a sector-wide basis rather than a jurisdictional one. This serves to illustrate the drivers upon the licensing frameworks of different jurisdictions. National regulators are taking the initiative in respect of introducing regulation for constellations; however, these discussions are not occurring in isolation. There is still a vital role for international dialogue and consultation between States on the way to manage the impact of constellations, especially in NGSO. This discussion will now evaluate the discussions that are occurring within these international fora.

8 The United Nations Committee on Peaceful Uses of Outer Space and Satellite Constellations

The five space treaties capture high-level principles of space law that States have affirmed through their signature and ratification. It is then national regulators that have clearly taken these principles and embedded them into domestic regimes and built upon them. The space treaties empower States to develop their own regulatory frameworks to authorise and supervise their own space activities. This does not mean, however, that space law is now developing solely within the confines of the jurisdiction of States. The United Nations Committee on the Peaceful Uses of Outer Space was founded at the outset of human activity in outer space (see Lyall & Larsen, 2018, pp. 14–18 for details of the formation and operation of UNCOPUOS). As discussed above, one of the growing concerns articulated by States through UNCOPUOS is over the registration of satellites within constellations. In 2022, the UNCOPUOS Legal Subcommittee published a document entitled Registration of Large Constellations and Mega constellations (see UNCOPUOS LSC, 2022a. This source is hereafter referred to as the RLC report) which was created through the Working Group on the Status and Application of the Five United Nations Treaties on Outer Space.

The RLC report provides crucial areas of consensus within and amongst States. First is the point that large constellations have technical distinctions such that, 'at present, large constellations are typically "assembled" incrementally, that is, a few satellites are launched at a time, whereas megaconstellation launches are dedicated to the constellation and comprise large batches of 30–60 mass-produced satellites. This difference in tempo and numbers is likely to directly influence whether a State modifies its registration practices' (UNCOPUOS LSC, 2022a, p. 5). In practical terms, there is not a real distinction between large, mega, or any other type of constellations as smaller constellations from 2 to 50 satellites could still go up in increments or in batches.

The United Nations Committee on the Peaceful Uses of Outer Space (UNCOPUOS) recognises that 'satellite constellations have been an integral part of space activities for nearly six decades. Constellations for communications, disaster prevention and management, Earth Observation, meteorology, national security, navigation, science and technology development are ubiquitous and are among the foundations of modern-day civilization' (UNCOPUOS LSC, 2022a, pp. 1–2). Most satellite constellations are on-orbit in Low Earth Orbit with navigation satellite constellations in Medium Earth Orbit.

According to the RLC report (UNCOPUOS LSC, 2022a, p. 2), 'almost all [...] constellations are operated by non-governmental entities and provide commercial communications or Earth Observation services'. This can be corroborated from open-source data, which also shows that Low Earth Orbit constellations are predominately made up of communications and Earth Observation satellites. Furthermore, the US (with over 25 constellations) and China (with over 20 constellations) have the most satellite constellations in Low Earth Orbit. The US and UK have constellations with large numbers of satellites per constellation whilst China has many smaller constellations. The US has the greatest number of satellites within a constellation, with the Starlink constellation having over 5800 satellites on-orbit as of May 2024.

As was mentioned above, the UNCOPUOS Legal Subcommittee Member States have included more discussion on registration recently. According to the Report of the Legal Subcommittee at its 62nd session in 2023, 'the Subcommittee noted that it was important to enhance the practice of registration, in particular, with regard to large constellations and megaconstellations' (UNCOPUOS LSC, 2023, p. 12). Based on the interest of enhancing registration across States, the United Nations Office for Outer Space Affairs (UNOOSA) is launching the 'Registration Project: supporting the implementation of treaty obligations related to the registration of objects launched into outer space' to further support implementation of the Registration Convention (UNCOPUOS LSC, 2023, p. 12).

The views expressed by the Member States of UNCOPUOS was that registration regarding constellations should be in conformity with obligations of liability put forth in the Liability Convention and regarding the use of the radio frequency spectrum put forth in the ITU Radio Regulations (see UNCOPUOS LSC, 2023). With the growing concern over registration of constellations, the RLC report gives some insight into the status of registration vis-à-vis constellations. This document encapsulates the notion that constellations are not a novel activity and additionally, per Article VI of the Outer Space Treaty, it is the States that are still responsible for their activities and the activities of their non-State actors including owners and operators of constellations, irrespective of size.

9 The ITU and the Management of Constellations

An oft-overlooked aspect of the operation of constellations is the relationship between the law as connected to activities in space and the broad span of telecommunications law. If the UNCOPUOS represents the key law-making forum for international space law, the central institution for the regulation of the telecommunications industry is the International Telecommunications Union which handles the filing of the use of the radio frequency spectrum for satellites and ground stations. It is the Radio Regulations which sit under the framework of the ITU Constitution and Convention which establishes the rule relating to the use of radio frequency spectrum for space systems (ITU Constitution, 2022, Article 44).

The Radio Regulations give more granular tenets regarding satellites and radio usage. They emphasise the importance of preventing and halting harmful interference over the radio frequency spectrum. While many of the Radio Regulations do not differentiate between satellites and constellations, there are certain Resolutions from World Radio Conferences that do specifically apply to satellite constellations using radio frequencies. As the ITU distinguishes between GSO and NGSO, the focus of this discussion will be on NGSO (including Low Earth Orbit) as this is where most constellations reside.

Article 1 of the Radio Regulations provides clarification of the definitions that are used within the Radio Regulations. As already established under international space law, a satellite in a constellation (or its component parts thereof) is a space object. The terms 'satellite constellation', 'large constellation', or 'mega constellation' are, therefore, used colloquially and within the discussions of the ITU but at present have no formal definition. The definitions then have different communication elements which, when read together provide another definitional element that aids our understanding of how satellite constellations fit into the overall picture of the ITU and the interplay between telecommunications law and space law.

The term 'satellite system' is defined in the ITU Radio Regulations (ITU Radio Regulations, 2020, 1.111) as 'a space system using one or more artificial earth satellites'. A space system (ITU Radio Regulations, 2020, 1.110) is 'any group of cooperating earth stations and/or space stations employing space radio-communication for specific purposes'. A station (ITU Radio Regulations, 2020, 1.61) is 'one or more transmitters or receivers or a combination of transmitters and receivers, including the accessory equipment, necessary at one location for carrying on a radiocommunication service, or the radio astronomy service'. Correspondingly, a space station (ITU Radio Regulations, 2020, 1.64) is 'a station located on an object which is beyond, is intended to go beyond, or has been beyond, the major portion of the Earth's atmosphere'. From these particulate definitions, satellites and satellite constellations alike are satellite systems for the purpose of the Radio Regulations as they all have space stations, Earth stations, or ground stations as forming part of their telecommunications activities.

Article 4 of the Radio Regulations stipulates the assignment and use of radio frequencies. Article 4 covers a lot of topics in detail—there are 24 paragraphs to this Article—but the key point is that Member States of the ITU 'shall endeavour to limit the number of frequencies and the spectrum used to the minimum essential to provide in a satisfactory manner the necessary services' (ITU Radio Regulations, 2020, Vol. 1, Article 4.1, p. 31) and shall avoid and prevent harmful interference. Article 4.1 should be read alongside the ITU Constitution's Article 44 where the RF spectrum and orbits are demarked as limited natural resources and that the spectrum should be used in an equitable manner (ITU Constitution, 2022, Article 44). It may be that, at some point in the future, the number of satellites in a constellation could become so great that it appears to be in violation of Radio Regulation Article 44 if, for example, a certain (large) number of satellites are used when a smaller number could have achieved the same outcome.

Article 5 of the Radio Regulations discusses frequency allocations based on regions and there are also Tables of Frequency Allocations based on region, frequency, and type of service. All satellites, including constellations, will be allocated frequencies based on this Article. Article 8 of the Radio Regulations (ITU Radio Regulations, 2020, Vol. 1, Article 8, p. 193) indicates the obligation to file for radio frequencies and have all filings recorded on the Master International Frequency Register (MIFR). The MIFR is maintained by the ITU and is filed by operators with support from their national communications office or department; for example, in the UK, the Office of Communications (Ofcom) supports satellite frequency filings for UK operators, again irrespective of whether this is for an individual satellite or constellation. This register should work in congruence with the registration process through the Registration Convention. Each satellite of a constellation should be registered through the UNOOSA registers, with the ITU, and held on national registries as well.

Article 9 of the Radio Regulations (ITU Radio Regulations, 2020, Vol. 1, Article 9, pp. 195–207) includes the procedures for effective coordination using the

International Frequency Information Circular (BR IFIC) or directly to the ITU Radio Bureau. Here the onus is on the operators to coordinate with their national regulator and add their intended frequency, and to check for potential harmful interference with current or planned satellite frequency activities against their own activities. This coordination helps to alleviate the possibility of harmful interference. This coordination procedure is further articulated in Radio Regulations Article 11 which gives instructions on notification and recording of frequency assignments (ITU Radio Regulations, 2020, Vol. 1, Article 11, pp. 211–224).

Article 15 of the Radio Regulations deals exclusively with interferences (ITU Radio Regulations, 2020, Vol. 1, Article 15, pp. 237–241). Section 1 sets out what is meant by interference, how to report infringements, and procedures in the case of harmful interference. The Radio Regulation Articles highlighted here are not bespoke to NGSO nor to constellations; indeed they are not confined to satellites and space systems. Nonetheless, they should be applied to satellites, including satellites in constellations. Having covered the main provisions of the Radio Regulations it becomes clear that, as with sui generis space law, there is nothing that applies specifically and uniquely to satellites working as part of a constellation.

Constellations are examined and dealt with in the context of World Radio Conference (WRC) Resolutions (ITU, 2019). In 2019, at the WRC, Resolution 35 was introduced. It is entitled 'a milestone-based approach for the implementation of frequency assignments to space stations in a non-geostationary-satellite system in specific frequency bands and services' (ITU, 2019, p. 222. Hereafter known as WRC-19 Resolution 35). WRC-19 Resolution 35 considers that because 'filings for frequency assignments to [NGSO] systems composed of hundreds to thousands of [NGSO] satellites have been received by the ITU since 2011, in particular in frequency bands allocated to the fixed-satellite service (FSS) or the mobile-satellite service (MMS)' (ITU, 2019, p. 222) there should be a milestone-based approach taken to filings for constellations.

WRC-19 Resolution 35 considers that 'in defining the timeline and objective criteria for the milestone-based approach, there is a need to seek a balance between the prevention of spectrum warehousing, the proper functioning of the coordination mechanisms and the operational requirements related to the deployment of a [NGSO] system' (ITU, 2019, p. 222). What this means is that the milestone-based approach works to ensure equitable use of the radio spectrum as well as to avoid 'paper satellites' or satellites that have been filed prematurely to secure specific frequencies (which the Resolution terms as spectrum warehousing).

WRC-19 Resolution 35 states that 'filings for frequency assignments to non-geostationary-satellite (NGSO) systems composed of hundreds to thousands of [NGSO] satellites have been received by ITU since 2011' (ITU, 2019, p. 222). The ITU does not mention 'large' or 'mega' constellations in WRC-19 Resolution 35, but the filings do suggest that large or megaconstellations for Low Earth Orbit or Medium Earth Orbit have been composed of hundreds to thousands of satellites. If the filing comes from the US, and taking the US definition of large constellation, then 100 to 1000s would constitute a large constellation or perhaps even a megaconstellation. There is not a set definition for 'megaconstellation', however, 'according to advance publication information submitted to the [ITU] and information provided to national regulators and the media, the number of satellites in a constellation now ranges from several to more than 300,000' (UNCOPUOS LSC, 2022a, p. 2).

Article I of the Outer Space Treaty calls for the use of outer space to be 'for the benefit and in the interests of all countries [and] shall be free for [...] use by all States without discrimination of any kind, on a basis of equality and in accordance with international law' (OST, 1967, Article I). It can be inferred from Article I that satellites, and by extension constellations, are legitimate uses of outer space by States, if they are conducted on the principle of equality and conform to international law. Regarding equitable use and international law, Article 44 of the ITU Constitution and Convention affirms that 'radio frequencies and any associated orbits [...] are limited natural resources and that they must be used rationally, efficiently and economically, in conformity with the provisions of the Radio Regulations, so that countries [...] may have equitable access to those orbits and frequencies' (ITU Constitution, 2022, Article 44). Together these tenets drive the freedoms and limitations of use, although it remains to be seen how States and operators combine to ensure equitable access to this limited resource or whether national interests and economic gains will trump these principles.

10 The Environmental Dimension of Constellations

Tied to concerns about the equitable use of LEO is a more general concern regarding the increase in the number of satellite constellations in LEO. This raises inevitable environmental concerns that will also require a combination of regulation and guidance for States and private operators (Boley & Byers, 2021). These concerns revolve around the generation of space debris, light pollution, and their potential impact on astronomical observations (Newman & Napier 2020). The deployment of large numbers of satellites, even if nominally working together, increases the risk of collisions and the generation of space debris (Newman & Williamson, 2018). Mitigating this risk requires constellation operators to engage in responsible satellite design and adhere to best practices for end-of-life disposal(s). This is an area where there has been considerable movement in respect of so-called soft laws, which are non-binding political or technical agreements that are useful in shaping behaviours and establishing norms (Freeland & Zhao, 2020).

A key soft-law agreement, promulgated through UNCOPUOS (at a time when the use of constellations was starting to become a serious concern) is the Guidelines for the Long-Term Sustainability of Outer Space Activities of the Committee on the Peaceful Uses of Outer Space (also known as the Long-Term Sustainability Guidelines or LTSG). These guidelines are meant for operators and policymakers and are 'grounded in the understanding that the exploration and use of outer space should be conducted in a way so as to ensure the long-term sustainability of outer space activities [and are] aimed at preserving the space environment' (UNOOSA, 2021, p. 2). Section B entitled 'Safety of Space Operations' (UNOOSA, 2021, pp. 19–29) speaks to operators and is where the LTSG could apply specifically to constellation operations. This section reiterates the importance of limiting space debris, having end-of-life procedures, registering and tracking objects, as well as considerations for design and overall operations of space objects.

One area of growing concern is space debris and non-functioning satellites. SDMG Guideline 6 asks actors to consider limiting the long-term presence of space objects in Low Earth Orbit at the end of the mission life (UNOOSA, 2010, p. 3). This leads to calls for end-of-life procedures, which would cover constellations. A statement published by the Inter-Agency Space Debris Coordination Committee (IADC) in 2017 reiterates this point by arguing, 'it is clear that significant improvements in the reliability of the disposal function at end of life will be needed for the new constellations compared with that currently demonstrated by space systems on orbit' (Inter-Agency Space Debris Coordination Committee [IADC], 2017, p. 6). Further suggested is that constellations should follow the SDMG with some 'technical guidance on how to best comply with them' (IADC, 2017, p. 7) such as recommendations in constellation design, spacecraft design, and operations (IADC, 2017, pp. 7–10). Again, the SDMG and the IADC Statement are non-binding, voluntary instruments. However, these documents can be applied to State and non-State actors and States can choose to incorporate them into their national space regulations and licensing procedures which in turn would make them binding requirements on actors within their jurisdiction(s).

As well as the risk to the physical environment of Earth's orbit, large constellations have created difficulties in respect of light pollution for ground-based astronomy since the arrival of Starlink in Low Earth Orbit. At the 61st Legal Subcommittee of UNCOPUOS in 2022, some delegations expressed views regarding satellite constellations and radio, optical, and infrared astronomy as well as the impact of constellations on the dark and quiet skies (UNCOPUOS LSC, 2022b, p. 32). The Scientific and Technical Subcommittee (STSC) of UNCOPUOS noted in 2023 the 'various national and international efforts [including] the development of regulations and legal frameworks, the establishment of dark sky conservation areas and radio quiet zones, research on technologies to mitigate light pollution and monitoring of the impact of satellite constellations on astronomy' (United Nations Committee on the Peaceful Uses of Outer Space Scientific and Technical Subcommittee [UNCOPUOS STSC], 2023, pp. 39–40). Furthermore, in 2023, UNCOPUOS LSC held a symposium on the legal aspects of the dark and quiet skies which also considered astronomy vis-à-vis constellations (UNCOPUOS LSC, 2023, p. 5). Whilst at the international level there is dialogue happening about dark skies, astronomy, and the impact of constellations within UNCOPUOS, there is still a noticeable lack of representation from non-State actors, the commercial space industry broadly, and specifically those owning and operating satellite constellations.

Finally, the International Institute of Space Law (IISL) issued a report in 2023 on 'Light Pollution of the Night Sky from a space law perspective' which was presented to the UNCOPUOS Symposium on dark and quiet skies (UNCOPUOS LSC, 2024). In this report, the Outer Space Treaty was analysed and applied to the rights of astronomy vis-à-vis satellites. The argument suggested that Article I of the Treaty includes the text 'there shall be freedom of scientific investigation in outer space' (OST, 1967, Article I). The report suggests that this could extend to ground-based optical and radio astronomy (UNCOPUOS LSC, 2024, p. 4). This is by no means certain, nonetheless, as per Article IX of the Outer Space Treaty which holds that States 'shall conduct all their activities in outer space [...] with due regard to the corresponding interests of all other States Parties to the Treaty' (OST, 1967, Article IX), the argument has been made that private and commercial owners and operators of satellite constellations should have due regard towards those conducting astronomy and at the very least engage in consultation to ensure both interests are protected (Rotola & Williams, 2021, p. 547).

11 Conclusion

With a focus on satellite constellations, this chapter has analysed the legal dimensions of an area of space activities that is going to become increasingly prominent in the not-too-distant future. As the establishment of the necessary infrastructure in NGSO showcase, the significant financial rewards available are large. The Starlink satellite network service is already beginning to exceed expectations in respect of its profitability (Erwin, 2024), and this will surely serve as an incentive for other providers of internet from space. National regulators will receive ever increasing applications for approval and licensing of both large and small constellation systems and the issues raised, regarding space debris, light pollution, and congestion of certain orbits will become ever more pronounced.

What can be seen from the international binding law and non-binding law discussions set out in this piece is that constellations are not entirely novel problems regarding international space and telecommunications law. Constellations consisting of numerous satellites are currently dealt with as single satellite entities and interconnectivity is not considered within Article VII of the Outer Space Treaty or within the Liability Convention. Constellations are a collection of space objects and, irrespective of being component parts of a larger collective mission, their use is bound by the same international regime as single satellites.

It is perhaps noticeable that no recommendations have been made in this discussion in respect of a new treaty to reflect the changing nature of space activities vis-à-vis constellations. It is contended that such an approach has two fundamental flaws. First, the tensions that affect current geopolitics means agreement between the main space powers on this area is highly unlikely. Second, the ossification of rules and regulations at the current stage of technological development would mean the production of a treaty would be moribund.

Instead of the creation of a new treaty, it is averred that the current developments, whereby national regulators, and international fora such as the ITU and UNCOPUOS take a much more dynamic approach to regulation is the correct way to proceed. Looking at constellations as a space system, and consulting with stakeholders for their views on the regulatory requirements is more likely to provide a responsive framework which includes the needs of commercial operators and takes account of questions of sustainability. By examining failure rates of individual satellites within the system and discussing the systemic problems of RF spectrum interference, international bodies can inform and influence the direction taken by national regulators.

This is not to say that the regulation of constellations is problem-free. Regulators are criticised by commercial operators for imposing excessively encumbering requirements. Astronomers and advocates for space sustainability argue that regulators are not paying sufficient attention to the issues faced by terrestrial astronomy as well as consideration of the broader environmental questions posed by constellations. Significant questions remain in respect of liability for damage caused in space and these are only exacerbated when large numbers of satellites operate collectively augmented with elements of autonomy in the decision-making process. It is suggested that international discussions producing a political (if not legally) binding agreement as to how to deal with collisions would be a welcome development. Such an agreement would perhaps provide guidance as to the contours of fault when a collision involved a constellation(s). It would also add a layer of soft law to the existing liability regime.

In drafting new regulations regarding constellations, States are going to continue to respond to pressure from their domestic industrial base. There is also clearly the challenge posed by 'over-mighty' multinational companies, whose wealth (be it collectively or in the hands of a billionaire owner) means they may seek to override regulations that do not suit them. In such a case, the only recourse is to trust that States will respond punitively to such confrontation. There is a role for an international body such as the ITU to act as a guarantor of good behaviour. The ITU controls global RF spectrum access, and this is one of the only pressure points that exist to influence actors to behave in a responsible fashion. In the absence of a binding treaty, and with developing technology, ever-cheaper access to space, and a planet craving more connectivity, this could be a key bulwark against constellations overwhelming key orbits around the Earth.

References

Abashidze, A., Chernykh, I., & Mednikova, M. (2022). Satellite constellations: International legal and technical aspects. *Acta Astronautica, 196*, 176–185.

Bielicki, D. M. (2020). Legal aspects of satellite constellations. *Air and Space Law, 45*(3), 245–264.

Boley, A. C., & Byers, M. (2021). Satellite mega-constellations create risks in Low Earth Orbit, the atmosphere and on Earth. *Scientific Reports (Nature Publisher Group), 11*(1). https://doi.org/10.1038/s41598-021-89909-7

Carpanelli, E. (2024). Unweaving the tangled web: The due regard obligation under Article IX of the Outer Space Treaty. *Air and Space Law, 49*(1), 35–58.

Code of Federal Regulations. (n.d.-a). 47 CFR 25.143. https://www.ecfr.gov/current/title-47/chapter-I/subchapter-B/part-25/subpart-B/subject-group-ECFR9754837c510e730/section-25.143

Code of Federal Regulations. (n.d.-b). 47 CFR 5.64. https://www.ecfr.gov/current/title-47/chapter-I/subchapter-A/part-5/subpart-B/section-5.64

Commercial Space Launch Act. 51 U.S.C. § 50901 et seq. (1984).

Convention on International Liability for Damage Caused by Space Objects (Liability Convention) 1972, 961 UNTS 187.

Convention on Registration of Objects Launched into Outer Space (Registration Convention) 1976, 1023 UNTS 15.

Daeknick, C., Klinghoffer, I., Maritz, B., & Wiseman, B. (2020). *Large LEO satellite constellations: Will it be different this time?* McKinsey. https://www.mckinsey.com/industries/aerospace-and-defense/our-insights/large-leo-satellite-constellations-will-it-be-different-this-time

Dennerley, J. A. (2018). State liability for space object collisions: The proper interpretation of 'fault' for the purposes of International Space Law. *The European Journal of International Law, 29*(1), 281–301.

Dennerley, J. A. (2022). Managing the risks associated with space debris. In M. A. Pozza & J. A. Dennerley (Eds.), *Risk management in outer space activities. An Australian and New Zealand perspective*. Springer.

Doumitt, A., & Speckman, L. (2023). *State of Play LASERCOM KEY TO BUILDING INTERNET IN SPACE Government and Private Sector Poised to Scale*. The Aerospace Corporation. https://aerospace.org/sites/default/files/2023-05/FY23_12205_SOP_Lasercom%20Ppr_r10.pdf

Erwin, S. (2024, May 9). Starlink soars: SpaceX's satellite internet surprises analysts with $6.6 billion revenue projection. *SpaceNews*. https://spacenews.com/starlink-soars-spacexs-satellite-internet-surprises-analysts-with-6-6-billion-revenue-projection/

Federal Communications Commission (FCC). (2023). *FCC Space Bureau and Office of International Affairs to launch next week*. FCC website. https://docs.fcc.gov/public/attachments/DOC-392418A1.pdf

Federal Communications Commission (FCC). (2024, May 2). *Space Bureau seeks to refresh the record on proposed rules pertaining to orbital debris mitigation*. FCC website. https://docs.fcc.gov/public/attachments/DA-24-412A1.pdf

Fernholz, T. (2024, March 15). *Aethero wants to bring Edge Compute into orbit*. https://payloadspace.com/aethero-wants-to-bring-edge-compute-into-orbit/#:~:text=How%20it%20works%3A%20Aethero%20builds,gains%20traction%20in%20the%20market

Foust, J. (2024, January 26). FCC reaffirms orbital debris mitigation rules. *SpaceNews*. https://spacenews.com/fcc-reaffirms-orbital-debris-mitigation-rules/

Freeland, S., & Zhao, Y. (2020). Rules of the "space road:" How soft law principles interact with customary international law for the regulation of space activities. *Journal of Space Law, 44*(2), 405–432.

Henry, C. (2018, September 11). Telesat says ideal LEO constellation is 292 satellites, but could be 512. *SpaceNews*.

Howell, E., & Pultarova, T. (2024, February 20). Starlink satellites: Facts, tracking and impact on astronomy. *Space.com*. https://www.space.com/spacex-starlink-satellites.html

Indian Space Research Organisation (ISRO). (2023). *Indian Space Policy – 2023*. ISO website. https://www.isro.gov.in/media_isro/pdf/IndianSpacePolicy2023.pdf

Inter-Agency Space Debris Coordination Committee (IADC). (2017, September). *IADC Statement on Large Constellations of Satellites in Low Earth Orbit*. IADC-15-03.

International Organization for Standardization (ISO). (2023). ISO 24113:2023. *Space systems — Space debris mitigation requirements*.

International Organization for Standardization (ISO). (2024). SO/TS 6434:2024. *Space systems — Design, testing and operation of a large constellation of spacecraft*.

International Telecommunication Union (ITU). (2019). *World Radiocommunication Conference 2019* (WRC-19) Final Acts.

International Telecommunication Union (ITU). (2020). *Radio Regulations*.
International Telecommunication Union (ITU). (2022). *Constitution and Convention of the International Telecommunication Union*.
Kerrest, A., & Smith, L. J. (2009). Article VII. In S. Hobe, B. Schmidt-Tedd, & K.-U. Schrogl (Eds.), *Cologne commentary on space law* (Vol. 1, pp. 126–145). Carl Heymanns Verlag.
Land Remote Sensing Policy Act. H.R.6133. (1992).
Lüders, R. D. (1961). Satellite networks for continuous zonal coverage. *Journal of the American Rocket Society, 31*, 179–184.
Lyall, F., & Larsen, P. B. (2018). Introduction: Actors, history and fora. In F. Lyall & P. B. Larsen (Eds.), *Space Law: A treatise* (2nd ed.). Routledge.
Marchisio, S. (2009). Article IX. In S. Hobe, B. Schmidt-Tedd, & K.-U. Schrogl (Eds.), *Cologne commentary on space law* (Vol. 1, pp. 169–188). Carl Heymanns Verlag.
Martin, A.-S., & Freeland, S. (2021). The advent of artificial intelligence in space activities: New legal challenges. *Space Policy, 55*, 101408.
McConville, M., & Chui, W. H. (2017). Introduction and overview. In M. McConville & W. H. Chui (Eds.), *Research methods for law* (2nd ed.). Edinburgh University Press.
National Aeronautics and Space Administration. (2019). *U.S. government orbital debris mitigation standard practices*. https://orbitaldebris.jsc.nasa.gov/library/usg_orbital_debris_mitigation_standard_practices_november_2019.pdf
Newman, C., & Cheney, T. (2023). Barriers and gateways to cleaning up Earth Orbit: The legal, economic, and political dimensions of debris remediation. *Air and Space Law, Special Issue, 48*, 113–136.
Newman, C. J., & Napier, L. (2020). Battle for the night sky – from telescopes to ad-breaks. Room. *Space Journal of Asgardia, 2*(24).
Newman, C., & Williamson, M. (2018). Space sustainability: Reframing the debate. *Space Policy, 46*, 30–37.
Newman, C. J., Dinsley, R., & Ralston, W. (2021). Introducing the law games: Predicting legal liability and fault in satellite operations. *Advances in Space Research, 67*(11), 3785–3792.
Peldszus, R., & Faucher, P. (2019). European space surveillance and tracking support framework. In *Handbook of space security*. Springer.
Rotola, G., & Williams, A. (2021). Regulatory context of conflicting uses of outer space: Astronomy and satellite constellations. *Air and Space Law, 46*(4/5), 545–568.
Shepardson, D. (2022, November 3). U.S. telecom regulator launching new space bureau. *Reuters*. https://www.reuters.com/business/media-telecom/us-telecom-regulator-launching-new-space-bureau-2022-11-03/
Snyder, A. (2024, May 5). Congestion in Earth's orbit is getting even worse. *Axios*. https://www.axios.com/2024/05/05/satellites-crowded-orbit-spacex#
Tabeta, S. (2024, January 10). China to launch 26,000 satellites, vying with U.S. for space power. *Nikkei Asia*. https://asia.nikkei.com/Business/Aerospace-Defense-Industries/China-to-launch-26-000-satellites-vying-with-U.S.-for-space-power
Thangavel, K., Sabatini, R., Gardi, A., Ranasinghe, K., Hilton, S., Servidia, P., & Spiller, D. (2024). Artificial intelligence for trusted autonomous satellite operations. *Progress in Aerospace Sciences, 144*, 100960.
The Communications Act. 47 U.S.C. § 151 et seq. (1934).
Treaty on Principles Governing the Activities of States in the Exploration and Use of Outer Space, Including the Moon and Other Celestial Bodies (Outer Space Treaty) 1967, 610 UNTS 205.
UK Space Agency. (2024). *Consultation on orbital liabilities, insurance, charging and space sustainability*. https://www.gov.uk/government/consultations/consultation-on-orbital-liabilities-insurance-charging-and-space-sustainability/consultation-on-orbital-liabilities-insurance-charging-and-space-sustainability#section-1%2D%2D-matters-to-address-in-the-shorter-term

United Nations Committee on the Peaceful Uses of Outer Space Legal Subcommittee. (2022a, February 2). *Registration of large constellations and megaconstellations*. UN Doc A/AC.105/C.2/L.322.

United Nations Committee on the Peaceful Uses of Outer Space Legal Subcommittee. (2022b, April 19). *Report of the Legal Subcommittee on its sixty-first session, held in Vienna from 28 March to 8 April 2022*. UN Doc A/AC.105/1260.

United Nations Committee on the Peaceful Uses of Outer Space Legal Subcommittee. (2023, April 13). *Report of the Legal Subcommittee on its sixty-second session, held in Vienna from 20 to 31 March 2023*. UN Doc A/AC.105/1285*.

United Nations Committee on the Peaceful Uses of Outer Space Legal Subcommittee. (2024, April 16). *Report of the International Institute of Space Law on the results of its Working Group on Light Pollution of the Night Sky from a space law perspective*. UN Doc A/AC.105/C.2/2024/CRP.28.

United Nations Committee on the Peaceful Uses of Outer Space Scientific and Technical Subcommittee. (2023, February 27). *Report of the Scientific and Technical Subcommittee on its sixtieth session, held in Vienna from 6 to 17 February 2023*. UN Doc A/AC.105/1279.

United Nations Office for Outer Space Affairs (UNOOSA). (2010). *Space debris mitigation guidelines of the committee on the peaceful uses of outer space*.

United Nations Office for Outer Space Affairs (UNOOSA). (2021). *Guidelines for the long-term sustainability of outer space activities of the committee on the peaceful uses of outer space*.

Vasisht, D., Shenoy, J., & Chandra, R. (2021, August 9). *Proceedings of the 2021 ACM SIGCOMM 2021 Conference* (pp. 151–164). https://dl.acm.org/doi/abs/10.1145/3452296.3472932

von der Dunk, F. G. (2010). *Too-close encounters of the third party kind: Will the liability convention stand the test of the Cosmos 2251-Iridium 33 collision?* Space and Telecommunications Law Program Faculty Paper No. 28. https://digitalcommons.unl.edu/cgi/viewcontent.cgi?article=1027&context=spacelaw

Weeden, B. (2019). *US Policy and Capability for SSA*. Secure World Foundation. https://swfound.org/media/206348/weeden-us-policy-and-capabilities-for-ssa.pdf

Wood, L. (2003). Satellite constellation networks. In Y. Zhang (Ed.), *Internetworking and computing over satellite networks*. Springer.

Christopher J. Newman, BA(Hons), PhD, FRSA. Chris is a Professor of Space Law and Policy at Northumbria University at Newcastle in the United Kingdom. He is active in the teaching and research of space law and has published extensively on the legal and ethical underpinnings of space governance.

J. Lauren Napier, BS, MA, PhD. Lauren is an Assistant Professor in the Northumbria Law School at Northumbria University.

Patent Law in Outer Space

Art Cotterell

1 Introduction

Encased in a glass display cabinet in the lobby of the World Intellectual Property Organization (WIPO) in Geneva, the specialist United Nations (UN) agency for intellectual property (IP), is what at first appears to be an unassuming piece of rock, until closer inspection reveals an inscription that simply reads: 'A Piece of the Moon'. This lunar remnant serves as a tangible and prescient reminder from Earth's nearest celestial neighbour of the inextricable relationship between intellectual property (IP), innovation, and space exploration. After all, without the advances made in research and development (R&D) during the Project Apollo era, this 105 gram sample would still be in situ on the near side of the Moon, over 380,000 km away.

During the 1960s, the 'Space Race' symbolised Cold War geopolitical tensions between the United States of America (US) and the then Union of Soviet Socialist Republic (USSR) (Lai, 2021). Over a half a century since the Moon landing, space is no longer the exclusive domain of space-faring nations. Rather, space is big business. The transition from 'old space', dominated by government space programs, to 'NewSpace', characterised by private enterprise, accelerated following the end of the nationalistic monopoly on launch capabilities in the US (Paikowsky, 2017). SpaceX exemplifies this shift. Reduced launch costs have supported the rapid

The views of the author are the authors' alone and are intended to provide commentary and general information, and do not represent the views of any organisation. This chapter should not be relied upon as a substitute for professional legal advice or for any other purpose. Some sections of this chapter reproduce material from the author's forthcoming doctoral thesis.

A. Cotterell (✉)
The Australian National University, Canberra, Australia
e-mail: Art.Cotterell@anu.edu.au

J. A. Dennerley, M. A. Pozza (eds.), *The Business of Outer Space*, Space Law and Policy, https://doi.org/10.1007/978-981-95-2034-3_5

growth of the space economy (World Economic Forum, 2024), including the deployment of Earth observation (EO) satellites to monitor the 'vital signs of the planet', like methane emissions, to help combat climate change (NASA, 2024). Public-private partnerships are also increasing, dispersing risks and rewards across stakeholders (Rausser et al., 2023). Beyond dominant space-faring nations, emerging space-faring nations are also seeking to secure the private and public benefits of space, including stimulating innovation and driving economic growth (Samanga, 2023; Shabbir et al., 2021).

The World Economic Forum (WEF) (2024, p. 4) predicts that the value of the space industry to the global economy lies in 'connecting people and goods' and will grow from US$630 billion to US$1.8 trillion by the year 2035 alone. This will be driven by space-based or space-enabled technologies for digital communications; EO services; and position, navigation, and timing (PNT) services, among others. Future commercial uses of space are also predicted to include in-space manufacturing and increased R&D, estimated to contribute up to US$2 billion towards this figure (2024, pp. 16–17). The microgravity environment has been leveraged aboard the International Space Station (ISS) to conduct over 3000 experiments, advancing medical research and healthcare for life on Earth (NASA, 2020, 2022a). Indeed, microgravity advances the discovery and development of new pharmaceuticals as it eliminates 'convection, sedimentation, and buoyancy that warp and disrupt physical and chemical processes on Earth', enabling faster and higher quality R&D (Giulianotti & Low, 2020; NASA, 2022b). For example, during the COVID-19 pandemic, research on an antiviral drug was conducted aboard the ISS (NASA, 2022c).

From a commercial perspective, the entrance of these new non-State actors and the increasing private use of outer space raises pressing questions as to whether private interests are sufficiently protected under the current law and what gaps exist in the legal framework. IP is a central concern in this context. Writing as early as 2004, WIPO concluded: the 'importance of establishing a legal regime that effectively protects intellectual property in outer space cannot be overemphasized' that 'assures a fair and competitive environment', especially considering the vast sums of investment required for R&D (World Intellectual Property Organization [WIPO], 2004, p. 5). This sharp warning, that the protection and enforcement of IP in outer space requires greater legal clarity lest there be a chilling effect on innovation, has been ringing for decades, primarily among scholars and, in recent years, an IP industry body and a few national IP offices (Blackman, 2023; International Trademark Association [INTA], 2022; WIPO, 2004; van Traa-Engelman, 1991; Luxenberg & Mossinghoff, 1985; Saragovitz, 1975).

At the outset, it is also important to make a distinction 'between activities carried out in outer space and activities relating to outer space which are carried out on the territory of a country or on the territories of several countries' (WIPO, 2004, p. 10). The latter, terrestrial legal context is relatively clearer, and is governed by existing national patent laws. The legal uncertainty to date exists around activities conducted in outer space, which is the focus of this chapter. Despite this uncertainty, the commercial space sector has grown apace, seemingly unimpeded by these concerns. The possibility of inventing in outer space is no longer relegated to the realms of science fiction. The first known patents were filed in 2018 with the United States Patents and

Trademark Office (USPTO) from commercial research conducted within the microgravity environment aboard the ISS (Gebhardt, 2018). Yet, the lack of clarity surrounding IP may become a barrier as increasingly complex, multi-partner activities occur off-Earth.

Planning for multiple commercial research space stations and cooperative permanent bases on the lunar surface are underway (Jones, 2024; Secure World Foundation, 2024). The space economy is tethered to, and services Earth, but the future could see the emergence of a space-for-space economy that bypasses Earth entirely (Weinzierl & Sarang, 2021). These varied activities beyond Earth will increase opportunities to invent and infringe in outer space, requiring clarity in the law to enable protection and the fair settling of inevitable disputes over IP. Humanity's propensity towards innovation and ingenuity has existed since time immemorial and this will continue off-Earth. Due to the importance of invention and innovation in the space context, discussions on IP generally revolve around patents. As a result, this chapter will focus on patents in space, but many of the issues raised have applicability across other IP rights, like trademarks and designs.

This chapter will first briefly introduce what a patent is before discussing the commercial relevance of patent rights and their terrestrial legal framework, including the foundational principle of territoriality and why that matters in the outer space context. Next, the chapter will provide an overview of the history of IP in outer space from the Project Apollo era to its contemporary role in accelerating the commercial growth of the space industry at the turn of the millennium.

The next section will consider if, and the extent to which, the intersection of the international space law and terrestrial patent law frameworks, supplemented by domestic patent law, can provide legal clarity on patent protection in outer space. Discrete, proven international cooperative projects such as the ISS will also be instructive, as the underpinning Intergovernmental Agreement (IGA) contains a dedicated provision on IP, which supported the filing of the first patents from the ISS. Discussion will then turn to the future and consider options to improve legal certainty in this area. It will conclude with considering options to elevate and advance this issue through international cooperation, including the need for a forum coordinated by WIPO with the UN Committee on the Peaceful Uses of Outer Space (COPUOS), to at least get this topic back on the agenda and bring the international community together.

2 Centrality of Patents to the Space Sector: Project Apollo to the Commercial Era

Outer space and IP have had an interconnected relationship since the early days of the 'Space Race' due to US national security concerns during the Cold War era. Contrary to perceptions that private sector R&D in space technology is new, history shows otherwise. Up to 90% of R&D funding for Project Apollo was directed towards acquiring products and hardware from private entities, rather than developing them in-house at the National Aeronautics and Space Administration (NASA) (Launius & McCurdy, 2018). Yet, this was a tightly controlled relationship by NASA.

One critical area where NASA exercised strict authority was through its contracting practices with the private sector on IP. Section 305 of the National Aeronautics and Space Act of 1958 (the *Space Act*) was central to this restrictive regulatory approach, providing that any invention made in the performance of any work under any contract with NASA was the exclusive property of the US. If an invention was patentable, the patent would issue to the US unless the NASA Administrator chose to waive those rights. (s 305(2) of the *Space Act*). Even the Commissioner of Patents could not issue a patent without first consulting NASA if the invention had 'significant utility' for space activities (s 305(2)(c)). Section 305 granted the NASA Administrator extensive automatic title-taking powers over federally funded inventions, justified on national security grounds (Kraemer, 1999; Parrish, 2013).

This stringent approach was driven by Cold War anxieties. If privately held, such IP could be inaccessible to the US in a conflict—or worse, fall into enemy hands, namely the Soviet Union (Kraemer, 1999). These national security concerns were existential: the 'Space Race' had 'nuclear roots' (Gainor, 2020, p. 69), and technologies developed for space had dual-use potential, including applications for intercontinental ballistic missiles (ICBM) with nuclear warheads attached. For the US, it was about retaining ownership over inventions that had dual-use application for civilian and military purposes and guarding them against foreign acquisition.

The subsequent three decades saw a continuation of this approach to IP. A shift began to occur in the 1980s, catalysed by a thawing of geopolitical tensions over the Cold War and the rise of neoliberalism. The US government announced a series of successive policies, laws, and regulatory approaches to encourage and accelerate the commercial utilisation of outer space, including on patents (Kraemer, 2001). In 1983, President Ronald Reagan signed a Memorandum on Government Patent Policy, articulated further in a subsequent executive order, to 'promote the commercialization [...] by granting to all contractors, regardless of size, the title to patents made in whole or in part with Federal funds' with the quid pro quo that the US government would receive 'royalty-free use' (Reagan, 1983, 1987; Dickerson, 2007). This broader patent policy was not specific to NASA, but the space agency was firmly within sights.

The Commercial Space Launch Act of 1984 formally ended the US government's monopoly on launch activities, opening the door to private launch providers (Piera, 2004). The Space Act was amended to require NASA to 'seek and encourage the fullest commercial use of space' (NASA, 2014). This shift was not just ideological; it was also pragmatic. NASA's push to support commercialisation was heavily influenced by financial constraints and delivery pressures (Launius & McCurdy, 2018). Projects like what became the ISS, first announced in 1984, were over-budget and behind schedule. With the *Challenger* disaster in 1986, public confidence decreased while scepticism towards large-scale ambitious space missions increased (Launius, 2003).

Despite these pro-business reforms, the NewSpace economy did not take off—either literally or figuratively—immediately. The 1990s and early 2000s marked a transitional period from the Cold War era, shaped by a confluence of factors including industry downsizing and consolidation, export control violations, and regulatory uncertainty (Cornell, 2011). Access to space remained prohibitively costly and risky. Despite increasing international cooperation—most notably through the ISS—the sector was not yet driven by intense commercial competition.

In response to this confluence of factors, NASA launched the Commercial Orbital Transportation Services (COTS) program in 2006, which was heralded as ushering in a 'new era in commercial spaceflight' (Lindenmoyer cited in NASA, 2014, p. 99). COTS enabled private entities to compete to deliver cargo—and eventually crew—to LEO, specifically to and from the ISS, with the aim of making these services more cost-effective. Under the program, NASA provided seed funding, per-launch payments, and the promise of being a first customer, in exchange for companies sharing in the financial outlay (Launius & McCurdy, 2018).

COTS marked a departure from the restrictive procurement contracts of the Project Apollo era and moved towards a new model of public-private partnership between NASA and the commercial sector (NASA, 2014, p. 103). Instead of using the traditional procurement contracts, COTS relied on Space Act Agreements (SAAs)—a more flexible legal mechanism available under the *Space Act* that had been underutilised up to that point (Dickerson, 2007, p. 347). SAAs gave NASA a 'commercial-like freedom to tailor each agreement to the specific needs of the partner and the mission' (2007, p. 348), including greater flexibility around IP ownership.

Effectively, SAAs rebalanced negotiating power over IP in favour of commercial entities. The prior system, under which NASA had title-taking rights to inventions, risked deterring private sector engagement. By contrast, the SAAs changed the incentive structure. The commercial space sector was 'on the brink of a revolution', driven in part by NASA's new pro-business stance (2007, p. 341). SpaceX became the first company to sign a SAA under the COTS program. In 2012, the start-up launched the *Falcon 9*, carrying the *Dragon* spacecraft; this was the first uncrewed commercial space capsule to dock with the ISS (Moskowitz, 2012). SpaceX now serves a growing range of commercial and government clients beyond NASA, with an estimated value of US$350 billion (Sheetz, 2024). In the years since, the space industry has expanded exponentially, with COTS—and its 'commercial friendly' IP clauses—a key early accelerate (NASA, 2014, p. 22).

3 Commercial Relevance of Patents

3.1 The Value-Add of Patents: From Market Exclusivity to Capitalisation

Understanding the value of a patent is critical to appreciating why legal clarity for commercial entities is important. A patent is a private right granted to inventors, providing a time-limited, exclusive monopoly to commercially exploit an invention, with the prospect of recouping the R&D costs, establishing market dominance and thus gaining a competitive advantage beyond the life of the patent. The term of protection for a patent is generally 20 years from filing date of the application. Patents provide a legally enforceable right to pursue enforcement against an infringing third party. Infringement can occur, for example, through developing another product that falls within the scope of a patented invention, counterfeiting, reverse engineering, or breaching the terms in a license agreement. Once a patent is granted, an owner can decide how best to commercialise the patent in alignment with their business strategy, which can entail manufacturing, licensing, selling, or otherwise transferring ownership of the patent.

A lot can occur during that period of exclusivity, making it important to leverage the monopoly. Intangible assets like patents have been reported to comprise up to 90% of the S&P 500 market value (Ocean Tomo, 2023). Hence, IP can increase market capitalisation and be more valuable than a commercial entity's tangible assets. A patent portfolio can help secure investment from venture capital and private equity firms, signal the maturity of small and medium-sized enterprises, and generate licencing revenue (Häussler et al., 2012; Hoenig & Henkel, 2015; Zhou et al., 2016). An audit of IP assets, liabilities, and risks forms part of the due diligence prior to investing (PwC, 2022)

Securing venture capital funding significantly influences a start-up's patenting strategy and the size and quality of its patent portfolio (Sander et al., 2016; Balsmeier & Woerter, 2017). Patent rights can increase market capitalisation when looking towards future mergers and acquisitions (M&As). A driving force for M&As is the acquiring entity's desire to integrate valuable IP from a competitor to improve products and industry concentration (Lamb, 2002). Indeed, M&As have been taking off, among younger companies looking to expand capabilities and gain competitive advantage, with a new wave of consolidation anticipated (Rainbow, 2023, 2025; Foust, 2025).

It is important to consider practical steps businesses can take to protect, manage, and commercialise their intangible assets, both now and into the future. An IP strategy is a key corporate governance tool that must align with—and adapt alongside—other guiding documents like a business plan (WIPO, n.d.-a). Ultimately, an IP strategy is about 'managing IP *according to business strategy*' (emphasis added) (Smith & Hansen, 2002, p. 366). A strong IP strategy can boost in-house R&D, competitive advantage, and market value (Roy, 2013)—and critically, it should not be siloed within the legal team. Executive input is essential. As has been noted, 'IP lawyers need to better understand business decisions and business managers need to better understand IP laws' (Holgersson & van Santen, 2018, p. 44). The strategy itself is important, but so is the process: the conversations, planning, and ongoing refinement that (re)shape it. With legal uncertainty around patents in outer space, staying current with developments is key for keeping an IP strategy relevant.

4 The Territorial (and Terrestrial) Legal Framework

4.1 *From the International Patent Law Framework to National Laws*

Understanding the international patent framework is critical to comprehending current attempts to extend national patent laws into outer space via the existing international space law framework and domestic amendments, as well as proposals for future reform. Multilateral treaties form the legal backbone of the international patent law framework by providing minimum standards of protection and enforcement. These treaties include: the Paris Convention for the Protection of Industrial Property (Paris Convention) (Paris Convention for the Protection of Industrial Property, 1883), the Patent Cooperation Treaty (PCT) (Patent Cooperation Treaty, 1970), and the Agreement on Trade-Related Aspects of Intellectual Property Rights (TRIPS Agreement) (Agreement on Trade-Related Aspects of Intellectual Property Rights, 1869). The latter is administered by the World Trade Organization (WTO), while the former two are administered by WIPO, a UN specialised agency. Global uptake of all three treaties is widespread. In brief, these agreements operate as follows: upon signing one of these treaties, a State must enact domestic laws to comply with its international obligations.

The Paris Convention, adopted in 1883, was the first major international treaty to establish principles for reciprocal IP protection among States, including patents. At the time, however, the technological context was vastly different: aeroplane flights were still experimental and even hot air balloons attracted headlines for their novelty (Anderson et al., 2015; Kim, 2004). As advances in transportation and communication facilitated the movement of people, commerce, and ideas across borders, the fragmented and uneven domestic approaches to IP protection created a need for a unifying law; the Paris Convention was the outcome (Duncan, 2022).

Notably, it was in the same year that Konstantin Tsiolkovsky, the ‘father of modern rocketry’, published *Free Space*, regarded as one of the earliest works to discuss ‘the problems of classical mechanics in a space free from gravity and resistance forces’ (Kosmodemyansky, 2000, pp. 6, 14). Tsiolkovsky remains one of the most influential visionaries on the ‘nuts and bolts’ of space travel, including his rocket equation (NewScientist, 2007, p. 48). And, just as Tsiolkovsky’s theories and designs continue to inform spaceflight in the twenty-first century, so too does the Paris Convention endure—having laid the groundwork for the modern international IP system and remaining embedded in subsequent multilateral agreements.

While the Paris Convention introduced principles and procedural mechanisms—such as national treatment and the right of priority—it did not establish minimum standards for substantive patent protection. What it did achieve, however, was the beginning of what Pinheiro-Machado (2017, p. 11) describes as ‘intellectual property rights as a global regulatory apparatus’, rather than as primarily a domestic matter. The TRIPS Agreement, which entered into force over a century later in 1995, did introduce minimum standards for IP protection and enforcement.

Administered by the WTO, adherence to its provisions is obligatory for WTO membership, and, by extension, participation in the international trade regime (WTO, n.d.). Under Article 27.1, patents must be granted for inventions that meet specific criteria—novelty, inventiveness, and industrial applicability. The minimum term of protection is 20 years from the filing date (Article 33).

Despite these minimum standards, considerable variation remains in how national laws interpret key substantive requirements, such as what satisfies the inventive step criterion (Correa, 2020, p. 266). Furthermore, the scope of 'prior art'—essentially the body of publicly available knowledge used to assess whether an invention is new or inventive—is not consistent across jurisdictions, which can lead to different outcomes for the same invention across different nations. Hence, TRIPS is understood as a minimum standards agreement, *not* a 'harmonizing instrument' (2020, p. 265). Efforts to harmonise substantive patent law have long stalled within WIPO (2020, p. 15).

This variation stems in part from the fact that national or regional patent offices are responsible for examining, granting, and administering registered IP rights, including patents, in accordance with their domestic laws. Member States to the TRIPS Agreement retain the flexibility to adopt higher standards of protection within those frameworks, including through bilateral and regional agreements, such as free trade agreements. These strengthened standards—often referred to as 'TRIPS-Plus' agreements—reflect the continuing plurality of national approaches to patent protection, even under shared international treaty obligations. These agreements, however, have been widely criticised as eroding the policy space and limiting the flexibilities afforded to developing countries under the TRIPS Agreement, particularly with respect to public health safeguards like compulsory licensing and access to generic medicines (Ruse-Khan, 2011).

It must be emphasised that all of the above highlights the fundamentally territorial nature of patent rights, meaning they are generally only protected and enforceable within the jurisdiction where the patent was granted, and are subject to the laws of that jurisdiction. Inventors must apply for protection in multiple jurisdictions to secure comprehensive protection for their inventions. While the PCT, which was adopted in 1970 and entered into force in 1978, streamlines the procedural aspects of seeking patent protection across multiple jurisdictions through a single international application, this does not result in a 'world patent' automatically protected universally (WIPO, n.d.-b). Rather, the PCT acts as a centralised filing route for applicants to initiate the process across contracting States, with each national patent office retaining the authority to examine and grant patents based on its own substantive laws.

This foundational principle of territoriality poses a significant challenge for the operation of patent law into outer space: patent law operates at the national level and is thus dependent on territorial borders to function. Outer space, by contrast, exists without such borders. 'Outer space' is not a jurisdiction. Existing international patent treaties do not contain any explicit provisions on outer space. The following sections will consider current and future attempts to overcome this issue, as well as related legal challenges with extending patent law into outer space.

5 Existing Legal Protection for Patents in Outer Space

5.1 International Space Law Framework

While none of the international patent treaties refer to outer space, the same applies to the international space law framework: none of the treaties specifically contain a provision on patents or IP more broadly (Chen & Zhao, 2022). Before discussing how national patent laws nonetheless find anchorage in the framework, this section will introduce the relevant treaties. The *Treaty on Principles Governing the Activities of States in the Exploration and Use of Outer Space, including the Moon and Other Celestial Bodies*, referred to as the Outer Space Treaty (OST) (Outer Space Treaty [OST], 1967), was adopted by the UN General Assembly and entered into force in 1967. Often referred as the 'Magna Carta' of space, this foundational multilateral agreement has received widespread ratification (Jakhu, 2017, p. 13). It contains high-level principles including on the exploration and use of outer space for the benefit and in the interests of all nations, freedom of scientific investigation, the non-appropriation of outer space, and the prohibition on placing weapons of mass destruction in outer space, among others.

Four additional treaties were negotiated between 1968 and 1979 through the United Nations Committee on the Peaceful Uses of Outer Space (UNCOPUOS) that expand upon and the OST: Agreement on the Rescue of Astronauts, the Return of Astronauts and the Return of Objects Launched into Outer Space (Rescue Agreement, 1968); Convention on International Liability for Damage Caused by Space Objects (Liability Convention, 1972); Convention on Registration of Objects Launched into Outer Space (Registration Convention, 1975); and Agreement Governing the Activities of States on the Moon and Other Celestial Bodies (Moon Agreement, 1979). Collectively these are known as the Five Treaties and have not been supplemented by any further binding multilateral instruments—at least through UNCOPUOS.

In the absence of further binding multilateral instruments, space law has evolved through a hybrid system of normative and non-normative sources—ranging from the extraterritorial application of some national laws, to private contracts, to non-binding soft laws and voluntary standards, among others (Israel, 2019; Lyall & Larsen, 2024). Still, the overarching principles of the OST continue to influence contemporary approaches to law-making in outer space. This is particularly evident in the NASA-led Artemis Accords to return humans to the Moon, which affirms and is 'rooted in' this foundational treaty (Deplano, 2021, p. 814; Neef, 2021).

The Five Treaties were negotiated in a largely 'anticipatory' and 'preparatory' fashion, given that human activity in outer space was then limited and technological capabilities rapidly evolving (Malagar & Magdoza-Malagar, 1999, p. 331). For example, when the first two treaties were concluded, no human had yet landed on the Moon. Moreover, these treaties emerged during a period of geopolitical urgency and the spectre of a nuclear war, and were intended to ensure that outer space would be demilitarised and dedicated to peaceful purposes. The OST is therefore often characterised as an 'arms control' or 'non-armament treaty' (West, 2024, p. 223).

The treaties ‘barely contemplate’ the use of outer space by commercial entities as opposed to States (de Zwart, 2021, p. 146). The OST contains only one provision directly relevant to private actors: Article VI, which states that State Parties bear international responsibility for national activities in space, whether conducted by governmental or non-governmental entities, and are required to authorise and continuously supervise the latter (OST, Article VI). This provision also spoke to the ideological battle that was playing out in the Cold War dynamic between communism and capitalism. The Soviet Union was ‘squarely’ opposed to any private activities, whereas the US was a ‘champion of private enterprise’ (von der Dunk, 2011, p. 3). Unsurprisingly, patents and the exclusive monopoly they provide were not mentioned.

That does not mean that these foundational treaties are ‘irrelevant’ to considerations of patents in space (Leepuengtham, 2017, p. 13). In fact, the exact opposite applies. The two treaties most relevant to patents, and IP generally, are the OST and the Registration Convention. The OST contains a provision, which when read alongside the Registration Convention, can be interpreted as extending national patents laws extraterritoriality into space. A key provision is Article VIII of the OST, which states:

> A State Party to the Treaty on whose registry an object launched into outer space is carried shall retain jurisdiction and control over such object, and over any personnel thereof, while in outer space or on a celestial body. (OST, Article VIII)

To break this down: under Article II of the Registration Convention, each launching State must maintain a national registry of objects it launches into outer space—such as EO satellites—and must furnish this to the UN with information including the launch date and location, orbital parameters, and general function of the space object. These obligations are closely linked to Article VIII of the OST, which confers jurisdiction and control over a registered space object to the State of registry. Hence, Bhat (2010, p. 7) describes the OST, when read with the Registration Convention as creating a ‘special regime for the exercise of jurisdiction’. In practice, this means that if a space object is registered by, say, Australia, Australian law—including patent laws—could apply to that object and its operations in outer space. Hence, the selection of a State of registry is a strategic commercial decision, since it could determine the applicable IP laws.

Still, the operative word here is ‘could’. Whether this framework reliably enables the extension of national patent law into space remains debated. WIPO recognised the position in the literature that ‘the applicability of national intellectual property law on space objects registered by the State is doubtful’ (2004, p. 11), in the absence of domestic provision. The US provides one such example. Under the United States Code 35 U.S.C. § 105, any invention ‘made, used or sold in outer space on a space object or component thereof under the jurisdiction or control of the United States’ is deemed to be ‘made, used or sold within the United States for the purpose of this title’ (United States Code, 2024). By contrast, Australia’s Patents Act 1990 (Cth) contains no provision explicitly extending its application to outer space, and the definition of ‘patent area’ in Schedule 1 does not include outer space. As will be discussed, the majority of nations have not amended their laws, but this should be considered.

It is also important to clarify that under Article I of the Registration Convention, a ‘launching State’ may be: (a) the State that launches the object; (b) procures the launch; (c) allows launch from its territory; or (d) hosts the launch facility. Article II allows multiple launching States to agree among themselves which one will serve as the registering State. This opens the door for ‘creative jurisdictional arrangements when there are multiple launching States’ (Ro et al., 2011, p. 222).

That, however, is not the only possibility that is left open. This approach introduces risk. Parallels are drawn with the ‘flag of registration’ principle from international maritime law. Under this principle, the law that applies to a ship is determined by the flag it flies (Coles & Watt, 2009, p. 1). In practice, this gives rise to what is known as a ‘flag of convenience’ (2009, p. 23): a ‘jurisdictional loophole’ that allows actors to register ships in jurisdictions where regulatory requirements are minimal or less costly (Malmen, 2021, p. 92). As a result, flag selection becomes a key business decision, as it influences liability and compliance (Hoffman et al., 2005).

A similar regulatory dynamic could emerge in outer space. This same ‘flag of convenience’ loophole could be exploited in the context of patent law (Jimenez, 2016). For example, a commercial actor anticipating potential patent infringement may choose to register its space object in a launching State where patent protection has not been secured or enforcement options are weaker, potentially avoiding liability for infringement. As Lee warns, this kind of forum shopping could lead to ‘regulatory competition’ among States, eroding patent protection and triggering a ‘race to the bottom’. Pannell (2016, p. 752) similarly cautions that ‘economic pressure’ could push companies to adopt flag of convenience strategies, which could create challenges that extend far beyond patent law. For example, efforts to circumvent regulatory oversight related to environmental standards for orbital debris mitigation. As more States qualify as launching States—recall the broad definition under the Registration Convention—a trend could emerge where States are incentivised to lower regulatory thresholds to attract commercial space operators. This risks fostering a permissive regulatory environment where competitiveness is prioritised over compliance and profit margins over the public interest.

To help mitigate this, IP lawyers Davidson and Sicard (2023) recommend companies adopt defensive IP strategies by securing ‘a broad footprint of patent protection in most of the spacefaring nations’, including the US, China, and across Europe. This also requires proactive monitoring of both established and emerging space nations to future-proof patent protection. Ultimately, however, this fragmented legal environment exists because ‘outer space’ cannot be designated as a territory for the purpose of protection. Instead, protection must be obtained through individual national patent systems, even though the PCT offers some procedural efficiencies for international filings.

Even if this approach does extend national IP laws into aspects of outer space, there is no guarantee that terrestrial legal frameworks are fit-for-purpose beyond Earth—either now or in the foreseeable future. For example, current laws do not account for new patent eligibility challenges that may arise from the unique R&D

conditions of a microgravity environment (Leepuengtham, 2017). Gaps in legal definitions also remain. This approach only applies to 'objects' 'launched into outer space' from Earth. As Bhat (2010, pp. 13–14) notes, using registration as a 'connecting factor' may result in 'limited coverage', particularly as new technologies allow for in-orbit launches or transfers between celestial bodies, making 'the place of registration [...] ambiguous'. A future space-for-space economy—where goods and services are produced and used entirely off-Earth—could bypass these legal connections altogether (Weinzierl & Sarang, 2021).

This uncertainty is compounded by debates over whether key principles in the OST are compatible with patent law. For example, Article II declares that outer space is 'not subject to national appropriation by claim of sovereignty, by means of use or occupation, or by any other means'. This reflects general norms also found in treaties, including for international maritime law (Storr, 2021). The scope of this non-appropriation principle is contested. One view holds that Article II does not inherently conflict with IP rights, since it applies to tangible territory, not intangible rights like patents (Lockridge, 2006, p. 328). An opposing view argues that the principle is 'categorical and omni-comprehensive', potentially broad enough to encompass even temporary patent monopolies, thus raising questions about the compatibility of patents with the non-appropriation principle (Avveduto, 2019, p. 238). Overall, Avveduto concludes, 'commercial development and innovation in outer space will either require an update of international space law principles or a conscious disregard of its provisions' (2019, p. 203). That said, the practical application of patent law aboard the ISS suggests these concerns can be reconciled. The Intergovernmental Agreement (IGA) governing the ISS has functioned since 2001 without apparent conflict between national IP systems and the OST. In fact, the first known patents based on R&D conducted aboard the ISS were filed in 2018 to the USPTO (Gebhardt, 2018). No publicly known legal objections were raised.

5.2 International Space Station

Any discussion of patents in outer space must consider the ISS. The ISS provides a concrete, operational context that offers valuable lessons for the future. Further, it highlights the need for commercial actors to understand how international agreements may affect R&D in space when multiple partners are involved. Since the year 2000, the ISS has been a permanently crewed structure in Low Earth Orbit (LEO), comprising laboratory modules and habitation quarters (NASA, 2023). Participating partners are the US, Canada, Japan, Russia, and the member states of the European Space Agency (ESA). The ISS is governed by a complex, three-tier level of agreements, consisting of an Intergovernmental Agreement (IGA) signed in 1998 (U.S. Department of State, 1998); Memorandums of Understanding; and implementing arrangements. The IGA acts as the 'overarching umbrella for all legal aspects' (von der Dunk, 2009, p. 150).

The IGA represented several legal firsts for space governance. It was the 'first major international legal instrument to interface' with the earlier Cold War-era international space law framework (Avveduto, 2019, p. 224). Relevantly, it also marked 'the first time that the major space powers instituted an international patent jurisdiction based upon the "floating island" concept', through Article 21, a dedicated IP provision (Pannell, 2016, p. 747). As government funding challenges increased, commercial use of the ISS research infrastructure became a necessity (von der Dunk, 2009, p. 152). This, in turn, triggered a legal necessity: to incentivise commercial interest and investment, the application of IP laws aboard the ISS became a 'fundamental issue' (O'Brien, 1987, p. 39) and 'the single most important area of law applicable to activities aboard' (Young, as cited in Vahrenwald, 1993, p. 318).

The IGA thus is a test case for the extraterritorial application of domestic patent law, including in relation to early US attempts to extend its patent regime into outer space through 35 U.S.C. § 105 (United States Code, 2024). Taken together, these legal innovations—and the real-world filing of patents arising from ISS-based research—now offer a rare, functioning precedent for patent protection in outer space.

Article 21 of the IGA begins by defining IP by reference to the Convention Establishing the World Intellectual Property Organization, to non-exhaustively cover patents, trademarks, copyrights, and industrial designs (see U.S. Department of State, 1998). Yet, the singular focus on patents within subsections (3) and (6) highlights that inventions were a central concern. Critically, Article 21(2) addresses the problem of territoriality by establishing 'a number of floating pieces of quasi territory of the different states' (von der Dunk, 2009, p. 152). Article 21(2) reads:

> Subject to the provisions of this Article, for purposes of intellectual property law, an activity occurring in or on a Space Station flight element shall be deemed to have occurred only in the territory of the Partner State of that element's registry, except that for ESA-registered elements any European Partner State may deem the activity to have occurred within its territory. For avoidance of doubt, participation by a Partner State, its Cooperating Agency, or its related entities in an activity occurring in or on any other Partner's space Station flight element shall not in and of itself alter or affect the jurisdiction over such activity provided in the previous sentence. (U.S. Department of State, 1998)

In effect, this provision seeks to hermetically seal jurisdiction over IP matter to the Partner State that has registered the relevant flight element. While this provision does not claim territorial sovereignty, it anchors legal authority in a territorial proxy: the registry of the flight element, which is deemed to determine the applicable jurisdiction. Thus, the physical structure of the ISS becomes 'decisive' in determining jurisdiction for IP (Vahrenwald, 1993, p. 321). Article 21(3) introduces a narrow exception, allowing nationality to serve as an alternate basis for determining jurisdiction. All partners (except Canada) have permanently stationed, registered flight elements under Article 5 of the IGA.

This provision means, for the purposes of IP law, an activity occurring in or on a registered flight element is deemed to have occurred in the territory of the Partner State that registered it. As a result, that Partner State's national IP law applies. For example, an invention made aboard the US-registered *Destiny* laboratory module is deemed to have occurred in the US. In the case of ESA, an activity aboard an ESA-registered element like the *Columbus* laboratory module is deemed to have occurred in all European Partner States represented by ESA (Balsano & Wheeler, 2006, p. 68). Subsections (4) and (5) apply specifically to ESA-registered elements. Where IP is protected in more than one ESA Member State, infringement can only be pursued in a single national jurisdiction. Moreover, a licence granted in one European Partner State must be recognised across all others.

This approach overcame several negotiating challenges. None of the Partner States had to cede jurisdiction to a single partner, since each partner applies its own domestic IP laws to its registered elements. This also meant there was no need to harmonise national patent laws. Article 21(2), as Lockridge (2006, p. 334) explains, 'acknowledges both the validity of [IP] rights in outer space and the continued acceptance of territoriality as the primary jurisdictional basis for the prescriptive reach of a nation's [IP] laws'. Nevertheless, as Meyer (1988, p. 338) pointed out during the conceptualisation of the ISS governance framework 'the extent of the applicability of domestic law aboard a space station' remains uncertain. This is unless States amend their patent legislation to explicitly cover space-based activity. Similar concerns have been raised in relation to the regime inferred for national patent law extension from the OST and Registration Convention, as discussed earlier.

Importantly, this approach helps reconcile the foundational territoriality of patent law with the OST's prohibition on national appropriation. Through Article 21(2), no Partner State is asserting sovereignty in outer space. Rather, as Chen and Zhao (2022, p. 6) explain, 'jurisdiction and control serve as a link or connection to determine which IP law applies to space objects or prescribe IPRs conferment and infringement rules about space activities'. In this sense, it constitutes 'functional sovereignty', whereby a State has 'jurisdiction and control over the movable property of space objects legally for a limited functional purpose' versus asserting sovereignty over outer space itself (2022, p. 5). This may establish a workable precedent for future space stations.

Preserving patent novelty aboard the ISS has also been a practical concern, given the visibility and monitoring of on-board activities. This issue will become increasingly important as commercial ventures expand into space, including proposed lunar stations. Since novelty is essential to patentability, avoiding premature disclosure is critical. Although Article 21 does not address this explicitly, Article 19(3) of the IGA imposes confidentiality obligations, requiring partners to protect proprietary rights and technical data marked as confidential (Sattler, 2003, p. 72). As Sattler notes, this reflects a shared 'understanding that the protection of proprietary data and inventions are critical factors in a successful commercial participation aboard the ISS' (2003, p. 74). Similar confidentiality safeguards are also found in the ISS Crew Code of Conduct, which has also been cited as helping to preserve novelty (Leepuengtham, 2017, p. 71).

6 Extending Domestic Patent Laws

6.1 US as the First Mover

Having examined the international legal framework, it is now necessary to consider how States have approached this issue domestically. While relatively few nations have enacted specific provisions extending patent law into outer space, those that have offer useful insights into possible—albeit fragmented—approaches. This section explores the domestic frameworks of the US, Russia, France, Germany, and Italy, which are nations that have introduced some form of provision relating to patents in space, often in connection with the ISS. It also considers the positions of India and China, two major spacefaring powers that have not yet enacted such reforms.

The US was the first nation to legislate the extraterritorial reach of its patent law, passing the Patents in Space Act of 1990, codified as 35 U.S.C. § 105 (United States Code, 2024). The aim was to encourage private investment in commercial space ventures by creating a more stable and certain legal environment for patent protection in space (Malmen, 2021). This amendment preceded the ISS IGA but was motivated, in part, by ongoing planning for this cooperative endeavour. WIPO views 35 U.S.C. § 105 as 'an explicit provision establishing a link between the three key elements: inventions, jurisdiction and territory', but noted arguments that 'the applicability of national [IP] law on space objects registered by the State is doubtful' (2004, p. 11). In this sense, the US approach can be seen as domestically codifying that approach in the OST and Registration Convention.

In brief, 35 U.S.C. § 105 provides that 'any invention made, used or sold in outer space on a space object or component thereof under the jurisdiction or control of the US shall be considered to be made, used or sold within the US for the purposes of this title' (United States Code, 2024). Yet, the extraterritorial reach of US patent law under 35 U.S.C. § 105 is 'not unqualified' (Avveduto, 2019, p. 235). Notably, subsection (a) contains an exception for activities 'otherwise provided for in an international agreement' (United States Code, 2024). This reflects the cooperative nature of many space missions. This may mean that the provision does not apply to the ISS, as the US is a signatory to the ISS IGA; this could trump 35 U.S.C. § 105 by virtue of this exception.

6.2 Approaches of Other Nations in the Context of the International Space Station

The majority of nations have not amended their domestic laws to explicitly address patent protection in outer space. Among the limited number that have, the resulting provisions are often less comprehensive than the US model, and inconsistencies emerge in both their drafting and scope. In Russia, an ISS partner, space legislation refers back to the Civil Code for IP protection related to the ‘development of space technology and equipment’, although it remains unclear whether this extends to inventions created in outer space (Doldirina, 2015).

Among European partners to the ISS, France also adopted a ‘quasi-territorial approach’ to patent law (Doldirina, 2015, p. 983), similar in spirit—but narrower in scope—than the 35 U.S.C. § 105 provision. French law under Article L611-1 of its Intellectual Property Code extends protection to ‘inventions made or used in outer space, including on celestial bodies or in or on space objects under national jurisdiction pursuant to Article VIII’ (Intellectual Property Code, France, 2024). By contrast, Germany and Italy did not adopt a general provision, but instead incorporated the IGA into their national laws, thereby extending their patent regimes to ESA-registered ISS modules (Balsano & Wheeler, 2006, p. 67).

These legislative developments occurred prior to and around the time the ISS became operational in 2000. Since then, no unified EU approach to IP in space has emerged. This is unsurprising, given the persistent challenges surrounding patent harmonisation within the EU (de Lange, 2021). In 2023, the European Commission announced plans for a comprehensive EU Space Law intended to ‘avoid and remove fragmentation and barriers across the single market caused by the heterogeneity or lack of national space legislations’ (European Commission, 2023). The proposal focused on safety, sustainability, and resilience, but did not explicitly address IP.

6.3 Two Major Space-Faring Powers Worth Monitoring: India and China

India, now an emerging space-faring power, has not yet enacted legislation extending its patent law into outer space. However, the now-lapsed Space Activities Bill 2017 offers insight into its early thinking. Clause 25(2) proposed that ‘any form of intellectual property right developed, generated, or created onboard a space object in outer space shall be deemed to be the property of the Central Government’ (Indian Space Research Organisation, 2017). Indeed, this mirrored NASA’s historical approach under Section 305 of the Space Act, which vested title to federally funded inventions in the US government. The draft Bill, intended to regulate India’s growing commercial space sector, was criticised for potentially deterring private innovation, particularly among start-ups (Saikia & Deb, 2024; Gohil, 2021).

In 2023, India released its first National Space Policy, aimed at expanding private sector participation in its nascent space economy (Indian Space Research Organisation [ISRO], 2023). As Goenka (2025) observes, this policy ‘needs to be buttressed with comprehensive legislation’ and notes that ‘building a robust intellectual property (IP) regime’ is among the aims of the Indian National Space Promotion and Authorisation Centre (IN-SPACe). IN-SPACe is an independent government body tasked with policy implementation and is focused on ‘[c]reating a stable and predictable regulatory framework to provide a level playing field to

Non-Government Entities in the space sector' (ISRO, 2023, p. 5). This shift suggests that any future space law may abandon the automatic title-taking model in favour of a more commercial-friendly approach, potentially drawing on the U.S. 35 U.S.C. § 105 model.

China, by contrast, has not enacted any legislation extending patent protection into outer space, nor has it published a draft akin to India's. Its patent regime remains strictly territorial, with no explicit extraterritorial provisions. Like most nations, China relies on Article VIII of the OST, which grants jurisdiction and control over registered space objects. China, however, has taken significant steps to improve IP protection, introducing various laws and regulations that are applicable to space-based activities aboard spacecraft (Chen & Zhao, 2022).

As Zhao (2015, p. 204) explains, while 'it is preferable to have more specific rules for a special environment such as outer space', China's existing legal regime already offers a 'solid foundation for further development of the rules for the protection of intellectual property arising out of space activities'. More recently, Zhang (2025, p. 33) notes that although China lacks a unified national space law, it does have a legal and policy foundation, albeit one consisting of 'fragmented multisectoral departmental regulations'. If international participation in China's Tiangong space station expands, the IP issues involved may become more pressing. In this regard, the ISS IGA may serve as a useful reference model for developing a framework agreement.

Though there has been limited legislative movement since the ISS era, this may change as commercial activity accelerates across both established and emerging space powers. The resulting patchwork of national approaches creates legal uncertainty, particularly for private actors operating across jurisdictions. For companies and investors, it is essential to understand differences in domestic law, the role of international agreements, and the implications of selecting a particular launching State. In the absence of a harmonised global framework, Article VIII of the OST continues to operate as a quasi-territorial mechanism, linking national jurisdiction and control to registered space objects. Over the long term, a comprehensive multilateral solution may be ideal to provide a coherent and functional regime for governing patents in outer space.

7 Looking to the Future for Patents in Space

7.1 From Satire to Signals from the IP Industry

On a recent April Fool's Day, a LinkedIn post began gaining traction, announcing 'Breaking News in the Patent World' with the creation of an 'Interplanetary Patent Office' to administer IP in outer space (Watrin, 2023). A reader steeped in the literature would be forgiven for initially believing this was a genuine announcement. While such ideas once seemed speculative—or merely satirical—attention is now seriously turning to the intersection between patents and outer space, not only in academic commentary but also within the IP industry and select IP offices.

For example, in 2022, the International Trademark Association (INTA) released its IP in Space white paper (International Trademark Association [INTA], 2022). This was a landmark moment, as it was the first time an international IP body publicly put forward detailed, forward-looking proposals on this topic. Whether these proposals gain enduring traction remains to be seen.

International Trademark Association (INTA) is an influential member-based organisation comprising more than 6600 entities, representing around 38,000 professionals across 18 jurisdictions. Its mandate is to promote the advancement of trademarks and intellectual property to 'foster consumer trust, economic growth and innovation' (INTA, 2025). While INTA primarily focuses on trademarks, its report explicitly acknowledged the broader importance of other IP rights, including patents. Accordingly, many of its recommendations are relevant beyond trademark protection (INTA, 2022, pp. 8–9).

Recognising the challenges inherent in negotiating a binding multilateral instrument, INTA proposes an incremental, staged approach to developing and implementing 'concrete and practical legal approaches to reaching a workable IP system in space' (2022, p. 8). After all, treaty-making can proceed at a glacial pace: the most recent treaty adopted by WIPO Member States in 2024 took more than two decades from the start of negotiations in 2001 (WIPO, 2024). If that timeframe were applied to space—think of the technological advances in 20 years.

As the then INTA President noted in the foreword to the report:

> [I]t will take time to create the appropriate legal frameworks for protection of IP off the surface of the Earth. It is therefore imperative that the IP community, and anyone interested in supporting and further developing the legal incentives and protections for entrepreneurial innovation, start planning now how to protect IP in space. (INTA, 2022, p. 5)

In the short term (by 2030), the report proposes multilateral actions such as enabling the 'creation of a new territory called "Outer Space" that could be designated within an international application' for a trademark under the Madrid Protocol' (2022, p. 8)—or a patent under the PCT. It calls for the establishment of a new Outer Space Intellectual Property Office. At the national level, INTA encourages nations to extend the scope of their IP laws and consider adopting legislation inspired by 35 U.S.C. § 105. In its next decadal plan (by 2040), INTA proposes expanding existing international space treaties, including via the adoption of an Additional Protocol on IP to the OST (2022, p. 9). Its long-term goal (by 2050) is the negotiation of a new multilateral treaty for the protection and enforcement of IP in space (2022, p. 9).

In the absence of such a comprehensive legally binding framework, INTA also recommends that commercial entities adopt interim protective measures. These include using private contracts and legal agreements to 'legally connect parties launching into outer space' (2022, p. 8). Clauses specifying venue, jurisdiction, and dispute resolution mechanisms—such as arbitration or mediation—are recommended, with sample language provided in the report (2022, pp. 26–27). As noted earlier, securing 'a broad footprint of patent protection in most of the spacefaring nations' is recommended, given the unresolved legal issues (Davidson & Sicard, 2023). To further safeguard IP rights, US inventors are advised to 'manufacture and register' their space objects within the US and launch from US-operated spaceports. This approach aligns with the strategic use of the flag of registration as a business decision. This 'broad footprint' strategy is relevant for inventors outside the US.

7.2 A Snapshot of Long-Standing Proposals in the Literature

Proposals in the literature similarly reflect a long-standing interest in providing greater legal clarity around patent rights in outer space. Broadly, these approaches fall into two main tracks: the negotiation of a new, legally binding multilateral instrument under international law (or amendments to existing treaties), and/or the extension of domestic patent laws to supplement the current international framework (see, e.g., Bhat, 2010; Jimenez, 2016; Davidson, 2019). One enduring proposal is the creation of a dedicated patent regime for outer space. In 2004, WIPO cited the perspective of one expert who, from a 'business perspective', suggested:

> [W]hile recognizing the difficulties to overcome the existing national and territorial legal framework, the best solution [is] to declare space and its accessories (for example, launch sites and vehicles) as a single territory with a single and uniform law and with a single and universal enforcement body. […] many of the practical difficulties that arise from the commercial application of space technologies stem from the very principle of territoriality and differences among national intellectual property law. (WIPO, 2004, p. 22)

This statement captures the key elements that recur across the literature—and were echoed in the INTA white paper. Central to these proposals is the establishment of 'outer space' as a distinct, new territory to better resolve issues of territoriality. Such a model would streamline how applicants, particularly commercial entities, protect patents in space. Instead of seeking protection across multiple launching States and navigating forum shopping and enforcement challenges, an applicant would file once within the newly designated territory of 'outer space'.

7.3 Analysis of Some Legal Challenges

There are significant legal and practical hurdles to such a proposal, and too many to canvass here. Most fundamentally, 'outer space' remains undefined in international law. While the OST governs its exploration and use, the drafters left the term 'outer space' itself undefined: an issue that has long existed (Malagar & Magdoza-Malagar, 1999, p. 317). The UNCOPUOS Legal Subcommittee continues to debate its definition, with no clear resolution (United Nations Office for Outer Space Affairs [UNOOSA], 2020).

Establishing 'outer space' as a 'single territory' would likely encounter both legal and political challenges. The ISS IGA negotiations are instructive here:

determining applicable jurisdiction required extensive negotiation, ultimately leading to 'a number of floating pieces of quasi-territory of the different states' (von der Dunk, 2009, p. 152). While the ISS provides a precedent, future stations operated by commercial actors—not nation-states—would pose even more complex legal and governance questions. Nor would this solve patent law issues comprehensively.

A further key question arises: where would a 'single and universal enforcement body' be situated? At present, national or regional patent offices are responsible for examining and granting applications. Would an Interplanetary Patent Office be more than just an April Fool's Day joke after all? One option is the establishment of a specialist subcommittee within UNCOPUOS, thereby leveraging its existing mandate to administer international space law instruments (Jimenez, 2016; Davidson, 2019). Alternatively, WIPO, given its subject-matter expertise in intellectual property, could be engaged in some capacity. However, each institution faces clear limitations, despite both operating under the aegis of the UN. UNCOPUOS lacks technical expertise in IP, while WIPO has limited experience with the complexities of space law. Furthermore, even the theoretical prospect of a single body overseeing both the grant and enforcement of patents raises concerns about institutional neutrality and conflicts that would require addressing.

Beyond institutional functions, enforcement itself presents a range of practical challenges. Monitoring infringement in outer space—whether in LEO, on the lunar surface, or even one day on Mars—would be logistically and financially prohibitive, at least for the foreseeable future. These constraints raise enforcement concerns that go beyond the establishment of legal norms and emphasise the need for a pragmatic, rather than a purely technical, legal approach.

The negotiation of a 'single and uniform' substantive patent law for outer space would also create challenges. While the TRIPS Agreement provides minimum standards for patent eligibility, States retain considerable discretion to exceed these and impose 'TRIPS-Plus' provisions—and not without controversy (Ruse-Khan, 2011). Despite this baseline, harmonisation of patent law has yet to be achieved on Earth, remaining a contentious and unresolved issue (Correa, 2020). Indeed, the topic has been subject to international debate since the adoption of the Paris Convention in the 1880s. Over a century later, WIPO's last attempt to negotiate a treaty on substantive patent law was suspended in 2006 due to disagreements over key issues, including what constitutes patentable subject matter, among others (WIPO, n.d.-c). Given this history, reaching agreement on a uniform patent regime for outer space is unlikely to be any less fraught.

This also raises questions around the criteria for patentability in space. Leepuengtham (2017, pp. 65–80) canvasses several: What standard of novelty should apply? Could altering an Earth-based experiment in microgravity suffice? Should the prior art base differ between terrestrial and space-based inventions? For inventive step, who qualifies as the person skilled in the art? The invention may not be replicable on Earth due to the unique microgravity environment of space. Further, what if the inventor is a non-human? As research conducted on future space stations and lunar bases will likely involve artificial intelligence (AI), this may further limit what can be patented. In brief, there are more questions than answers and highlight the challenges of developing laws for an emerging field.

Given these challenges, alternative models have been proposed to streamline procedural processes, echoing several of INTA's recommendations. These include enabling the designation of 'outer space' under the PCT or adopting an Additional Protocol to an existing treaty within either the space law or IP frameworks (Doldirina, 2015; Jimenez, 2016; Leepuengtham, 2017). Such approaches are seen as procedural rather than substantive—aimed at clarifying conflict-of-laws issues without harmonising substantive patent law—and may be more politically feasible, at least in theory.

Such challenges lead back to national law as a stop-gap solution, despite limited momentum since the ISS, with respect to amendments to domestic patent law. The legislative focus has largely shifted to other outer space activities and issues, such as space resource utilisation (space mining) and orbital debris mitigation (Dey & Jagadanandan, 2024; Smith et al., 2024). A 2013 UN General Assembly resolution acknowledged this trend towards State-level intervention, stating that, as commercial space activity increases, 'appropriate action at the national level is needed' to address regulatory gaps left by the international space law framework (United Nations General Assembly, 2013, p. 1). In this regard, the US provision remains the most comprehensive model available for policymakers considering extraterritorial extensions of domestic patent law.

Indeed, 35 U.S.C. § 105 has been described as 'a model for other domestic space patent law', allowing other nations to 'assess its application and usefulness' (de Zwart, 2021, p. 152). Significantly, WIPO (2004, p. 11) notes that 35 U.S.C. § 105 establishes 'a link between the three key elements: inventions, jurisdiction and territory'. In the absence of a model law, domestic amendments of this kind risk producing a patchwork of inconsistent—and potentially conflicting—legal regimes. Nonetheless, they point to the longer-term need for renewed international dialogue—and eventually coordination—on the intersection of space and patent laws in light of growing commercial activity off-Earth. INTA's position is that 'The question is not "If" IP protection in space will happen, but "when"' (2022, p. 5). As the following section explores, whatever the approach(es) taken to patents in outer space, this will require sustained international engagement and cooperation.

7.4 *Why International Cooperation Still Matters*

For any multilateral approach to be feasible—whether a binding or non-binding instrument—it must first be placed on the international agenda. At present, it is not. This omission is not unique to patents in space. Whereas space law-making in the Cold War era centred on treaty-making, contemporary approaches increasingly rely on national legislation, non-binding soft law, and private contracts (Israel, 2019). As Lyall and Larsen (2024, p. 18) observe, UNCOPUOS may now 'take a back seat' as multilateralism is supplemented by 'private and domestic law solutions for particular problems'. However, this multilateral inertia is a 'crisis' that is a 'system-wide phenomenon across all areas of global governance' (Tepper, 2022, p. 506).

Despite its imperfections, multilateralism ostensibly enables consensus-building and balancing of competing interests. Sometimes more successfully than others. By contrast, unilateral domestic law-making risks entrenching inward-facing national interests, while private law centres commercial priorities. As Sharma (2025) warns, while corporations cannot claim sovereignty in outer space in the traditional sense, they can 'wield outsize influence'. Hence, there is a need for 'cooperation over corporate dominance'. After all, that influence will not be evenly distributed: it will likely be exercised by large actors like SpaceX, not necessarily by start-ups or emerging space nations whose interests' risk being overlooked.

The question of patents in outer space must ideally—and perhaps optimistically—be internationalised, not only nationalised. If the future lies in a treaty or protocol—however far off—that will require time, coordination, and trust-building. Despite geopolitical tensions and rivalries in space—not least the purported 'Space Race' between the US and China—cooperation remains essential, even and especially in times of conflict (Cotterell, 2024a). At the 2024 UN Summit of the Future, world leaders reaffirmed their 'commitment to the United Nations, the international system and international law' (United Nations General Assembly, 2024). Action 56 of the Pact for the Future committed to 'strengthen international cooperation for the exploration and use of outer space for peaceful purposes and for the benefit of all humanity' (United Nations, 2024).

All multilateral proposals, whether in the academic literature or put forward by industry, will require sustained cooperation to reconcile diverse and sometimes competing interests. One recent bilateral initiative on IP in space occurred in late 2023 between the USPTO and the Canadian Intellectual Property Office (CIPO) and included an industry roundtable with commercial stakeholders (Blackman, 2023). Two key themes emerged: the importance of international cooperation and the value of a whole-of-government approach. The latter reflects a growing recognition that space policy cannot remain siloed within specialist agencies. For nations to coordinate effectively at home and engage meaningfully in international fora, it is essential to adopt a 'space mainstreaming' approach, which is defined as 'integrating considerations of space technologies and capabilities across a broader range of government departments and agencies, rather than limiting them to a specialised, siloed domain of policy development and decision-making' (Cotterell, 2024b, p. 1). After all, space is a critical enabler of economic, environmental, foreign policy, national security, and social policy priorities. For patents in space, this means that, as a starting point, domestic IP and space agencies must establish open channels of communication and information sharing—and consider jointly engaging stakeholders external to government.

Such bilateral engagement is a positive step. Having said that, these conversations must expand to include nations with aspirational or emerging commercial space industries, particularly from developing nations in the Global South. Likewise, the needs and capabilities of commercial stakeholders vary considerably, and this may also differ depending on the geographic location. A bootstrapped start-up navigating early-stage R&D faces markedly different challenges than a growing SME, an established NewSpace company or a legacy aerospace prime. To this end, the USPTO (United States Patent and Trademark Office [USPTO], 2024) 'dialogue' on IP and space commercialisation recognised this, with a dedicated focus on 'opportunities for small and medium-sized enterprises and startups'. Public-private partnerships may also introduce new complexities around IP ownership and strategy, including questions about open versus closed innovation models (Rausser et al., 2023). All these distinctions are important when considering patents in space—this is more than just a matter of legal clarity on territoriality.

As in other emerging technology domains like AI, the law struggles to keep pace with innovation (Akpobome, 2024). According to Marchant (2011, p. 23), this 'pacing problem' exists because, first, 'many existing legal frameworks are based on a static rather than dynamic view of society and technology' and second, 'legal institutions are slowing down with respect to their capacity to adjust to changing technologies'. In this context, there is now an opportunity to pick up the pace and proactively map and model possible legal approaches—likely there will be more than one.

It is worth reiterating that IP is currently absent from the formal agendas of UNCOPUOS and WIPO. The last in-depth review of IP law in space by WIPO was in 2004, prompted by a request from the Organisation for Economic Co-operation and Development (OECD) (WIPO, 2004). Prior to that, WIPO's Program and Budget for the 1996–1997 biennium mandated for its International Bureau to study the 'desirability and feasibility of adopting rules and/or recommending principles' on IP in space, leading to a 1997 meeting of participants from several space agencies (WIPO, 1997, p. 4). Meanwhile, past efforts at UNCOPUOS to include IP on its Legal Subcommittee's agenda at the millennium's start did not garner sufficient support (WIPO, 2004).

International space law and international IP law-making remain under the auspices of two distinct UN bodies—UNCOPUOS and WIPO—that have little direct interaction. This needs to change. A joint forum could help bridge this divide, opening communication channels, fostering information sharing and importantly bring the international community. In fact, Balsano and Smith (1997) called for such coordination before the start of the twenty-first century. Such cross-institutional dialogues are not without precedent: during the COVID-19 pandemic, WIPO, the WTO, and World Health Organization (WHO) engaged in trilateral cooperation, in recognition of the 'intersection of public health, intellectual property and trade' (World Health Organization [WHO], 2021).

WIPO is currently coordinating the WIPO Conversations on IP and emerging technologies, a series designed to be 'an open, inclusive, multi-stakeholder forum intended to provide stakeholders with a leading, global setting to discuss the impact of frontier technologies on all IP rights and to bridge the existing information gap in this fast moving and complex field' (WIPO, 2025). Its 2023 WIPO Conversation on Generative AI drew over 5000 participants from more than 160 countries across the Global North and South, spanning government, industry, academia, and civil society (WIPO, 2023). Outer space is not currently one of the proposed topics for conversation, but there is merit in making it one.

A dedicated WIPO Conversation on IP and Outer Space could serve as a practical and politically feasible next step. To be clear, this is not a forum for negotiation. Indeed, the forum's strength would lie in its distance from any requirement for consensus on a legal instrument. Rather, the purpose would be to enable discussion, knowledge-sharing, and foundational awareness-raising among diverse stakeholders and interests. Such a forum could introduce and consider policy topics, such as access to and transfer of space-based technologies, alongside technical questions on legal design. A WIPO-led conversation would not resolve legal questions—nor should it. Its value would stem from providing time and space for enquiry on this topic, and contributing to ongoing dialogue, issue identification, and information exchange. At the very least this would place this topic on the international agenda. Multilateralism may be slow and imperfect, but it remains an essential tool for bringing the international community together.

To return to that small fragment of the Moon on display at WIPO: it is a reminder of how far human ingenuity and innovation can reach, and now, of how far legal, regulatory, and governance frameworks still have to travel to keep pace. Commercialisation is already well underway and will likely continue to grow. In that context, international cooperation on this issue must be a proactive choice. If patents are to support innovation in space and on Earth for the benefit of all humankind, the time to engage is now.

References

Agreement Governing the Activities of States on the Moon and Other Celestial Bodies (Moon Agreement) 1979, 1363 UNTS 3.

Agreement on the Rescue of Astronauts, the Return of Astronauts and the Return of Objects Launched into Outer Space (Rescue Agreement) 1968, 672 UNTS 119.

Agreement on Trade-Related Aspects of Intellectual Property Rights (TRIPS Agreement), Annex 1C of the Marrakesh Agreement Establishing the World Trade Organization 1869 UNTS 299.

Akpobome, O. (2024). The impact of emerging technologies on legal frameworks: A model for adaptive regulation. *International Journal of Research Publication and Reviews, 5*(10), 5046–5060.

Anderson, D., Graham, I., & Williams, B. (2015). *Flight and motion: The history and science of flying*. Routledge.

Avveduto, R. (2019). Past, present, and future of intellectual property in space: Old answers to new questions. *Washington International Law Journal, 29*(1), 203–236.

Balsano, A. M., & Smith, B. (1997). Intellectual property and space activities: A new role for COPUOS? In G. Lafferranderie & D. Crowther (Eds.), *Outlook on space law over the next 30 years* (pp. 363–371). Brill Nijhoff.

Balsano, A. M., & Wheeler, J. (2006). The IGA and ESA: Protecting intellectual property rights in the context of ISS activities. In F. G. von der Dunk & M. M. T. A. Brus (Eds.), *The International Space Station: Commercial utilisation from a European legal perspective* (pp. 63–86). Brill.

Balsmeier, B., & Woerter, M. (2017). *Measuring the spillovers of venture capital* (CESifo Working Paper No. 6623). CESifo. https://www.econstor.eu/bitstream/10419/171087/1/cesifo1_wp6623.pdf

Bhat, B. (2010). Inventions in outer space: Need for reconsideration of the patent regime. *Journal of Space Law, 36*, 1–22.
Blackman, C. (2023). *Viewpoints: IP in space with thought leaders Vidal and Georgaras*. Licensing Executives Society USA and Canada. https://www.lesusacanada.org/viewpoints-ip-in-space-with-thought-leaders-vidal-and-georgaras/
Chen, Z., & Zhao, Y. (2022). Intellectual property protection in outer space: Conflict in theory and application in practice. *Space Policy, 61*, 101484.
Coles, R., & Watt, E. (2009). *Ship registration: Law and practice* (2nd ed.). Informa.
Convention on International Liability for Damage Caused by Space Objects (Liability Convention) 1972, 961 UNTS 187.
Convention on Registration of Objects Launched into Outer Space (Registration Convention) 1975, 1023 UNTS 15.
Cornell, A. (2011). Five key turning points in the American space industry in the past 20 years: Structure, innovation, and globalization shifts in the space sector. *Acta Astronautica, 69*(11–12), 1123–1131.
Correa, C. M. (2020). *Trade related aspects of intellectual property rights: A commentary on the TRIPS Agreement* (2nd ed.). Oxford University Press.
Cotterell, A. (2024a). Space isn't all about the race: Rival superpowers must work together for a better future. *The Conversation*. https://theconversation.com/space-isnt-all-about-the-race-rival-superpowers-must-work-together-for-a-better-future-240543
Cotterell, A. (2024b). The case for 'space mainstreaming' to advance national priorities. *Australian Centre for Space Governance*. https://www.spacegovcentre.org/_files/ugd/ed2eed_224cf01716c247799585e5ed2efde2f7.pdf
Davidson, A. M. (2019). To explore outer space: The intellectual property frontier for patents. *Hofstra Law Review, 47*(3), 889–920.
Davidson, K., & Sicard, K. (2023). Extraterrestrial law: Protecting patents in outer space and on celestial bodies. *IPWatchdog*. https://ipwatchdog.com/2023/08/20/extraterrestrial-law-protecting-patents-outer-space-celestial-bodies/id=164862/
de Lange, D. (2021). EU patent harmonization policy: Reconsidering the consequences of the UPCA. *Journal of Intellectual Property Law & Practice, 16*(10), 1078–1090.
de Zwart, M. (2021). Intellectual property, innovation and new space technology. In G. W. Austin, A. F. Christie, A. T. Kenyon, & M. Richardson (Eds.), *Across intellectual property: Essays in honour of Sam Ricketson* (pp. 144–157). Cambridge University Press.
Deplano, R. (2021). The Artemis Accords: Evolution or revolution in international space law? *International and Comparative Law Quarterly, 69*(3), 701–728.
Dey, A., & Jagadanandan, J. (2024). Study on space debris mitigation under the national space laws. *University of Bologna Law Review, 9*, 45.
Dickerson, T. B. (2007). Patent rights under Space Act Agreements and procurement contracts: A comparison by the examination of NASA's Commercial Orbital Transportation Services (COTS). *Journal of Space Law, 33*, 341–370.
Doldirina, C. (2015). Intellectual property rights in the context of space activities. In F. von der Dunk (Ed.), *Handbook of space law* (pp. 949–994). Edward Elgar.
Duncan, L. (2022). The key historical influences leading to the Paris Convention for the Protection of Industrial Property of 1883. In P. S. Morris (Ed.), *Intellectual property and the law of nations, 1860–1920* (pp. 15–54). Brill.
European Commission. (2023). *Targeted consultation on EU Space Law*. Defence Industry and Space. https://defence-industry-space.ec.europa.eu/newsroom/consultations/targeted-consultation-eu-space-law_en
Foust, J. (2025). Industry executives predict "more thoughtful" new wave of space deals. *SpaceNews*. https://spacenews.com/industry-executives-predict-more-thoughtful-new-wave-of-space-deals/
Gainor, C. (2020). The nuclear roots of the space race. In A. C. T. Geppert, D. Brandau and T. Siebeneichner (Eds.), *Militarizing outer space: Astroculture, dystopia and the Cold War* (pp. 69–91). Palgrave Macmillan.

Gebhardt, C. (2018). First patents filed from commercial research on Space Station, crew readies for busy period. *NASA Spaceflight*. https://www.nasaspaceflight.com/2018/08/first-patents-filed-commercial-research-iss-crew-busy-period/

Giulianotti, M. A., & Low, L. A. (2020). Pharmaceutical research enabled through microgravity: Perspectives on the use of the International Space Station US National Laboratory. *Pharmaceutical Research, 37*, 1–4.

Goenka, P. (2025). *How strategic vision and innovation is boosting India's space economy*. World Economic Forum. https://www.weforum.org/stories/2025/01/strategic-vision-innovation-boosting-india-space-economy/

Gohil, M. S. (2021). Need for comprehensive and robust Indian space laws. *ILI Law Review, Summer Issue*, 47–70.

Häussler, C., Harhoff, D., & Mueller, E. (2012). To be financed or not... – The role of patents for venture capital financing (ZEW Centre for European Economic Research Discussion Paper No. 09-003). *Zentrum für Europäische Wirtschaftsforschung*. https://d-nb.info/1189739720/34

Hoenig, D., & Henkel, J. (2015). Quality signals? The role of patents, alliances, and team experience in venture capital financing. *Research Policy, 44*(5), 1049–1064.

Hoffman, J., Sanchez, R. J., & Talley, W. K. (2005). Determinants of vessel flag. In K. Cullinane (Ed.), *Shipping economies* (pp. 173–190). Elsevier.

Holgersson, M., & van Santen, S. (2018). The business of intellectual property: A literature review of IP management research. *Stockholm Intellectual Property Law Review, 1*(1), 44–63.

Indian Space Research Organisation (ISRO). (2023). *Indian space policy – 2023*. https://www.isro.gov.in/media_isro/pdf/IndianSpacePolicy2023.pdf

Indian Space Research Organisation. (2017). *The Draft Space Activities Bill, 2017*. https://prsindia.org/files/bills_acts/bills_parliament/1970/Draft%20Space%20Activities%20Bill%202017.pdf

Intellectual Property Code, France. (2024). https://www.wipo.int/wipolex/en/legislation/details/22588

International Trademark Association. (2025). *About INTA*. https://www.inta.org/about/

International Trademark Association (INTA). (2022). *IP in Space*. https://www.inta.org/wp-content/uploads/public-files/perspectives/industry-research/221207_ipinspace_report.pdf

Israel, B. R. (2019). Space resources in the evolutionary course of law making. *American Journal of International Law Unbound, 113*, 114–118.

Jakhu, R. S. (2017). Evolution of the Outer Space Treaty. In A. Lele (Ed.), *50 years of the Outer Space Treaty: Tracing the journey* (pp. 13–19). Pentagon Press.

Jimenez, J. F. (2016). Patents in outer space: An approach to the legal framework of future inventions. *Journal of the Patent and Trademark Office Society, 98*(3), 447–468.

Jones, A. (2024). Looking ahead to the next 25 years of private space stations. *Space.com*. https://www.space.com/commercial-space-stations-next-25-years

Kim, M. G. (2004). Balloon mania: News in the air. *Endeavour, 28*(4), 149–155.

Kosmodemyansky, A. (2000). *Konstantin Tsiolkovsky: His life and work* (X. Danko, Trans.). University Press of the Pacific. (Original work published in Russian).

Kraemer, S. K. (1999). *NASA, monopolies, and the Cold War: The origins and consequences of NASA patent policy, 1958–1996* [Conference paper]. Annual Meeting of the Society for the History of Technology, United States. https://www.hq.nasa.gov/office/codez/plans/R&D/SHOTOCT99.html

Kraemer, S. K. (2001). Federal intellectual property policy and the history of technology: The case of NASA patents. *History and Technology, 17*(3), 183–216.

Lai, A. K. (2021). *The Cold War, the Space Race, and the law of outer space: Space for peace*. Routledge.

Lamb, R. B. (2002). The role of intellectual property and intangible assets in mergers and acquisitions. In L. Bryer & M. Simensky (Eds.), *Intellectual property assets in mergers and acquisitions* (pp. 2.1–2.45). Wiley.

Launius, R. D. (2003). Public opinion polls and perceptions of US human spaceflight. *Space Policy, 19*(3), 163–175.

Launius, R. D., & McCurdy, H. E. (2018). Introduction: Partnerships for innovation. In R. D. Launius & H. E. McCurdy (Eds.), *NASA spaceflight: A history of innovation* (pp. 1–32). Palgrave Macmillan.

Leepuengtham, T. (2017). *The protection of intellectual property rights in outer space activities*. Edward Elgar.

Lockridge, L. W. (2006). Intellectual property in outer space: International law, national jurisdiction, and exclusive rights in geospatial data and databases. *Journal of Space Law, 32*(2), 319–360.

Luxenberg, B., & Mossinghoff, G. J. (1985). Intellectual property and space activities. *Journal of Space Law, 13*(1), 8–21.

Lyall, F., & Larsen, P. B. (2024). *Space law: A treatise* (3rd ed.). Taylor & Francis Group.

Malagar, L. B., & Magdoza-Malagar, M. (1999). International law of outer space and the protection of intellectual property rights. *Boston University International Law Journal, 17*(2), 311–366.

Malmen, L. (2021). Exploitation of space and patent law: How the current legal system ineffectively protects private companies in the commercial space industry. *Santa Clara Journal of International Law, 20*(1), 80–101.

Marchant, G. E. (2011). The growing gap between emerging technologies and the law. In G. E. Marchant, B. R. Allenby, & J. R. Herkert (Eds.), *The growing gap between emerging technologies and legal-ethical oversight* (pp. 19–33). Springer.

Meyer, C. (1988). Protecting inventors' rights aboard an international space station. *Journal of the Patent and Trademark Office Society, 70*(5), 332–347.

Moskowitz, C. (2012). SpaceX launches private capsule on historic trip to space station. *Space.com*. https://www.space.com/15805-spacex-private-capsule-launches-space-station.html

NASA. (2014). *Commercial orbital transportation services: A new era in spaceflight*. https://www.nasa.gov/wp-content/uploads/2016/08/sp-2014-617.pdf

NASA. (2020). *20 breakthroughs from 20 years of science aboard the International Space Station*. https://www.nasa.gov/missions/station/20-breakthroughs-from-20-years-of-science-aboard-the-international-space-station/

NASA. (2022a). *Five space station research results contributing to deep space exploration*. https://www.nasa.gov/missions/station/five-space-station-research-results-contributing-to-deep-space-exploration/

NASA. (2022b). *The benefits of microgravity (μg)*. https://www.nasa.gov/missions/station/the-benefits-of-microgravity/

NASA. (2022c). *Using microgravity to combat COVID-19*. https://www.nasa.gov/missions/station/iss-research/using-microgravity-to-combat-covid-19/

NASA. (2023). *International Space Station*. https://www.nasa.gov/reference/international-space-station/

NASA. (2024). *Climate change: Vital signs of the planet*. https://science.nasa.gov/climate-change/

Neef, R. (2021). Artemis Accords: A new path forward for space lawmaking? *Adelaide Law Review, 42*(2), 569–580.

New Scientist. (2007). Space's influential thinkers. *New Scientist, 195*(2620), 48–51.

O'Brien, J. E. (1987). The U.S./International Space Station. *Journal of Space Law, 15*(1), 35–42.

Ocean Tomo. (2023). *Intangible asset market value study*. https://oceantomo.com/intangible-asset-market-value-study/

Paikowsky, D. (2017). What is new space? The changing ecosystem of global space activity. *New Space, 5*(2), 84–88.

Pannell, W. C. (2016). Pirate battles in outer space: Preventing patent infringement on the 8th sea. *University of Memphis Law Review, 46*(3), 733–761.

Paris Convention for the Protection of Industrial Property (Paris Convention) 1883, 828 UNTS 305.

Parrish, B. (2013). Commercializing space: Intellectual property concerns with Space Act Agreements. *Journal of Air Law and Commerce, 78*, 651–684.

Patent Cooperation Treaty (PCT) 1970, 1160 UNTS 231.

Patents Act 1990 (Cth).

Piera, A. (2004). Intellectual property in space activities: An analysis of the United States patent regime. *Air and Space Law, 29*(1), 42–58.

Pinheiro-Machado, R. (2017). *Counterfeit Itineraries in the Global South: The human consequences of piracy in China and Brazil.* Routledge.

PwC. (2022). *Mergers and acquisitions: The 5 stages of the M&A transaction.* https://www.pwc.com/mt/en/publications/tax-legal/mergers-and-acquisitions-5-stages-of-MA-transaction.html

Rainbow, J. (2023). Young space firms are driving acquisition activity. *SpaceNews.* https://spacenews.com/young-space-firms-are-driving-acquisition-activity/

Rainbow, J. (2025). Space M&A poised for takeoff in 2025. *SpaceNews.* https://spacenews.com/space-ma-poised-for-takeoff-in-2025/

Rausser, G., Choi, E., & Bayen, A. (2023). Public–private partnerships in fostering outer space innovations. *Proceedings of the National Academy of Sciences, 120*(43), e2222013120.

Reagan, R. (1983, February 18). *Memorandum on government patent policy.* The American Presidency Project. https://www.presidency.ucsb.edu/documents/memorandum-government-patent-policy

Reagan, R. (1987, April 10). *Executive Order 12591: Facilitating access to science and technology.* National Archives. https://www.archives.gov/federal-register/codification/executive-order/12591.html

Ro, T. U., Kleiman, M. J., & Hammerle, K. G. (2011). Patent infringement in outer space in light of 35 U.S.C. § 105: Following the white rabbit down the rabbit loophole. *Boston University Journal of Science and Technology Law, 17*(2), 202–235.

Roy, D. (2013). Intellectual property strategy for competitive advantage. *International Journal of Intellectual Property Management, 6*(1–2), 36–61.

Ruse-Khan, H. G. (2011). The international law relation between TRIPS and subsequent TRIPS-plus free trade agreements: Towards safeguarding TRIPS flexibilities? *Journal of Intellectual Property Law, 18*(2), 325–385.

Saikia, K., & Deb, P. (2024). Intellectual properties derived in space exploration: Issues and scopes. *Journal of Intellectual Property Rights, 29*(2), 127–132.

Samanga, R. (2023, November 15). *Who woke the sleeping giant? Africa's emerging space programs take off.* Stimson Center. https://www.stimson.org/2023/who-woke-the-sleeping-giant-africas-emerging-space-programs-take-off/

Sandner, P., Dufter, C., & Geibel, R. (2016). Does venture capital investment lead to a change in start-ups' intellectual property strategies? *American Journal of Industrial and Business Management, 6*(12), 1146–1173.

Saragovitz, H. M. (1975). The law of intellectual property in outer space. *IDEA: The PTC Journal of Research and Education, 17*(1), 86–98.

Sattler, R. (2003). U.S. commercial activities aboard the International Space Station. *Air and Space Law, 28*, 66–78.

Secure World Foundation. (2024). *Lunar space cooperation initiatives.* https://www.swfound.org/publications-and-reports/lunar-space-cooperation-initiatives

Shabbir, Z., Sarosh, A., & Nasir, S. I. (2021). Policy considerations for nascent space powers. *Space Policy, 56*, 101414.

Sharma, A. V. (2025, March 17). Starlink and international law: The challenge of corporate sovereignty in outer space. *EJIL: Talk!.* https://www.ejiltalk.org/starlink-and-international-law-the-challenge-of-corporate-sovereignty-in-outer-space/

Sheetz, M. (2024, December 11). SpaceX valuation surges to $350 billion as company buys back stock. *CNBC.* https://www.cnbc.com/2024/12/11/spacex-valuation-surges-to-350-billion-as-company-buys-back-stock.html

Smith, J. H., Rathnasabapathy, M., & Wood, D. (2024). The political and legal landscape of space debris mitigation in emerging space nations. *Journal of Space Safety Engineering, 11*(4), 697–709.

Smith, M., & Hansen, F. (2002). Managing intellectual property: A strategic point of view. *Journal of Intellectual Capital, 3*(4), 366–374.

Storr, C. (2021). 'Space is the only way to go': The evolution of the extractivist imaginary of international law. In S. Chalmers & S. Pahuja (Eds.), *Routledge handbook of international law and the humanities* (pp. 290–301). Routledge.

Tepper, E. (2022). The big bang of space governance: Towards polycentric governance of space activities. *New York University Journal of International Law and Politics, 54*(2), 485–555.

Treaty on Principles Governing the Activities of States in the Exploration and Use of Outer Space, Including the Moon and Other Celestial Bodies (Outer Space Treaty) 1967, 610 UNTS 205.

U.S. Department of State. (1998). *Agreement among the Government of Canada, Governments of Member States of the European Space Agency, the Government of Japan, the Government of the Russian Federation, and the Government of the United States of America concerning cooperation on the Civil International Space Station*. https://www.state.gov/wp-content/uploads/2019/02/12927-Multilateral-Space-Space-Station-1.29.1998.pdf

United Nations General Assembly. (2013, December 16). *Resolution adopted by the General Assembly on 11 December 2013*. A/RES/68/74.

United Nations General Assembly. (2024, October 2). *United Nations adopts ground-breaking Pact for the Future to transform global governance* (GA/12641). https://press.un.org/en/2024/ga12641.doc.htm

United Nations Office for Outer Space Affairs (UNOOSA). (2020). *Historical summary on the consideration of the question on the definition and delimitation of outer space* (A/AC.105/769/Add.1). United Nations. https://www.unoosa.org/res/oosadoc/data/documents/2020/aac_105/aac_105769add_1_0_html/AC105_769Add01E.pdf

United Nations. (2024). *Pact for the future, global digital compact and declaration on future generations*. https://www.un.org/sites/un2.un.org/files/sotf-pact_for_the_future_adopted.pdf

United States Code, 35 U.S.C. § 105.

United States Patent and Trademark Office (USPTO). (2024). *Dialogue on intellectual property and space commercialization*. https://www.uspto.gov/about-us/events/dialogue-intellectual-property-and-space-commercialization

Vahrenwald, A. (1993). Intellectual property on the space station "Freedom". *European Intellectual Property Review, 15*(9), 318–326.

van Traa-Engelman, H. (1991). The commercial exploitation of outer space: Issues of intellectual property rights and liability. *Leiden Journal of International Law, 4*(2), 293–304.

von der Dunk, F. G. (2009). Space law in the age of the International Space Station. In L. Codignola, K. U. Schrogl, A. Lukaszczyk, & N. Peter (Eds.), *Humans in outer space: Interdisciplinary odysseys* (pp. 148–161). Springer.

von der Dunk, F. G. (2011). The origins of authorisation: Article VI of the Outer Space Treaty and international space law. In F. G. von der Dunk (Ed.), *National space legislation in Europe: Issues of authorisation of private space activities in the light of developments in European space cooperation* (pp. 3–28). Martinus Nijhoff.

Watrin, H. (2023, March 29). Staggering news in the world of patents [LinkedIn post]. *LinkedIn*. https://www.linkedin.com/feed/update/urn:li:activity:7047764293483716608/

Weinzierl, M., & Sarang, M. (2021, February 12). The commercial space age is here. *Harvard Business Review*. https://hbr.org/2021/02/the-commercial-space-age-is-here

West, J. (2024). Arms control and the myth of peaceful uses in outer space. In P. J. Blount (Ed.), *The Oxford handbook of space security* (pp. 223–247). Oxford University Press.

World Economic Forum. (2024). *Space: The $1.8 trillion opportunity for global economic growth*. https://www3.weforum.org/docs/WEF_Space_2024.pdf

World Health Organization. (2021). *Directors General of WHO, WIPO and the WTO agree on intensified cooperation in support of access to medical technologies worldwide to tackle the COVID-19 pandemic*. https://www.who.int/news/item/24-06-2021-directors-general-of-who-wipo-and-the-wto-agree-on-intensified-cooperation-in-support-of-access-to-medical-technologies-worldwide-to-tackle-the-covid-19-pandemic

World Intellectual Property Organization. (1997). *Meeting of consultants on inventions made or used in outer space*. https://www.wipo.int/documents/d/patents/docs-en-topics-outer-space-meeting-of-consultatnts_inventions_space_1997.pdf

World Intellectual Property Organization. (2004). *Intellectual property and space activities*. https://www.wipo.int/documents/d/patents/docs-en-topics-outer-space-ip_space_wipo-contribution_oecd_2004.pdf

World Intellectual Property Organization. (2023). *8th WIPO conversation wraps up, igniting discussions on generative AI's impact on intellectual property*. https://www.wipo.int/about-ip/en/frontier_technologies/news/2023/news_0002.html

World Intellectual Property Organization. (2024). *WIPO member states adopt historic new treaty on intellectual property, genetic resources and associated traditional knowledge*. https://www.wipo.int/pressroom/en/articles/2024/article_0007.html

World Intellectual Property Organization. (2025). *WIPO Conversation on intellectual property and frontier technologies*. https://www.wipo.int/en/web/frontier-technologies/frontier_conversation

World Intellectual Property Organization. (n.d.-a). *A step-by-step strategy checklist for SMEs*. https://www.wipo.int/en/web/business/checklist

World Intellectual Property Organization. (n.d.-b). *FAQs: Patents*. https://www.wipo.int/en/web/patents/faq_patents

World Intellectual Property Organization. (n.d.-c). *Draft Substantive Patent Law Treaty*. https://www.wipo.int/patent-law/en/draft_splt.htm

World Trade Organization. (n.d.). *TRIPS: Frequently asked questions*. https://www.wto.org/english/tratop_e/trips_e/tripfq_e.htm

Zhang, L. (2025). China's space station and international law-making. *Acta Astronautica, 232*, 32–38.

Zhao, Y. (2015). *National space law in China: An overview of the current situation and outlook for the future*. Brill.

Zhou, H., Sandner, P. G., Martinelli, S. L., & Block, J. H. (2016). Patents, trademarks, and their complementarity in venture capital funding. *Technovation, 47*, 14–22.

Art Cotterell, LLB (Hons), BSW, Grad Dip Legal Practice, PhD Candidate, is a research associate with the Australian National University's School of Regulation and Global Governance (RegNet). Cotterell is affiliated with the Australian Centre for Space Governance and is admitted as a lawyer in the Supreme Court of the Australian Capital Territory.

Space Industry System-of-Systems Risk Considerations

Aaron Young and Bradley Robb

1 Introduction

The prelude to this book series, 'Risk Management in Outer Space Activities: An Australian and New Zealand Perspective' (Pozza & Dennerley, 2022), surveyed multiple areas of risk consideration for space activities, from space debris to cyber-security. The book sheds light on a variety of risks, hazards, and risk management approaches relevant to space endeavours, with a central theme being the importance of understanding one's context for risk and employing a structured assessment approach accordingly. This chapter continues that work by underscoring the need for space actors within the emerging space industry to fundamentally understand their risk context and understand their contribution to stabilising the broader space ecosystem through proper risk practices.

The Global Risks Report, produced by the World Economic Forum, highlights the staggering growth in space investment over the last 10 years (World Economic Forum, 2022). This is reflected in the European Space Agency's (ESA) Annual Space Environment Report of 2021, which shows an exponential growth in the number of space objects launched into orbits between 1960 and 2020 (European Space Agency [ESA], 2021). This increase in space-based activities, particularly

The views of the authors are the authors' alone and are intended to provide commentary and general information, and do not represent the views of any organisation. This chapter should not be relied upon as a substitute for professional legal advice or for any other purpose.

A. Young (✉)
ALARP Solution, Canberra, Australia
e-mail: aaron.young@alarpsolutions.com.au

B. Robb
ALARP Solutions, Adelaide, Australia

J. A. Dennerley, M. A. Pozza (eds.), *The Business of Outer Space*, Space Law and Policy, https://doi.org/10.1007/978-981-95-2034-3_6

from new commercial and private space actors, is resulting in a rapidly expanding and diversifying space industry. This includes a variety of capabilities designed to meet an increasing consumer demand for different space products and services, such as satellite broadband to Earth observation data.

From an industry perspective, the delivery of most space-based capability involves the design, build, and use of complex systems-of-systems (SoS). A system-of-systems comprises multiple interrelated and interdependent equipment, elements, or parts (such as systems, subsystems, assemblies, components, etc.) that work together to accomplish specific outcomes. In the space industry context this can include satellites, launch systems, ground stations, communications networks, and other related systems. For example, a rocket typically comprises four high-level systems, including: the structural assembly system, mission payload system, guidance system, and propulsion system (National Aeronautics and Space Administration [NASA], n.d.). These systems are integrated and work together to enable the rocket to work as intended. However, due to the complexity, interaction, and interdependence between the components in a system-of-systems context, risk considerations are crucial for ensuring the safety, reliability, and performance of such space systems, and ultimately, successful mission outcomes.

The authors of this chapter, having worked in risk and safety for many years in Australia and New Zealand, contend that there is significant opportunity in these two countries, and the wider region, to learn lessons from existing space actors in the industry and other adjacent industries such as aviation. These two countries are relatively new players in the evolving space industry, meaning they are in a unique position to implement lessons learnt from the wider global space and aviation industries and embed a positive risk culture in their respective space industry contexts.

This chapter introduces a hazard analysis activity used in the System Safety Engineering discipline known as System-of-Systems Hazard Analysis (SoSHA). As the name suggests, SoSHA is an activity that looks at the hazards associated with the integration of systems to understand the following:

- Whether the individual systems working together introduce new hazards and associated risks that do not exist when individual systems work in isolation.
- Where existing hazards and associated risks within individual systems are magnified through their integration with other/new systems.
- Where existing risk controls within individual systems are weakened or are no longer effective for that system, or the controls themselves introduce risk, when integrated with other systems.

As the next section will expand upon, in each of these cases, risk needs to be managed early and effectively, starting with an assessment of the risk in a system-of-systems context.

1.1 The System-of-Systems Context

A good operational definition for a hazard is that it is 'a source or a situation with the potential for harm in terms of human injury or ill-health, damage to property, damage to the environment, or a combination of these' (Department of Standards Malaysia, 2011, p. 3). In simplified terms, a hazard therefore is 'a potential source of harm'. Building on this, the current United States (US) Department of Defense (DoD) standard for System Safety describes SoSHA activities as a hazard analysis activity that is undertaken to review inter-relationships between systems to 'identify any unique SoS hazards' (Department of Defense [DoD], 2023, p. 72). It requires those who use the standard to have a detailed level of understanding as to the desired operational effect (outcome) of the SoS and to know how this can be achieved through the combined systems at the SoS level. Importantly, it places special focus on the human element of the system given the human is providing inputs and receiving outputs for some or all elements at the SoS level (DoD, 2023, p. 72). The standard categorises different safety analysis activities into task series for better understanding and implementation. Among these the 'Task Section 200—Analysis' series specifically focuses on various aspects of hazard analysis in the context of system safety, with the series outlining a structured approach to identifying, assessing, and mitigating hazards throughout the lifecycle of a system (DoD, 2023, pp. 44–77). Within this series, two activities that are particularly relevant to this chapter are 'Subsystem Hazard Analysis' (SSHA) (see Task 204 in DoD, 2023, pp. 52–54) and System Hazard Analysis (SHA) (see Task 205 in DoD, 2023, pp. 55–57).

SSHA is an activity that is typically undertaken by Original Equipment Designers and Manufacturers (OEDs and OEMs) of individual subsystems at the equipment level. For example, think of a rocket propulsion system, where the propulsion subsystem may itself include fuel tanks (for fuel storage), fuel, oxidisers, pumps, and so on. Furthermore, all the rocket's equipment typically comprise multiple additional components. In the case of the fuel pump, this would include the casing, valves, screws, pins, clamps, and hoses. These items undergo rigorous testing and analysis to identify and mitigate any risks associated with their design and build. However, in many cases, the designer and manufacturer of individual equipment and components within a subsystem are not the same organisation as the system design organisation. Nevertheless, new systems are often designed using existing and proven subsystem technology. There are many reasons for this, most notably the fact that it is often easier, cheaper, and quicker to use a proven design, particularly if it is already commercially available and performs the intended function to an acceptable level of performance and safety. In most cases, this approach is very effective, especially when time to market is a critical factor or where it is not in the best interest (or commercially viable) of an organisation to start designing and/or manufacturing its own components and equipment. In short, the rocket motor subsystem, while a system in its own right, comprises multiple components that when combined provide the functions of a rocket motor.

Next, SHA is the activity undertaken when various subsystems are integrated together to operate as a dedicated system. To illustrate using the previous example, the rocket motor subsystem is just one of many subsystems in the rocket. Other subsystems would include the guidance subsystem (onboard computer), communication systems, and payload subsystem, amongst others (see generally NASA, n.d.). In the example used here, the rocket is just one system within the overall SoS, with the others being systems such as the control tower, external communications, launch platform, ground infrastructure, the air space management system (air traffic control), and the external flight control system that monitors and controls the rocket once it leaves the platform. Additionally, there are typically other associated space systems the rocket and its payload may interact with. Consequently, one can begin to see the intricate and complex nature of space industry system-of-systems.

1.2 The Challenges with System-of-Systems Integration

The challenge with SoS integration is twofold. First, there is the issue of ensuring (proving or certifying) that the equipment, systems, subsystems, assemblies, and components are fit for purpose. This means that they must meet their intended functions and perform to a required standard. In the space industry, this is sometimes known as a system's 'Spaceworthiness'. Secondly, and most importantly, there is the issue of ensuring that individual systems, subsystems, equipment, assemblies, and components do not negatively interfere with the functions of other systems and their associated systems and parts. If they do, there is a chance new hazards will be introduced into the system, and/or the risks associated with existing hazards will be magnified. That is, the likelihood of the hazard eventuating increases, or the associated consequences of the existing hazard events are magnified even further.

There are various methods that designers use when undertaking SSHA and SHA. For relatively simple systems and subsystems, these approaches generally rely on an analysis of the physical interfaces between individual subsystems, equipment, components, and inputs from the natural and human-made environments. In more complex systems, an analysis of functional interfaces[1] and their dependencies is often also needed to confirm every individual subsystem, equipment, or component will function as intended when it is integrated and operating as a complete system.

To illustrate the challenges with SoS integration, one can look to the early days of designing the airbag system for cars, where designers proved the concept using CO_2 canisters as the source of gas that would inflate the airbag assembly. On its own, this was a good choice and suitable for achieving the intended function; however, it subsequently did not meet the performance requirements (inflate quickly

[1] Given that a function is an activity that is natural to something (a person, a physical object, a piece of software, etc.), a functional interface is the connections between the thing and other things including the environment.

enough) and thus was scrapped as a concept as it would have been ineffective from a performance point of view. To resolve this, the preliminary design changed from using CO_2 canisters to sodium azide [NaN_3] pellets. This change resulted in an increase in the inflation speed, the volume of gas produced, and the reliability of inflation. However, it inadvertently introduced several new hazards such as the production of sodium (Na) (which is highly flammable), and excess heat. While the problem of having a slow and unreliable inflation was resolved, it came with new and in many instances, greater safety risk to vehicle occupants, such as the threat of fire and exposure to hot gas and toxic residue post deployment. While the chemistry of using sodium azide was relatively well known and the designers eventually found a way to make the by-products less innocuous (in this case they found that adding silica to the compound made the less hazardous by-product of sodium silicate as well as producing the desired nitrogen gas), at the time they missed identifying several integration risks that ultimately led to latent failures in early airbag system designs. This example from the automotive industry serves to demonstrate how, in complex systems, seemingly fit for purpose system parts can fail upon integration—that is, introducing new hazards that were not present prior to the system's integration. Turning to the space industry, rockets, spacecraft, and satellites will comprise many more systems, subsystems, assemblies, and components that all must work together in harmony.

As previously alluded to, an understanding of the natural and human-made environment (the specific risk context) that a space object, such as a satellite, will be operating in is crucial for SSHA and SHA. Returning to the automotive example, in high temperature environments (such as that which may be experienced when a car is sitting in the hot sun for an extended period of time), research found that the sodium azide compound was prone to degradation. Further, depending on the metal casing used to contain the airbag and the inflation assembly, the chemical compound could also react with the casing material causing corrosion and introducing potential structural failures in the casing. Where corrosion occurred, it could result in the pellets oxidising, which could lead to a failure to inflate, a delayed inflation, or only a partial inflation upon activation. This required a thorough understanding of how temperatures on Earth could affect a car's airbag. Temperatures and environmental conditions in outer space and on other celestial bodies such as the Moon and Mars are wildly different to our planet, meaning spacecraft and satellite engineers must consider how different environments might impact upon various integrated systems in a space object. Returning once more to the automotive example, another design flaw subsequently revealed that if the airbag module was not bonded and earthed correctly, the airbag could inadvertently inflate due to the inflator assembly subsystem being exposed to electromagnetic fields.[2] The space environment mirrors

[2] There are examples of airbags inflating due to electrical interference from other electrical systems within the vehicle. In 2013, Toyota recalled more than 1 million vehicles across three models due to an issue where air bags could deploy accidentally without warning as a result of internal electrical interference (Interference Technology, 2013).

these sorts of conditions, as spacecraft systems and subsystems have long been subjected to the effects of solar flares.

System design is not an exact science, and the various vehicle recalls and design iterations to update the airbag system over the past 20 years are testament to this. Often, design flaws are latent, and the hazards are only realised under certain conditions which were unforeseen in the requirements setting and testing phases of the product design and build. Realistically, it is to be expected that not every foreseeable hazard condition will be understood during the initial design, and as the airbag example shows, as it has been rolled out across the automotive industry and incidents and systems failures have been recorded, various airbag designs have been refined further to address the previously unknown (latent) failure condition.

Industry examples such as the evolution of the airbag have led to a greater focus by designers on the effective application of SSHA and SHA. Individual systems and subsystems will invariably undergo rigorous analysis and significant testing, to provide a level of assurance that the design is safe and fit for purpose however, this does not normally occur at a system-of-systems level as there are no formal techniques for conducting an SoSHA. This chapter aims to convince the reader that this oversight needs to be corrected, and in Sect. 2, the authors will highlight what can go wrong when things such as SoSHA are not undertaken, are not prioritised, or are poorly executed. It will do this by analysing a series of common causes and symptoms of substandard SoS integration which can lead to complex SoS's failures. Section 3 will go on to examine several space missions that have gone wrong due to substandard SoS integration, and which resulted in mission failures or accidents, and discuss what the space industry can learn from these examples. Following this, Sect. 4 dives deeper into why technical integration issues can cause mission failure and accidents, and how SoS hazard and risk management techniques can help identify and alleviate certain hazards and issues and prevent such accidents and mission failures. Finally, in Sect. 5, the authors would like to recommend an approach that space actors can adopt in order to facilitate the identification and management of SoS risks across the lifecycle of space capabilities. This approach has been developed by ALARP Solutions, a risk and safety engineering consulting firm specialising in risk management and systems safety solutions (ALARP Solutions, 2024). The approach is designed to assist organisations better understand the risks that can arise when multiple systems are integrated.[3]

[3] This chapter does not endorse any specific approaches to System-of-Systems Hazard Analysis or the analysis of risks within the integration of complex systems. The content in this chapter should be considered as reference material and is not a substitute for professional engineering advice.

2 The Causes and Symptoms of Substandard System-of-Systems Integration

Substandard SoS integration is easy to identify retrospectively as one is often left dealing with the catastrophic consequences from accidents, mission failures, project cost and schedule over-runs, and delays in achieving system acceptance. In many cases, root cause analysis of what went wrong typically includes poor SoS integration which has created latent failures in one or more systems, or at the SoS level. Many of these can also be attributed to poor requirements definition (when decisions are made concerning what the system is to do and how it will achieve its requirements) and poor requirements management (when records or deviations from requirements are not appropriately documented or analysed).[4] The next subsection will describe and analyse six of the common causes and symptoms of substandard SoS integration.

2.1 Substandard System-of-System Definition

Having an exact, agreed-upon meaning for an SoS is essential for shared understanding and operational consistency. Clear, common definitions create a shared language between the designers and operators of systems and promote interoperability and functional consistency. The opposite of this is a poor SoS definition, which means not having a clear concept or understanding for how the various systems will come together to deliver the SoS's desired outcome. This typically arises where *functions* are not identified or are not allocated to individual systems correctly. If a system is designed in isolation, that is, it was never intended to be part of a broader SoS, then there is a fair chance that the system integration will be troublesome. An SoS requires not only a clear holistic understanding of how the unified parts work together to deliver an outcome, but also how the SoS's component parts function in and of themselves. Both of these insights must find their way into a comprehensible and endorsed SoS definition that can act as the single source of truth when communicating what the SoS is and what it does.

Using an air traffic network example that includes the procurement and replacement of an ageing voice air to ground communication system, a key requirement is that the radio must be able to communicate with all air navigation service providers (ANSPs). Even though the radio's role in the SoS concept is easily understood, detailed requirements still need to be elicited to enable the functional and physical

[4] The lifecycle of a capability, asset, system, or product, such as a spacecraft or satellite, is often articulated in phases whereby the early phases involve understanding the user needs, defining requirements, and identifying risks, which then move on to designing, building, and testing the space object. The later phases of the lifecycle relate to the object's operation and sustainment (upkeep and update), upgrade, and its eventual disposal.

integration of the radio into the aircraft and to enable reliable communication between the aircraft and the Air Traffic Controllers. More importantly, the requirements should address unique radio specifications (e.g., to ensure that other aircraft systems do not interfere with the radio and the radio does not interfere with other aircraft systems) such as the operating protocols that specify how to operate the radio (i.e., how to select frequencies, transmit in emergency mode, etc.).

2.2 Loss of Configuration Management

Systems do not remain the same over time. This is what configuration management tries to account for and is essential in an SoS context. The aim of configuration management is to ensure that all documentation relating to the system is maintained such that it accurately represents the system. This is incredibly important in order to track and monitor changes to a system over time. Configuration management applies to system requirements, design documentation (including standards and decisions made during the design process), and operational documentation (such as the operating manuals, maintenance publications, and field data records on usage and upkeep).

Loss of control of configuration management, in particular of the system baseline configurations, will often introduce risk into the SoS. Configuration management may well be conducted at the system level, but there may be nothing at the SoS level (i.e., individual systems may be changed, maintained, and well understood by individual teams, but if these teams operated in siloed environments, then the holistic SoS suffers).

Incremental evolution of individual systems, and therefore the SoS, is a natural phenomenon, caused itself by the desire to incorporate improvements in technology, or simply wanting to get more out of the system with minor changes to its design and settings. It is very important that systems that are subject to incremental evolution continually look at SoS hazards every time a system is upgraded. This is because the impact of changes on the SoS needs to be fully analysed and understood, particularly if the new capability exceeds what the SoS was originally designed to do, or if the SoS still has not achieved its intended operating capability. In the latter example, the full capability of the SoS may be limited and/or the SoS may need to be operated a certain way to address the known weaknesses.

Using the air traffic network example once more, consider a scenario where a radar at an aerodrome is replaced with a new one featuring improved functionality, thus offering better performance. However, a challenge may arise during the installation of the radar if the documentation for the original radar siting has been lost. Given the age of the system, operators may not understand why the old radar was placed in its original location. It might emerge that the ideal site—on top of a local hill—was dismissed years ago due to difficulties accessing the area. Since these access issues have long been resolved, installing the new radar on the hill would have been optimal, providing enhanced coverage without the limitations of blind spots. Unfortunately, a lack of consistent configuration management over time prevented operators from recognising the rationale behind the old radar's location, leading to the new radar being installed in the same, less optimal position with the same operating restrictions and hazards.

2.3 *Substandard Obsolescence Management*

Forecasting and planning for how an SoS might need to be upgraded or replaced over time is at the heart of obsolescence management. Obsolescence is where systems become outdated and can no longer be supported. This occurs for many reasons such as the OEM no longer being in business or deciding that it was no longer financially viable to continue to manufacture or support the system in question. It might also include the fact that the technology is simply too outdated and/or does not provide the level of performance required to meet the needs of the operator. Regardless, the impact that obsolescence can have on the SoS design can be tricky to navigate and to plan for.

The first challenge is determining when a system will become obsolete. Mitigating this risk requires disciplined failure and defect reporting (when the system has reached the end of its life) and robust engineering change management procedures to ensure the candidate systems for obsolescence are identified early and subsumed into a planned maintenance availability (update or upgrade) to minimise any disruption. The second challenge, and the one that introduces the most risk, is how the organisation sources and subsequently integrates a replacement system into the existing SoS design. If this is done with minimal design disclosure, or is made in haste, errors could be made in selecting the wrong product that ultimately prevents the SoS working as intended or could even introduce new latent hazards.

Turning to our air traffic network example, an environmental control subsystem within a ground control tower typically comprises a chilled water system. Its primary function is to cool the computer processors in order to make sure that they do not overheat when in operation. A secondary function of the system is that it provides cooling to occupants within the building. Obsolescence of the current chilled water system introduces a number of SoS risk. Firstly, if not identified early, the system may potentially go offline for an extended period of time as replacement parts are sourced and changed out. Secondly, if there is insufficient time to source a suitable replacement, the designer may be forced to integrate a non-optimal system as an immediate fix which has shortfalls in performance, and that could overstress the system resulting in a loss of the SoS performance or service.

Space actors must be aware that obsolescence presents great challenges for the ongoing operation and maintenance of space objects, particularly those that do not return to Earth such as satellites. These spacecrafts typically have an operational lifespan of about 15 years. Over the course of its lifespan, there is no mid-life upgrade or scheduled maintenance opportunities available to the operators of these space objects. For example, over the course of its lifespan, a satellite ground control station may be updated and upgraded many times, potentially replacing key systems and equipment every few years. All the while, the satellites that this ground station supports remain unchanged. System design engineers must ensure any changes to ground control station equipment that interface with the satellites will not impact upon the operation of the satellites.

2.4 Change to the SoS Operating and Support Intent

Sometimes an SoS will begin its life with a specific intent behind how it will operate and be supported, but this intent changes due to unforeseen circumstances. This may result in the SoS operating outside its design intent. Changes to the operating and support intent (which includes how an organisation intends to operate and support the SoS) that are not adequately managed can also introduce risk into the SoS. For example, consider a local metropolitan aerodrome that supports light aircraft and small commercial airline activity during weekdays between the hours of 06:00 and 20:00 (this is the context for its operating and support intent). Let's say that at a particular point in time, the aerodrome is considered as an option to land larger commercial aircraft from a nearby international airport while the major airport undergoes upgrades. During this time, the operating and support concept for the local aerodrome will need to change significantly over what it was initially designed for. Even though the communication, navigation, surveillance, and air traffic management systems (CNS-ATM) would still be able to perform the functions they were designed to do, there are other SoS integration issues and potential risks at play. For a start, if the original support concept for the aerodrome was to conduct maintenance on the aerodrome CNS-ATM systems in the late evenings, overnight, or on weekends, issues may be inadvertently introduced because there is now a risk that system maintenance may not be able to be undertaken like it was in the evenings or over the weekends. This is one of many SoS considerations that would need to be resolved. Others include the processing and movement of people inside the terminal, and the movement of people and public transport to and from the terminal. A detailed understanding of the operating and support concept is therefore critical to identifying exceptional risks for those times when the system is operated outside its design, operating, and support envelope, even if only for a short period of time.

2.5 Multiple Organisations Being Responsible for the Design and Supply of Different System-of-Systems Elements

Risk is often introduced into an SoS design when different elements of the system are designed and built by different organisations. This can result in the different system parts not being used in the manner in which they were initially designed.

Whilst international, industry, and technical standards are designed to offset some of these problems and harmonise the way in which technologies and products are used (by aligning like-minded industries to a consistent way of doing things), there are often multiple recommended standards that could be adopted and used (explored below). This means that the selection of an appropriate standard typically comes down to the inclinations of an individual organisation and may be driven by reasons of cost, historical biases, or process preferences.

It is important to note that many countries and commercial entities are now designing space systems and operating in a global space industry that does not have clear and unanimous international regulations for SoS design of space objects. Mandating compliance to prescriptive design, build, and integration standards may alleviate this issue, which is the case in industries such as the US nuclear industry (which follows very detailed prescriptive rules for design, build, and operations), and the international maritime industry(which adopts stringent design and build rule sets for ships via 1 of the 12 member organisations in the International Association of Classification Societies (IACS)) (International Association of Classification Societies, n.d.). This approach has many benefits and is based on many years of lessons learnt; however, it can lead to blind compliance and doing only what is required. This can also serve to inhibit novel and innovative ideas and placing these kinds of restrictions on to space actors might curtail the emergence of new space technology.

In large and complex SoS, there is rarely a single entity responsible for setting standards for the design and operation of every system element. The reality is that each organisation will have its own approach and methodology, particularly when they are building an SoS comprising many systems, all of which have a different design and operational intent. Additionally, the issue becomes magnified when respective design teams within an organisation are geographically displaced, speak different languages, use different units of measurement, and undergo different standards of training.

For Communication Navigation Surveillance and Air Traffic Management Systems (CNS-ATMS) in Australia and New Zealand, given the size of their industry, it makes no sense to design and build a new SoS from scratch, particularly given the benefits of acquiring affordable systems that have proven themselves in service in the UK, Europe, and the US over the course of many years. The CNS-ATM SoS adopted by the respective air navigation service providers (ANSPs) in Australia and New Zealand[5] typically comprises a collection of orphaned systems from many different original OEMs and countries. Not surprisingly, each has been designed to meet local regulations and meet local certification requirements, and in doing so, have developed, or adopted standards to suit these jurisdictions, however, they are rarely designed to integrate with other systems outside of their immediate system

[5]An air navigation service provider (ANSP) is a body that manages flight traffic on behalf of a country or a region. ANSPs can be private or public legal bodies. New Zealand has one ANSP named Airways. Australia has two ANSPs, Airservices Australia and the Royal Australian Air Force.

boundary. While Australia and New Zealand are happy to accept the individual systems through a process of recognition of prior certification with other affiliated International Civil Aviation Organization (ICAO) certification bodies, the context of operation of the systems is not always aligned to the Configuration Role and Environment (CRE) in which the system design was intended. This often results in operational restrictions.

2.6 Use of Different Standards in the Design of System-of-System Elements

Technical standards are established and documented norms and practices that specify how particular products, services, and processes should be designed, built, and operated so as to promote their consistent use, ensure the interoperability between goods and components, and/or facilitate compatibility between multiple parties (Oxford Reference, n.d.). Space industry supply chains are often international, complex, and diverse. This means that space actors wanting to undertake space activities, such as a design, build, and operation of a satellite, will often need to engage with, and navigate, a global interconnected network of governments and companies (for instance suppliers, manufacturers, and vendors who will provide a variety of hardware and software such as communications equipment, satellite electronics, power supply systems, etc.) from which to source the satellite's component parts and subsystems. Space organisations may also recruit staff and specialists from diverse educational and technical backgrounds, who may each have slightly different ways of working. Therefore, a significant challenge in integrating systems lies in the fact that often the SoS designers are not the designers of individual systems or their subsystems. As a result, systems will often be built using different technical standards, by different people, and to different design philosophies.

For example, while a Prime Systems Integrator (PSI) is often responsible for the design and integration effort, their role may be impeded and even impossible to achieve if the commercial and intellectual property environment prevents them from having control over constituent parts of the system. Commercial issues that can arise include the undefined assignment of accountability and responsibility for design and operations, unclear contractual arrangements between the principal and other contracted entities, the inability to resolve data, security, or intellectual property ownership issues, as well as multiple contracted design organisations each being engaged and responsible for their own system, subsystem, assembly, or component. Technical standards go some way to resolving these challenges by harmonising the ways of working between multiple parties involved in a system's design, build, test, operation, and maintenance.

Nevertheless, a reoccurring problem related to the absence of technical standards (or the lack of their consistent adoption and use) that the authors see time and time again surrounds the procurement of systems reliant on electrical power. More often than not, Australian and New Zealand system integrators procure systems from overseas vendors, particularly the UK, Europe, and the US. This becomes a challenge when integrating them into an SoS that was designed to meet, and be compliant with, Australian and New Zealand design electrical standards. To highlight the challenge, the Australian and New Zealand electrical power standard is 240V AC at 50 Hz, whereas the American standard is 115 VAC at 60 Hz. Therefore, a US system cannot simply be plugged into an Australian power supply, and, even where an adapter is used, if the US system was never designed to operate at 240V AC, technical risks are introduced that the system and SoS integrator must understand and rectify where necessary.

3 Overview of Significant Mission Failures and Accidents in the Space Industry

Space activities can be hazardous affairs. The history of spaceflight has several noteworthy examples of failed missions and serious accidents, some of which have resulted in fatalities. This section provides an overview of several historical examples of when things have gone wrong, and will outline some of the technical, engineering, and system-related factors that either contributed to these failures/accidents or which were overlooked. Specifically, these examples will explore system-of-systems risk challenges associated with space activities.

3.1 Space Shuttle Challenger Disaster (1986)

(i) *Background:* The 28th of January 1986 marked one of the most tragic days in the history of space exploration. This was the date when the Space Shuttle *Challenger* exploded shortly after its launch from the Kennedy Space Centre in Florida. The disaster led to the death of all seven crew members, which included five National Aeronautics and Space Administration (NASA) astronauts and two payload specialists (for details see Rogers et al., 1986).

(ii) *Cause*: The root cause of the disaster was eventually traced back to the failure of an O-ring seal housed in the right solid rocket booster (SRB), which is a launcher used to generate thrust during a spacecraft launch. Engineers from Morton Thiokol, an American company that had built the SRB, had concerns about the O-ring based on previous launches where the O-ring had eroded in warmer conditions. It was forecast that the air temperature was going to drop to −3 °C at the scheduled time of the launch on the morning of 28 January. The O-ring, which was not designed to handle these unusually frigid conditions, failed to properly seal. As a result, hot gases leaked from the SRB, leading to the structural failure of the external fuel tank and the subsequent breakup of the orbiter (for details see Rogers et al., 1986, Chapter 4).

(iii) *Impact*: The *Challenger* disaster had far-reaching consequences for US space exploration. The Space Shuttle Program was suspended for 32 months and led to the formation of the Rogers Commission,[6] a presidential commission appointed by then President Ronald Reagan to investigate the accident (see generally Rogers et al., 1986). The Commission's report highlighted serious flaws in NASA's decision-making and organisational processes, particularly concerning the management of known risks with the SRBs. Nobel prize-winning physicist Richard Feynman participated in the investigation. He noted that there was a significant disconnect between management estimates of risks to those of working engineers; where management estimated probability to failure to be in the range of 1 in 100,000, compared to the engineers' range of 1 in 100 (Feynman, 1986). The findings of the Rogers Commission ultimately resulted in a major overhaul in NASA's management structure and operational procedures to prioritise safety (see generally Rogers et al., 1986, pp. 252–255). Less tangibly but possibly more importantly, the disaster also had a significant impact on the public's perception of space exploration and still remains as a poignant reminder of the risks associated with space-related activities (see generally Rogers et al., 1986, p. 1).

(iv) *Lessons Learnt*: The integration of the SRBs into the shuttle design represented a complex undertaking as there were literally thousands of components, like the O-ring, that was designed specifically for an intended function and expected to operate in space conditions. The O-ring, a safety critical component was designed to seal sections of the SRB. While it was designed and built to withstand very strict engineering specifications, it was subsequently operated in conditions that were outside its intended operating environment. Analysis of the design by engineers likely considered the effects of unusually cold temperatures on individual components and the broader system, but this message was not understood by management (see generally Rogers et al., 1986). This failure underlined the importance of fully understanding the integration of individual components within a system down to the smallest widget. It also highlighted the need to test component interactions where possible, and finally, it highlighted the importance of management understanding the information that is presented to them and making every effort to fully understand the risks before they make a decision to proceed (for details see Rogers et al., 1986, Chapter 5).

[6] Named after the Commission's Chairman William P. Rogers.

3.2 Mars Observer *Mission Failure (1993)*

(i) *Background*: The *Mars Observer* mission was a significant NASA project with the aim of studying Mars from orbit. The observation satellite was launched from Earth on 25 September 1992 and proceeded on its journey to Mars without incident. However, just days before the spacecraft was due to enter the Martian atmosphere, on 21 August 1993, communications with the spacecraft were lost. The primary objectives of the *Mars Observer* were to study the Martian surface, the atmosphere, and the climate. The spacecraft was fitted with scientific instruments suitable to map the planet's topography, study its geology, and analyse its atmosphere (see generally Young et al., 2000).

(ii) *Cause*: An extensive investigation identified several credible causes for the failure (see Stephenson & Bernard, 1994). One example was a rupture of the spacecraft's fuel pressurisation system. It is likely that, if this was the cause, it occurred when propellant valves were opened in preparation for an orbital manoeuvre leading to a sudden loss of pressure. The resultant damage could have disabled the spacecraft's communication and control systems. Other potential causes included electrical power loss, loss of computational function, or transmitter failures (MARS Observer Mission Failure Investigation Board, 1993).

(iii) *Impact*: The loss of *Mars Observer* was a significant setback for Mars exploration at the time and led to NASA re-evaluating its approach to planetary missions, specifically in relation to risk management and spacecraft design. Following this incident, NASA adopted the 'faster, better, cheaper' approach for subsequent missions, which is extensively discussed in Howard E. McCurdy's book, *Faster, Better, Cheaper Low-Cost Innovation in the U.S. Space Program* (McCurdy, 2003). The aim of this strategy was to reduce system-of-systems integration issues by decreasing the complexity of individual missions and thus mitigate risks associated with more complex designs. This approach led to a series of successful Mars missions, including the *Mars Global Surveyor* and *Mars Pathfinder*, and played a critical role in shaping future missions.

(iv) *Lessons Learnt*: The *Mars Observer* combined multiple new technologies and systems, including its fuel pressurisation system, intended for a long-duration interplanetary missions. All the credible causes outlined in the subsequent investigation, including the possible rupture of the spacecraft's fuel pressurisation system, highlight the risks associated with the complex system-of-systems integration under the unforgiving conditions of space. The 'faster, better, cheaper' approach, as detailed in McCurdy's book (2003), underscores how reducing mission complexity can address these integration challenges and improve overall mission success. A direct conclusion from McCurdy's book is that, where possible, reducing complexity is a good first step in managing system-of-systems integration risks (McCurdy, 2003).

3.3 Ariane 5 *Launch Vehicle Failure (1996)*

(i) *Background*: The *Ariane 5* launch vehicle failure occurred on its maiden flight on 4 June 1996. This ESA rocket was designed to be an advanced and more capable successor to *Ariane 4* but exploded just over 30 s after liftoff (see generally Lions, 1996).

(ii) *Cause*: The root cause of the failure was ultimately traced to a software issue. Specifically, a data conversion from a 64-bit floating point integer to a 16-bit signed integer caused a processor trap (an exception) because of an overflow error (see generally Lions, 1996, p. 4). The problem originated from software that had been specifically designed for and used in *Ariane 4*; where it had functioned without issues due to the distinct flight characteristics of that rocket. However, *Ariane 5* had different flight characteristics that included greater acceleration and a trajectory that led to a horizontal velocity five times greater than that of *Ariane 4* (see generally Lions, 1996, p. 4). This led to unexpected and erroneous values that the older software could not handle. In this case, the rocket velocity exceeded the maximum allowable speed as represented by the 16-bit integer, resulting in the software handling error telling the computer to reboot which caused the rocket motor to swivel to its default starting position. This resulted in extreme forces on the vehicle that caused it to veer off course and break up, ultimately triggering the internal self-destruct feature (see generally Lions, 1996, 3.1 Findings).

(iii) *Impact*: Aside for the significant financial loss of USD370 million (Dowson, 1997), *Ariane 5* destroyed 4 ESA 'Cluster' satellites used for analysing the impacts of the solar wind on the Earth (ESA, n.d.). The incident highlighted the critical need for a comprehensive overhaul of software verification processes and risk management practices, advocating for the integration of proof-based system engineering and ensuring that software validation is approached within a broader system-wide engineering framework (Le Lann, 1996).

(iv) *Lessons Learnt*: The event highlighted a number of points that have since been learnt by space design engineers and software engineers across many industries. Firstly, software should not be relied upon for safety critical functions where other design solutions are available. Secondly, wherever possible, systems should be tested in realistic conditions. In the case of *Ariane 5*, the software was tested in a simulator only and not all software functions were or could be tested (Sommerville, 2004). Finally, designers should be careful when reusing proven software and be sure they understand its functions and limitations. In the case of *Ariane 5*, the software design team did not understand the limitations and never tested the software to see how it would perform under realistic conditions (see generally Lions, 1996, p. 12).

3.4 Mars Climate Orbiter *Crash (1999)*

(i) *Background*: The *Mars Climate Orbiter* was intended to serve two purposes. The first of these was to study Mars' atmosphere and provide detailed analysis of the Martian climate, weather patterns, seasonal changes, and atmospheric composition and dynamics. The second purpose was to serve as a communications relay for future Martian surface-based missions that would include landers and rovers. Unfortunately, the Orbiter was lost due to a navigation error as it attempted to enter Mars' orbit on 23 September 1999 (see generally NASA, 1999a, 1999b).

(ii) *Cause*: The navigation error which led to the loss of the Orbiter was caused by a unit conversion mistake. The *Mars Climate Orbiter*'s thruster data software was developed by Lockheed Martin to calculate thrust in imperial units, specifically pound-force second (lbf.s). However, the navigation software developed by the navigation team at NASA's Joint Propulsion Laboratory (JPL) was expecting impulse data to be in the metric units of Newton-seconds (N.s). This conversion error led to the navigation software interpreting thrust data to be approximately four times lower than it actually was (see generally NASA, 1999a, p. 16).

(iii) *Impact*: Aside from the loss of a $235.9 million spacecraft (see NASA, 1999b, p.6), the loss of the *Mars Climate Orbiter* set back NASA research and was a major blow to NASA's Mars program, prompting a thorough review of communication and procedural standards within NASA and amongst its contractors (see NASA, 2009).

(iv) *Lessons Learnt*: This incident was a clear example of a failure in integrating software and hardware systems with organisational processes. The discrepancy between metric and imperial units was a direct result of two systems (developed by different teams in different countries) that were not fully integrated in terms of specified and agreed units of measurement, communication protocols, and operational standards (see NASA, 2009).

3.5 Space Shuttle Columbia *Disaster (2003)*

(i) *Background*: On 1 February 2003, the Space Shuttle *Columbia* was completing its 28th space mission, which required the seven crew members to conduct around-the-clock scientific experiments. During re-entry into the Earth's atmosphere, and just 16 min before the space shuttle was scheduled to land, it tragically disintegrated, resulting in the loss of all seven crew members (see generally Columbia Accident Investigation Board, 2003; Smith, 2003).

(ii) *Cause*: The disaster was initiated by a piece of insulating foam that broke away from the left bipod ramp. The bipod is the point at which the space shuttle attaches to the external fuel tank and which contains the liquid hydrogen and liquid oxygen propellants for the shuttle's three main engines. The bipod ramp is designed to insulate the bipod from the super-cold temperatures of the liquid fuel and prevent icing. The break-away foam struck the leading edge of *Columbia*'s left wing, which resulted in damage to the Thermal Protection System, which is designed to manage the extreme heat of atmospheric re-entry. With the Thermal Protection System in a degraded state, it was not able to withstand the extreme temperatures of re-entry, which ultimately resulted in the shuttle's disintegration (see generally Columbia Accident Investigation Board, 2003; Smith, 2003, Chapter 3).

(iii) *Impact*: The initial impact of the tragedy was devastating, resulting in the loss of seven astronauts. The subsequent debris search and investigation involved thousands of people, which itself saw the loss of two searchers in a helicopter accident. The longer-term effects on the space shuttle program were pronounced, as space shuttle operations were delayed for 2½ years to address key safety issues. These included a redesign of the external tank to reduce the risk of foam shedding, implementation of more robust inspection and repair capabilities for the Thermal Protection System, upgraded imaging sensors to monitor launch and detect damage, and, most importantly, an overhaul of the safety culture within NASA and its management's decision-making processes (see Columbia Accident Investigation Board, 2003; Smith, 2003, Chapter 10).

(iv) *Lessons Learnt*: The *Columbia* disaster highlighted multiple integration issues across the shuttle's thermal protection system, sensor technology, and organisational decision-making processes. In his book, *The Failure of Risk Management*, Douglas Hubbard cites research in relation to the *Columbia* Space Shuttle Disaster by Judgment and Decision Making psychologist, Robin Dillon-Merrill (see Hubbard, 2020; Dillon & Tinsley, 2008). Dillon-Merrill revealed that previous near-miss events of a similar nature in the space shuttle program, events where shedding of external tank foam had occurred but not resulted in a disaster, were treated favourably from a risk perspective. So, rather than being treated as warnings of potential failures, these events were potentially misinterpreted as evidence of acceptable risk levels in a robust system. She also found that being exposed to 'some relatively unlikely risk', resulted in individuals being more tolerant of the risk even though the likelihood of the risk occurring had not changed (see Dillon & Tinsley, 2008; Hubbard, 2020). The reality is that a near miss should be treated as if the risk was actually realised and should form the foundation of lessons learnt and underpin a strong safety culture in every organisation. This organisational issue was also highlighted in the *Columbia* Accident Investigation Board report, where the authors state:

> We are convinced that the management practices overseeing the Space Shuttle Program were as much a cause of the accident as the foam that struck the left wing. The Board was also influenced by discussions with members of Congress, who suggested that this nation needed a broad examination of NASA's Human Space Flight Program, rather than just an investigation into what physical fault caused *Columbia* to break up during re-entry. (Columbia Accident Investigation Board, 2003, p. 11)

From a systems-of-systems risk perspective, the hazards associated with integrating multiple complex systems cannot be overstated. The *Columbia* disaster is a textbook example of these risks, highlighting the challenges involved in the integration of various complex systems, including the external fuel tanks, the Thermal Protection System, the shuttle itself, the monitoring systems, and even human elements within organisations.

4 Understanding the Challenges in Managing the Integration of Complex System

The above mission failures and accidents can be broadly grouped into the following two categories:

- Failure of organisational governance
- Failure of assets and/or services

4.1 Failures of Organisation Governance

Governance is the foundation upon which all effective and enduring enterprises are built. It directs and resources the systems, processes, and people that deliver an organisation's outcomes. Consequently, failures in governance often have profound and far-reaching impacts, manifesting through the realisation of technical risks. Myriad reviews have identified governance failures as a root cause of both organisational collapses and major crises.

Prominent examples include the Fukushima Daiichi Nuclear Disaster in Japan (2011), the Flint water crisis in Michigan (2014), and the Boeing *737 MAX* disasters (various years). In each case, governance failures were cited as a critical factor, ultimately leading to severe technical failures with devastating consequences for human life. In a sense, the governance failures created systemic latent risks that were only fully understood long after the events occurred.

The mission failures and accidents discussed in Sect. 3 further illustrate this point. For instance, the Space Shuttle *Challenger* disaster (1986) underscores how governance failures directly contributed to the tragedy. Specifically, the inability of engineers to effectively communicate their concerns or influence the decision to delay the launch resulted in the catastrophic loss of the shuttle shortly after take-off.

In recent years, governance failures have become increasingly visible, as evidenced by the collapse of several major organisations. In the context of system-of-systems integration, poor governance, such as unclear accountability and decision rights, can significantly hinder the ability to integrate systems across different accountable authorities.

4.2 Failures of Assets and/or Services

Failure of assets and/or services are generally far easier to identify as their impact is typically immediate. In some instances, the system-of-system design includes mitigations to prevent the escalation of a system or service failure leading directly to a major event, and at other times, just like the governance failures, which often manifest in technical failures, the impact is unrecoverable. Failure of assets and/or services is typically caused through one or more of the following conditions:

- Poor SoS requirements derivation and management: The *Mars Climate Orbiter* crash in 1999 is an example of this. An error in units of measurement caused the spacecraft to fly too close to Mars and burn up in its atmosphere.
- Poor integration and testing: The ongoing need to integrate new scientific instruments brought onto the International Space Station (ISS) is a constant issue. Resolving compatibility issues with the ageing ISS systems have resulted in many delays over a long period of time. Further, where issues cannot be fully resolved and the system is sent to the ISS anyway as there was no other option, the result is a decreased efficiency in the operation of the ISS. Likewise, an integration issue between the different communications systems (spacecraft, satellite, and ground terminals) used to control the *Mars Observer* in 1993 is suspected of being responsible for the spacecraft losing contact with the Earth. Even today, the integration of payloads on commercial satellites is a constant source of mission delay.
- Rushed implementation: This has long been a root cause of many major projects throughout the twentieth century. This is typically caused by an overly aggressive project schedule, funding constraints, or a poorly defined verification and validation program to fully test if the requirements have been met and the controls of the system are present, suitable, operating, and effective. When the complexity of systems comes into the equation, the stakes only get higher.
- Technical failure:
  - The *Hubble Space Telescope*'s Wide Field Camera 3 failure (2010), where a component failure resulted in the loss of one of the camera's detectors.
  - The failed *Ariane 5* launch (1996), where a software issue caused the rocket to veer off course and self-destruct.
  - The reduced performance of the *X-37B* spaceplane due to exposure to radiation (2020), where radiation exposure caused the spacecraft's systems to degrade and its mission to be shortened.
  - The loss of the Space Shuttle *Challenger* (1986), where a design flaw in the shuttle's O-ring seals led to a catastrophic failure.
  - *Kepler Space Telescope* (2013) where degradation of the spacecraft's batteries caused it to shut down and end its mission.

- Data/information integrity and security:
  - Compatibility issues with existing GPS caused incorrect positioning of the European Galileo navigation system (2016).
  - The *Mars Reconnaissance Orbiter*'s HiRISE camera data loss (2012), where a data storage issue caused a loss of some of the camera's images.
  - The loss of data during the *Solar and Heliospheric Observatory* (SOHO) mission (1998), where a data storage issue caused a loss of some of the spacecraft's data.
  - The theft of design schematics for the *X-37B* spaceplane (2018), where hackers stole sensitive information about the spacecraft's design.

In the context of the space industry, the above symptoms must be considered in the context of the following unique considerations:

- The potential for a minor failure to lead to complete mission failure and/or have catastrophic consequences. In a SoS, a failure in one system can have a ripple effect and lead to failures in other systems. This can be particularly problematic in space systems, where the failure of a single component can have severe consequences, such as the loss of a satellite or the failure of a mission.
- Effective communication and coordination between different systems and organisations. In the space industry, multiple organisations may be involved in the design, development, and operation of a single SoS. This can make it challenging to ensure that all stakeholders have a shared understanding of the system and its risks and can make it difficult to coordinate risk management activities. Specifically, SoSHA needs to be done by the entity that has full view of the SoS risk. This becomes a significant issue when that entity is a government, where adequate training and resources are not always a priority.
- Specific risks associated with the space environment. Space systems must operate in a harsh and unforgiving environment, with risks such as radiation, micrometeoroids, and extreme temperatures. These risks must be considered when designing and operating space systems, and appropriate mitigation strategies must be implemented.
- Complex regulations and legal requirements that govern the space industry. The space industry is heavily regulated, with laws and regulations covering issues such as safety, security, and the protection of the environment. Organisations must be aware of these regulations and comply with them in order to operate in the space industry.
- Time to complete analysis and risk management. Unfortunately, while many operators do understand the importance of doing proper comprehensive safety analysis, the activity is often given little to no time. Typically, in asset-based industries where organisations are procuring equipment (e.g., defence, rail, oil and gas and mining), the goal is to put the system to work as soon as possible.

5 The ALARP Solutions System-of-Systems Hazard Analysis Approach: Using SoS Analysis to Support Hazard and Risk Management in the Space Industry

In a complex system-of-systems, where multiple systems interact to achieve overarching objectives, understanding and managing the interdependencies and integration risks is crucial for system safety and effectiveness. The authors leverage a bespoke method involving the construction of an interdependencies matrix, which has proven highly effective in prompting consideration of these crucial factors. Below is an overview of the approach used to conduct a System-of-Systems Hazard Analysis (SoSHA) using techniques developed by ALARP Solutions.

5.1 Importance of SoSHA

SoSHA is essential for identifying and managing risks that arise from the interactions between various systems within an SoS. These interactions can often lead to complex behaviours and emergent risks that are not apparent when systems are considered in isolation. Effective SoSHA ensures that:

- System interactions are understood: This involves understanding how systems affect each other, which is vital for ensuring that the operation of one system does not inadvertently compromise the safety or functionality of another.
- Emergent risks are mitigated: By analysing the combined operations of interconnected systems, SoSHA identifies risks that emerge from these interactions, allowing for the implementation of controls before these risks can manifest in operational settings.
- Optimised system integration: SoSHA facilitates smoother system integration by highlighting potential conflicts and compatibility issues between systems early in the design and development phases.
- Enhanced system reliability and safety: By ensuring that all systems harmoniously work together without unforeseen disruptions, SoSHA contributes to the overall reliability and safety of the SoS.

5.2 Conducting SoSHA with the Interdependencies Matrix

The development of an 'Interdependencies Matrix' has been a cornerstone of the authors' approach to SoSHA. To demonstrate the methodology of an SoSHA, a high-level example of the infrastructure used to launch a communications satellite into a geostationary orbit will be used. For the purposes of this analysis, this SoS will be referred to as the Orbital Satellite Deployment System (OSDS).

Table 1 OSDS element descriptions

ID	Element	Element description
1	Launch vehicle (Rocket)	This system provides the propulsion needed to escape Earth's atmosphere and enter into an orbit. It consists of multiple stages, including boosters, main engines, and fuel tanks
2	Satellite payload	The satellite itself, which contains the instruments, sensors, or communication equipment that will perform the intended mission once in orbit
3	Launch Support and Integration System (LSIS)	This system prepares the satellite and launch vehicle for the mission. It includes the launch pad and tower, fuelling infrastructure, vehicle assembly infrastructure, fire suppression systems on the launch pad, among others
4	Ground control	This is the infrastructure on Earth used to control and communicate with the satellite throughout its mission, including ground stations and monitoring software

For context, the high-level elements comprising the OSDS and a description of each is provided below in Table 1. For this analysis, the elements have been kept overly simplistic and it is acknowledged that many more elements would comprise an SoS designed to place a satellite into orbit, for example, a communications system including a network of satellites that facilitate data transfer between various SoS elements—this has been done purposefully to focus on the SoSHA methodology.

5.3 SoSHA Methodology

To perform an SoSHA on the OSDS (or any SoS), the following tasks are to be performed:

1. Scope the analysis
2. Identify dependencies between SoS elements
3. Identify hazards, mishaps, causes, and consequences
4. Assess risk
5. Identify suitable risk controls
6. Review and monitor safety performance

5.3.1 Step 1: Scope the Analysis

For the purposes of this example, the SoSHA will be scoped to the SoS launch and delivery phase only. That is, only the activities of launching the satellite and placing it into orbit will be analysed. However, it is noted that a comprehensive SoSHA should include all stages (e.g., manoeuvre in orbit and re-entry at end of life) of the

SoS life cycle. Furthermore, when planning the analysis, it is also necessary to ensure the appropriate inputs are available. The primary inputs for the SoSHA are:

- A Functional Baseline (FBL) that details all required functions of the SoS.
- Previous system hazard analysis results which will inform the scope of previous analysis and may inform failure modes associated with individual systems that create SoS unsafe states.

5.3.2 Step 2: Map Relationships and Dependencies

This step requires the assessor to list the components both horizontally and vertically within a matrix and then list the dependencies between each component. Be sure to list the human as an element of the system too where this is appropriate. Inter-system dependencies are categorised as follows:

- Functional (FN): Functional dependencies are where one element of the SoS is reliant on an action or process of another. An example of a functional dependency is that the launch pad *secures* the rocket in preparation for launch. Functional dependencies are usually phrased as verbs to denote the action they perform.
- Physical (PHY): Physical dependencies are physical interactions between one element and another. For example, the satellite is housed inside the rocket during launch. These interactions often are associated with hazards when the materials, temperature, electromagnetic output, etc. of each element are incompatible with each other.
- Resource (RES): Resource dependencies are where multiple elements of the SoS share the same resource for their operation (bandwidth, memory, power, airspace, etc.). Hazards arise where there is a compromise of the resource between elements.
- Data/Information (DAT): Data or information dependencies are where elements rely on the information provided by other elements to perform their intended function. Hazards arise where there is anomalies or compromised data provided to elements.

An example of the dependency matrix for the OSDS is provided below in Table 2. As is shown, the dependency matrix lists how the element within the columns are dependent on the element listed within the rows. Table 2 is not a comprehensive list of dependencies; however, it provides examples for all dependency types necessary to teach the methodology.

5.3.3 Step 3: Identify Hazards, Mishaps, Causes, and Consequences

Once dependencies are identified, it is necessary to understand how these dependencies could fail which then leads to adverse consequences. To understand failure modes and the conditions that allow them, SoS hazards, their mishaps, mishap

Table 2 Dependency matrix for the OSDS

Element ID	Launch vehicle	Satellite payload	LSIS	Ground control
Launch vehicle	–	PHY: Contains satellite during launch FN: Secure satellite during launch FN: Protect satellite from aerodynamic forces and heat in launch FN: Release payload (satellite) once in orbit	PHY: Exert thrust on launch pad	DAT: Provide telemetry and system data to ground control
Satellite payload	Nil	–	Nil	DAT: Provide telemetry and system data to ground control
LSIS	PHY: Holds rocket in place PHY: Umbilical connections between launch pad and rocket FN: Directs exhaust heat away from rocket during launch FN: Fuel rocket RES: Provide power to rocket systems when on ground	Nil	–	DAT: Provide fuel transfer and environmental control data to ground control
Ground control	FN: Monitor system performance and telemetry	FN: Monitor satellite when released into orbit FN: Control satellite when released into orbit	FN: Monitor fuel transfer and environmental control when rocket is on the ground	–

causes, and consequences of each mishap must be determined. These properties make up what is known as a *causation profile*. A causation profile is akin to an *accident causation model* as it describes the undesirable event and associated adverse consequences and what led to the event in the first place, that is, what the hazard was, and what the causes and existing controls were in place to prevent or minimise the likelihood and consequence of the mishap if the hazard was realised.

Accident causation models are a useful tool for safety engineers as they enable those undertaking the analysis and assessment to describe all scenarios related to the realisation of the hazard (also known as a loss of control in some industries). Accident causation models are often presented visually using a bow tie model. When applied in a systematic way, analysis of an accident causation model (and presentation using a bow tie model) provides useful context to the user with respect to the design of the system, and the strength and adequacy of its hazard and accident controls. Where a design is weak and more can be done to eliminate or mitigate a risk (which is discussed in a subsequent step), application of hazard controls,[7] preventative accident controls,[8] or mitigative accident controls[9] using the *Design Order of Precedence* (see Department of Defense, 2023, pp. 13, 23) or *Hierarchy of Control* (see Safe Work Australia, n.d.; Health and Safety at Work Act 2015; Work Health and Safety Act 2011) is undertaken until the system owner deems the risk acceptable and/or, the risk has been minimised as far as is reasonably practicable. The definition of causation profile attributes is detailed below in Table 3.

ALARP Solutions uses two main activities to determine causation profile properties, which are the Functional Failure Analysis (FFA) and the Interface Failure Analysis (IFA). The concepts of both activities are described briefly below.

Functional Failure Analysis (FFA)

The FFA is used to identify unsafe SoS scenarios associated with failures of defined SoS functions. As the analysis is based on SoS functions, a list of functions must be provided as a key input to the analysis. This list of functions is usually provided through a Functional Baseline document during the development of the SoS. The

Table 3 Causation profile attribute definitions

Term	Definition
Hazard	A real or potential condition that could lead to an unplanned event or series of events (i.e., mishap) resulting in death, injury, occupational illness, damage to or loss of equipment or property, or damage to the environment (Department of Defense, 2023, p. 6)
Mishap	An event or series of events resulting in unintentional death, injury, occupational illness, damage to or loss of equipment or property, or damage to the environment (Department of Defense, 2023, p. 6)
Cause	One or several mechanisms that trigger the hazard without controls and could result in the realisation of a hazard or mishap
Control	A barrier that eliminates or minimises a root cause (threat) from leading to a hazard or accident depending on where it is placed in the system
Consequence	A resulting outcome stemming from a mishap which may include unintentional death, injury, occupational illness, damage to or loss of equipment or property, or damage to the environment

[7] Controls that prevent the onset of a hazard.

[8] The controls that prevent the onset of an accident.

[9] The controls that are used to prevent the escalation of an accident once it has occurred.

FFA primarily assesses three failure modes for each individual function to identify unsafe system scenarios, with these including:

- Function not provided
- Function performed when not required
- Function performed incorrectly

These failure modes allow causes, mishaps, and consequences to be identified which have occurred due to some functional hazard, ultimately leading to appropriate control development which will occur in later analysis steps. An example of an FFA for a single OSDS function is provided below in Table 4.

Interface Failure Analysis (IFA)

Like the FFA, each identified dependency identified within the dependency matrix (Table 2) is assessed to identify how failures of the dependency could generate unsafe system scenarios. The Interface Failure Analysis (IFA) assesses the same three failure modes as the FFA for each individual dependency to identify unsafe system scenarios, with these including:

- Dependency not provided
- Dependency performed when not required
- Dependency performed incorrectly

These failure modes allow causes, mishaps, and consequences to be identified which occur due to some physical or functional hazard, ultimately leading to appropriate control development which will occur in later analysis steps. An example of an IFA for one of the dependencies listed within Table 2 is provided below in Table 5.

5.3.4 Step 4: Assess Risk

At the conclusion of the FFA and IFA, a consolidated list of hazards, mishaps, causes, and consequences will have been developed to allow for the assessment of risk. Risk is the combination of the assessed severity of a risk event (mishap) and the probability (likelihood) that the mishap will occur. Risk assessment in the context of an SoSHA allows for detailed understanding of what could go wrong, how badly it could go wrong, how often it could go wrong, and then supports the prioritisation of treatments (control development) to either prevent a mishap from occurring in the first instance, or failing that, to mitigate or reduce the consequences if a particular mishap does occur.

There are various methods of assessing risk; however, the two most common are through the use of risk matrices (typically a qualitative approach) or quantitative assessments. Depending on the organisation's risk tolerance, and the industry the organisation is working in (i.e., applicable safety regulations they operate under), a risk assessment using Quantitative Risk Assessment (QRA) of hazards and their associated mishaps is often used to justify when a defined safety target level has

Table 4 OSDS Functional Failure Analysis (FFA)

Functional Failure Analysis							
REQ ID	SoS function	Failure mode	Analysis	Hazard	Mishap	Causes	Consequences
FN1-OSDS	**Deploy** satellite at the correct orbital height	Function not provided	The satellite is not deployed from the launch vehicle	Inability to deploy satellite correctly	Satellite not deployed	Failure in release mechanism (hardware); Failure in triggering release mechanism (software/electronic); Satellite propulsion failures	Wasted resources; mission failure
		Function provided when not required	The satellite is deployed at an incorrect time (during launch/at incorrect height/too late/too soon)	Inability to deploy satellite correctly	Uncoordinated satellite deployment	Vibration/EMI triggers deployment early or late; software failures trigger deployment when not required	Launch vehicle and satellite breakup (if satellite deployed during launch); mission failure
		Function provided incorrectly	The satellite is deployed incorrectly which may result in the satellite impacting the launch vehicle through to being unable to be in the correct orientation	Inability to deploy satellite correctly	Uncontrolled satellite deployment	Faulty release mechanism; satellite propulsion uncontrolled	Satellite/launch vehicle damage (if impact occurs); mission failure

Table 5 Interface Failure Analysis (IFA)

Interface Failure Analysis							
DEP ID	SoS dependency	Failure mode	Analysis	Hazard	Mishap	Causes	Consequences
DEP3-OSDS	FN: **Protect** satellite from aerodynamic forces and heat in launch	Dependency not provided	Satellite is not protected from aerodynamic forces and heat during launch	Inability to provide satellite protection	Satellite exposed to aerodynamic forces; satellite exposed to booster heat	Launch vehicle breakup; incorrect satellite deployment; satellite loaded in unprotected environment	Damaged/ destroyed satellite; mission failure
		Dependency provided when not required	Not applicable				
		Dependency provided incorrectly	Satellite protection is inadequate or insufficient. Same output as 'Dependency not provided'				

been achieved. While risk matrices are commonly used due to their simplicity and ease of use, they have significant limitations and can lead to misleading conclusions (see Hubbard, 2020, Chapter 8). Therefore, the authors recommend more quantitative and defensible methods for risk assessment where possible.

It is outside the scope of this chapter to discuss the merits of different risk assessment techniques, and the choice will largely be dictated by the organisation's risk and/or safety program. Note, however, that under Australian and New Zealand Work Health Safety legislation, all health and safety hazards in the workplace should be eliminated, and if they can't be eliminated, minimised so far as reasonably practicable (SFARP) (see Work Health and Safety Act 2011; Health and Safety at Work Act 2015). The "reasonably practicable" concept is effectively a legal test mandated by the legislation. It is precautionary in nature and focuses on risk reduction regardless of any set target, that is, regardless of your risk assessment, any risk targets set, and the effectiveness of your implemented controls, if there is something more you could do, and it is reasonable and practicable to do so, then do that also.

5.3.5 Step 5: Identify Suitable Risk Controls

Following risk assessment, suitable controls are identified and implemented to eliminate or minimise identified risks. The authors separate these controls into several key categories. Hazard controls focus on eliminating or reducing the likelihood of a hazard being realised, often through engineering solutions such as physical barriers or automated shut-off systems. Where hazards cannot be entirely eliminated, Preventative Accident Controls (PACs) or Preventative Consequence Controls (PCCs) are introduced to prevent accidents from occurring after a hazard has been realised. For example, backup power systems ensure critical functions remain operational, reducing the risk of system failure.

If an accident does occur, Mitigative Accident Controls (MACs) or Mitigative Consequence Controls (MCCs) are used to minimise the severity of consequences. These include measures such as emergency evacuation procedures, spill containment, and the use of Personal Protective Equipment (PPE). However, the effectiveness of any control can be compromised by escalation factors and deficiencies, which weaken or degrade safety measures. Deficiencies may range from partial failures, such as inadequate training or poorly maintained equipment, to complete failures, where critical systems do not function as intended. Addressing these deficiencies is also essential to maintaining the integrity of any risk control framework and ensuring that hazards remain effectively managed. Indeed, good risk practices, as outlined and promoted by International Organization for Standardization (ISO) in its ISO 31000:2018 Risk management—Guidelines (International Organization for Standardization, 2018), outline generally the following important actions:

- Start off by identifying all additional risk controls.[10]
- Assess the suitability and merit of each risk control as it relates to the impact it will make on the risk, that is, confirm the control should reduce the likelihood or consequence of the risk.

Under Australian and New Zealand Work Health and Safety legislation, it is necessary to prioritise the implementation of high-quality controls as stipulated through the *Hierarchy of Controls* (see Figure 1 from Safe Work Australia (n.d.) for a visual description of the hierarchy of control measures). Specifically, Persons Conducting a Business or Undertaking (PCBU) (Work Health and Safety Act 2011) are required to identify and implement Level 1 risk controls. These controls are those that *eliminate* hazards. If no reasonable or practicable Level 1 controls can be identified and implemented, Level 2 controls should then be considered. These controls are those that *substitute*, *isolate*, or *engineer out* the hazard. If the risk has still not been minimised so far as reasonably practicable, Level 3 controls must be considered. Level 3 controls are *administrative* in nature and include procedures, training, and supervision. If the risk has still not been reduced so far as reasonably practicable after application of Level 3 controls, Level 4 controls are to be considered. These *personal protection equipment* controls prevent direct exposure to the effects of the hazard-mishap event. If an incident were to occur that related to a given system, under Australian and New Zealand law, the organisation (PCBU) will be required to demonstrate they had done all things reasonably practicable to eliminate or minimise the risk. Therefore, it is a good principle for risk management and strict application of the *Hierarchy of Controls* for non-safety related risks provides organisations with a robust risk management process (see generally Safe Work Australia (n.d.)). Once all available and suitable controls have been identified, it is necessary to reassess the risk to determine any residual risk(s) associated with the SoS to inform appropriate review periods as discussed in the next step.

5.3.6 Step 6: Review and Monitor Safety Performance

Monitoring and review of implemented safety control performance provides assurance and opportunities to further reduce risk. Ongoing monitoring and periodic review should be clearly defined as a core component of the risk management process as stipulated through an organisation's Safety Management System (SMS). Usually, organisations stipulate that mishap risk should be periodically reviewed based on the assessed risk of that mishap (e.g., mishaps assessed with a risk level of 'High' should be reviewed frequently) or, after an incident has occurred.

Periodic review of mishaps provides an opportunity for risk to be mitigated further through the implementation of additional controls that may have been assessed as unsuitable in the past but because of technological developments or some other

[10] Additional risk controls are those as well as the risk controls inherent in the system before the initial risk assessment.

circumstances are now suitable, or identification of new controls that were not available at the time of the last assessment.

6 Conclusion

The integration of complex systems in the space industry presents risk management challenges that require a structured and proactive approach to hazard identification and mitigation. This chapter highlights how System-of-Systems Hazard Analysis offers an important framework for understanding and managing these risks, particularly in an industry where minor failures can lead to expensive and catastrophic consequences. The case studies presented highlight that system failures are often not isolated events but rather the result of poor integration, inadequate risk assessment, and governance failures. From the loss of the *Mars Climate Orbiter* due to unit conversion errors to the *Challenger* disaster's overlooked engineering concerns, these examples reinforce the critical need for early, rigorous, and continuous risk assessment in system-of-systems contexts.

Furthermore, the interdependencies between space systems, for example, satellites, launch vehicles, ground control networks, and human operators necessitate a broader perspective on risk that goes beyond the challenges of managing risk for individual systems. This chapter has demonstrated that risk assessment cannot be limited to individual system performance but must account for how systems interact, how failures propagate, and how organisational decision-making can inadvertently introduce vulnerabilities. To this end, the authors have presented a structured SoSHA approach to provide a roadmap for improving risk resilience in the context of space industry projects. By systematically identifying functional, physical, resource, and data/information dependencies, space actors can anticipate and mitigate emergent hazards before they lead to mission failures. As the space industry continues to expand, driven by new entrants, commercial investment, and an evolving regulatory landscapes, ensuring a strong risk culture, clear governance structures, and robust system integration methodologies will be fundamental to sustaining safe and successful space operations.

References

ALARP Solutions. (2024). https://www.alarpsolutions.com.au/

Columbia Accident Investigation Board. (2003, August). *Report of the Columbia Accident Investigation Board, Report Volume I*. https://ehss.energy.gov/deprep/archive/documents/0308_caib_report_volume1.pdf

Department of Defense. (2023). *Department of Defense Standard Practice System Safety*. MIL-STD-882E. https://safety.army.mil/Portals/0/Documents/ON-DUTY/SYSTEMSAFETY/Standard/MIL-STD-882E-change-1.pdf

Department of Standards Malaysia. (2011). *Occupational Safety and Health (OSH) Management Systems – Requirements* (First Revision). MS1722:2011.
Dillon, R. L., & Tinsley, C. H. (2008). How near-misses influence decision making under risk: A missed opportunity for learning. *Management Science, 54*(8), 1425–1440.
Dowson, M. (1997). The Ariane 5 software failure. *ACM SIGSOFT Software Engineering Notes, 22*(2), 84. https://doi.org/10.1145/251880.251992
European Space Agency. (2021). *ESA's Space Environment Report 2021*. https://www.esa.int/Space_Safety/Space_Debris/ESA_s_Space_Environment_Report_2021
European Space Agency. (n.d.). *Cluster factsheet*. https://www.esa.int/Science_Exploration/Space_Science/Cluster_factsheet
Feynman, R. P. (1986). Volume 2: Appendix F - Personal Observations on Reliability of Shuttle. In *Report of the PRESIDENTIAL COMMISSION on the Space Shuttle Challenger Accident*. https://www.nasa.gov/history/rogersrep/v2appf.htm
Health and Safety at Work Act 2015 (New Zealand). https://www.legislation.govt.nz/act/public/2015/0070/latest/DLM5976660.html
Hubbard, D. W. (2020). *The failure of risk management: Why it's broken and how to fix it* (2nd ed.). Wiley. https://doi.org/10.1002/9781119198536
Interference Technology. (2013, February 1). Toyota issues vehicle recall due to electrical interference. *Interference Technology*. https://interferencetechnology.com/toyota-issues-vehicle-recall-due-to-electrical-interference/
International Association of Classification Societies. (n.d.). https://iacs.org.uk/
International Organization for Standardization. (2018). *ISO 31000:2018 Risk management – Guidelines*. Switzerland.
Le Lann, G. (1996). *The Ariane 5 Flight 501 failure – A case study in system engineering for computing systems*. INRIA Report No. 3079. https://cgi.cse.unsw.edu.au/~cs2111/ClassicalB/PDF/the-ariane-flight-failure.pdf
Lions, J. L. (1996, July 19). *Ariane 5. Flight 501 failure*. Report by the Inquiry Board. https://esamultimedia.esa.int/docs/esa-x-1819eng.pdf
MARS Observer Mission Failure Investigation Board. (1993). *VOLUME I MARS OBSERVER Mission Failure Investigation Board Report*. https://spacese.spacegrant.org/Failure%20Reports/Mars_Observer_12_93_MIB.pdf
McCurdy, H. E. (2003). *Faster, better, cheaper. low-cost innovation in the U.S. Space Program*. Johns Hopkins University Press.
National Aeronautics and Space Administration. (1999a, November 10). *Mars Climate Orbiter. Mishap Investigation Board. Phase I Report*. https://llis.nasa.gov/llis_lib/pdf/1009464main1_0641-mr.pdf
National Aeronautics and Space Administration. (1999b, September). *Mars Climate Orbiter arrival*. Press Kit. https://mars.nasa.gov/internal_resources/812/
National Aeronautics and Space Administration. (2009, August). Lost in translation. *System Failure Case Studies, 3*(5). https://sma.nasa.gov/docs/default-source/safety-messages/safetymessage-2009-08-01-themarsclimateorbitermishap.pdf?sfvrsn=eaa1ef8_4
National Aeronautics and Space Administration. (n.d.). *Rocket parts*. https://www1.grc.nasa.gov/beginners-guide-to-aeronautics/rocket-parts/
Oxford Reference. (n.d.). *Technical standard*. https://www.oxfordreference.com/display/10.1093/oi/authority.20110803102805121
Pozza, M. A., & Dennerley, J. A. (2022). *Risk management in outer space activities. An Australian and New Zealand perspective*. Springer.
Rogers, W. P., Armstrong, N. A., Acheson, D. C., Covert, E. E., Feynman, R. P., Hotz, R. B., Kutyna D. J., Ride, S. K., Rummel, R. W., & Sutter, J. F. (1986, June 6). *Report of the Presidential Commission on the Space Shuttle Challenger Accident* (Vol. 1). https://ntrs.nasa.gov/api/citations/19860015255/downloads/19860015255.pdf
Safe Work Australia. (n.d.). *Managing risks*. https://www.safeworkaustralia.gov.au/safety-topic/managing-health-and-safety/identify-assess-and-control-hazards/managing-risks

Smith, M. S. (2003, September 2). *NASA's Space Shuttle Columbia: Synopsis of the Report of the Columbia Accident Investigation Board.* https://ntrs.nasa.gov/api/citations/20040040191/downloads/20040040191.pdf

Sommerville, I. (2004). *The Ariane 5 Launcher failure.* Software Engineering Case Studies. https://www.inf.ed.ac.uk/teaching/courses/seoc/2005_2006/resources/Ariane5failure.pdf

Stephenson, R. R., & Bernard, D. E. (1994, February 2). *JPL Mars Observer in-flight anomaly investigation.* https://ntrs.nasa.gov/citations/20060037745

Work Health and Safety Act 2011 (Australia). https://www.legislation.gov.au/C2011A00137/latest/text

World Economic Forum. (2022). *Global Risks Report 2022* (17th edn.). https://www.weforum.org/publications/global-risks-report-2022/

Young, T., Arnold, J., Brackey, T., Carr, M., Dwoyer, D., Fogleman, R., Jacobson, R., Kottler, H., Lyman, P., & Maquire, J. (2000, March 14). *Mars Program Independent Assessment Team Report.* https://ntrs.nasa.gov/api/citations/20000032458/downloads/20000032458.pdf

Aaron Young, MSc (Oceanography), BSc (Physics), Grad Dip (Meteorology), is a principal risk and safety consultant specialising in governance, risk, assurance, and metrics. He has over 30 years' experience in Defence and Defence industry projects.

Bradley Robb, BE (Aero), Grad Dip (Education), Grad Dip (Human Factors and Safety Management Systems), is a risk and safety management consultant and is the owner and managing director of ALARP Solutions.

MIX
Papier aus verantwortungsvollen Quellen
Paper from responsible sources
FSC® C105338

If you have any concerns about our products,
you can contact us on
ProductSafety@springernature.com

In case Publisher is established outside the EU,
the EU authorized representative is:
Springer Nature Customer Service Center GmbH
Europaplatz 3, 69115 Heidelberg, Germany

Printed by Libri Plureos GmbH
in Hamburg, Germany